The North Carolina Shore

and Its Barrier Islands

Living with the Shore
Series editors, Orrin H. Pilkey and William J. Neal

The Beaches Are Moving: The
Drowning of America's Shoreline
New edition
Wallace Kaufman and
Orrin H. Pilkey

Living by the Rules of the Sea
David M. Bush, Orrin H. Pilkey,
and William J. Neal

Living with the
Alabama-Mississippi Shore
Wayne F. Canis et al.

Living with the Coast
of Alaska
Owen Mason et al.

Living with the California Coast
Gary Griggs and Lauret Savoy et al.

Living with the Chesapeake Bay
and Virginia's Ocean Shores
Larry G. Ward et al.

A Moveable Shore: The Fate of the
Connecticut Coast
Peter C. Patton and James M. Kent

Living with the East Florida Shore
Orrin H. Pilkey et al.

Living with the West Florida Shore
Larry J. Doyle et al.

Living with the Georgia Shore
Tonya D. Clayton et al.

Living with the Lake Erie Shore
Charles H. Carter et al.

Living with Long Island's South Shore
Larry McCormick et al.

Living with the Louisiana Shore
Joseph T. Kelley et al.

Living with the Coast of Maine
Joseph T. Kelley et al.

Living with the New Jersey Shore
Karl F. Nordstrom et al.

The Pacific Northwest Coast:
Living with the Shores of Oregon
and Washington
Paul D. Komar

Living with the Puerto Rico Shore
David M. Bush et al.

Living with the Shore of Puget Sound
and the Georgia Strait
Thomas A. Terich

Living with the South Carolina Coast
Gered Lennon et al.

The North Carolina Shore and Its Barrier Islands

Restless Ribbons of Sand

Orrin H. Pilkey, William J. Neal, Stanley R. Riggs,
Craig A. Webb, David M. Bush, Deborah F. Pilkey,
Jane Bullock, and Brian A. Cowan

Duke University Press   Durham and London   1998

Living with the Shore Series

Publication of 21 volumes in the Living with the Shore series has
been funded by the Federal Emergency Management Agency.

Publication has been greatly assisted by the following individuals
and organizations: the American Conservation Association, an
anonymous Texas foundation, the Charleston Natural History
Society, the Office of Coastal Zone Management (NOAA), the
Geraldine R. Dodge Foundation, the William H. Donner Founda-
tion, Inc., the George Gund Foundation, the Mobil Oil Corpora-
tion, Elizabeth O'Connor, the Sapelo Island Research Foundation,
the Sea Grant programs in New Jersey, North Carolina, Florida,
Mississippi/Alabama, and New York, The Fund for New Jersey, M.
Harvey Weil, Patrick H. Welder Jr., and the Water Resources
Institute of Grand Valley State University. The Living with the
Shore series is a product of the Duke University Program for the
Study of Developed Shorelines, which was initially funded by the
Donner Foundation.

Contents

Figures, Tables, and Risk Maps

Figures

Tables

Risk Maps

Preface

Twenty years ago we produced *From Currituck to Calabash: Living with North Carolina's Barrier Islands,* a simple summary of North Carolina's coastal hazards and a citizens' guide to reducing vulnerability to the risks from such hazards. The book enjoyed wide distribution, going through several printings and two editions, and served as the model for twenty subsequent volumes of the Living with the Shore series. But "nothing stays the same," as they say, and since 1978 the coast has changed, rearranged by a series of hurricanes and northeasters. During the same period, our knowledge of barrier islands and our approach to evaluating coastal development risk has progressed and expanded as a result of new storm experiences, new construction trends, and improved islandwide risk-mapping techniques. Also during the same period, beach "cottages" have been replaced by beach "mansions" and multiple dwelling units during poststorm recovery periods, and North Carolina's approach to coastal zone management and legislation has evolved to work more closely with nature and to reduce future property losses. The shoreline engineering paradigm has shifted from an emphasis on shore-hardening structures to beach nourishment, and even to a policy of relocation in Nags Head and other towns. And we now realize that a whole-island view should prevail over a simple focus on the shoreline.

This book is the result of all our new knowledge. Although it updates and replaces *From Currituck to Calabash,* some original material remains because some things haven't changed. Nature still works in the same way. Development pressure in the coastal zone continues, especially on the high-risk barrier islands. People still want to build their houses in flood-prone areas, either out of ignorance or, in the case of some post-Fran examples, perhaps arrogance. The taxpayer-at-large is still picking up the tab for too many "donuts" in each disaster, only the "donut holes" now signify billions of dollars rather than millions! People still remove forest cover, level dunes, block overwash, or otherwise interfere with natural systems and contribute to worsening the impact from natural processes. Generations of previous jetties, groins, and seawalls (about 5 percent of North Carolina's developed shore is "stabilized") still contribute to local downdrift erosion problems. People still ask, "When is *someone* going to do something about *my* eroding beach?" and barrier-island problems still figure prominently in daily media reports and politics at all levels.

Sometimes we are so focused on one issue—to relocate or not to relocate a structure, to nourish or not to nourish a beach—that we overlook future hazards, such as flooding or earthquakes and their associated problems. To address the various changes in our knowledge, the specific lessons learned from recent storms, and natural processes and potential issues (which often stay the same), we produced a book that combines the mostly new with a little of the old.

Most significantly, the original authors, Dr. Orrin Pilkey, Duke University; Dr. William J. Neal, Grand Valley State University; and Dr. Stan Riggs, East Carolina University; are joined by new authors who bring an up-to-date view of the North Carolina coast and a breadth of experience in coastal hazard evaluation and mitigation.

Craig Webb's Duke University master's thesis, "Risk Mapping of North Carolina's Barriers," provided the core for chapter 7; and his thesis work provided the inertia behind this book. From 1993 to 1997 he was part of the Program for the Study of Developed Shorelines team that investigated such events as Hurricane Emily's impact on sound-side shorelines and property damage mitigation lessons from Hurricane Opal (1995) in Florida.

Dr. David Bush of the State University of West Georgia in Carrollton, Georgia, was a resident of North Carolina for many years and is a shoreline expert. His research while at Duke University focused on coastal hazards, risk assessment mapping, and property damage mitigation. He has experience with the U.S. Atlantic and Gulf coasts as well as the Caribbean, focusing especially on the Carolinas and Puerto Rico. His expertise was recognized in his appointment to the National Academy of Sciences postdisaster field study teams after Hurricanes Gilbert and Hugo. He was involved with planning for the U.S. Decade for Natural Hazard Reduction, and is the senior author of *Living with the Puerto Rico Shore* and *Living by the Rules of the Sea.*

The late Orrin Pilkey Sr.'s construction chapter was revised extensively by his granddaughter, Deborah, to include concepts and design recommendations based on the lessons of Hurricanes Andrew, Iniki, and Fran. Deborah Pilkey is a Ph.D. student in engineering at Virginia Polytechnic Institute and State University.

Jane Bullock, chief of staff of the Federal Emergency Management

Agency, and Brian Cowan, FEMA mitigation policy analyst, wrote the earthquake construction chapter. In their tenure with FEMA, these two authors have dealt with numerous hurricanes, earthquakes, and flood disasters.

One of the driving forces behind this book and the entire Living with the Shore series has been the support of the Federal Emergency Management Agency. Specifically, the FEMA officials who provided input for this latest volume are Gary Johnson, Jane Bullock, and Dick Krimm. The conclusions of this book, however, are those of the authors, based on various published reports and studies of record, and are not meant to reflect the views of any specific agency.

Amber Taylor drafted most of the figures for this book, as she has for all the recent volumes of the Living with the Shore series. Thanks to Debbie Gooch for typing several drafts. Dr. Rob Thieler, Dr. Rob Young, Susan Bates, Dr. Bill Cleary, Matt Stutz, Meg McQuarrie, Tracy Rice, Kathie Dixon, and Jill Rozicki helped with many tasks along the way. Sharlene Pilkey helped with the postdisaster recovery and cleanup ideas, based on her family's personal experience with Hurricane Fran. Thanks also go to Steve Benton, Rich Shaw, Evan Brunson, and Caroline Bellis of the North Carolina Division of Coastal Management and to numerous local officials, including Greg Loy, Bruce Bortz, and Don Bryan. As with the original book, we are indebted to those coastal residents who shared their experiences, insights, and concerns with the authors. Finally, thanks to Dr. John Wells and Dr. Charles Peterson, University of North Carolina at Chapel Hill, for the expression "restless ribbons of sand" from their U.S. Department of the Interior publication on barrier islands. The barrier islands of North Carolina are truly restless ribbons of sand.

William J. Neal
Orrin H. Pilkey
Series Editors
September 10, 1997

Preface to the Previous Editions

Some 2,500 years ago the citizens of Carthage, a Phoenician people, built a harbor along the shores of the Gulf of Tunis in North Africa. This harbor, from which Hannibal sailed to attack Rome, is still used today by small Arab fishing boats.

A few hundred years later and some twenty miles away, the Romans, a mightier people, built the seaport of Utica. North Africa was the breadbasket of the Roman Empire, and across the docks of Utica flowed huge quantities of food and treasure to be shipped to Rome. Today, a tourist standing atop the highest column in the ruins of Utica can no longer see the sea. The shoreline has moved 17 kilometers seaward, away from what was once the harbor.

The Carthaginians designed their structures to be compatible with nature. The Romans, the first practitioners of brute-force technology, chose to confront, alter, and destroy nature. What the Romans didn't realize was that in the long run, nature always wins at the shoreline. The sandy barrier island shoreline of the U.S. Atlantic and Gulf coasts is a dynamic, ever-changing environment that often does not interact well with the trappings of man. The exploitation of this dynamic coastal area is being carried out at an ever-increasing rate. First came the harbors and ports, which required channel maintenance; then came the seashore resorts, which attracted construction on the rapidly retreating shorelines. While earlier generations of Americans were like the Carthaginians—either wise enough to locate properly or resigned to watching their homes fall victim to shoreline retreat—modern island developers are more like the ancient Romans: with money, technology, and political clout, they attempt to stop shoreline retreat so as to extend the lifespans of buildings along the shore. The long-range result of such efforts, however, is economic and environmental calamity. This is visible along the New Jersey and southern Florida shorelines. They attest to the fact that man's success in harnessing nature for his own ends does not necessarily enhance his surroundings or the quality of his life.

We have written this book because we wish to help North Carolinians learn to live in harmony with nature at the shoreline and to understand fully the consequences of doing otherwise. This book is not meant to discourage development; we hope, rather, that it encourages proper, limited development. Although certain natural areas warrant protection from development, preservationism is an unrealistic philosophy to follow on all of the coast, especially since a development pattern has already been established on most of it. Unrestricted development, however, endangers coastal residents and island resources. The public should become aware of and concerned about our island resources in order to conserve them.

This book is an outgrowth of the 1975 book *How to Live with an Island*, by Orrin Pilkey Jr., Orrin Pilkey Sr., and Robb Turner. Although the first book dealt with development on a single island—Bogue Banks, near Morehead City, North Carolina—many of its principles were applicable to other islands. Thus the book was distributed from Cape Cod, Massachusetts, to Padre Island, Texas. Our primary purpose, however, was to affect development on the North Carolina shoreline. In this book we have applied our understanding of shoreline geology and engineering to every privately owned island in North Carolina—from Currituck to Calabash. William Neal, professor of geology at Grand Valley State College in Allendale, Michigan, spent nine months on sabbatical leave researching and writing much of the manuscript. His work was sponsored by the National Science Foundation Program in Science and Societal Problems. Dr. Stanley Riggs, who teaches geology at East Carolina University, has spent many months and years, "in fair weather and foul," studying the natural forces at work on the Outer Banks. His work has been supported largely by the Sea Grant Program and in part by the North Carolina Board of Science and Technology.

Like our earlier book, *From Currituck to Calabash* was published through the interest and efforts of Peter Chenery, director of the North Carolina Science and Technology Research Center. Doris Schroeder, director of communications for the Center, edited the original manuscript, rewriting and rearranging much of the material that we handed her; Betty Zatz, editorial assistant at the center, then edited it to its final form.

We were also aided by three Lindas: Linda Gerber, administrative secretary of the Duke geology department, who typed the original manuscript; Linda Caulder, secretary at the North Carolina Science and Technology Research Center, who typed the final printer's copy; and Linda Cooper, a UNC–Chapel Hill journalism student, who helped to index and edit the book. The figures throughout the book were drafted by Jim Hamm and Mark Evans; and most field photographs were taken by Jim Page.

We are especially grateful for the contributions of Drs. William Cleary and Paul Hosier of the University of North Carolina at Wilmington, Drs. Jay Langfelder and Stan Boc of North Carolina State University, and Lim Vallianos of the Army Corps of Engineers Wilmington district office.

In gathering data for this book we were helped by many people who live along the shore—so many, in fact, that it would be impossible to list them all here. We are grateful for their cheerful and enthusiastic cooperation, and the new insights and concerns that we acquired from them.

1 Lessons from the Lighthouse

The Cape Hatteras Lighthouse is North Carolina's most famous coastal landmark, and perhaps the world's most famous lighthouse (fig. 1.1). In addition to warning mariners of the treacherous waters of the "Graveyard of the Atlantic," for nearly 130 years this silent sentinel has stood watch over the constantly changing ribbons of sand that we know as the Outer Banks. Hatteras Light, like her sister lighthouses along the coast of the Carolinas, can teach us a range of lessons that go beyond the history of maritime safety and commerce. Lighthouses are the original hurricane-resistant construction; they are markers against which to measure coastal dynamics—how the coast changes, and how we respond to those changes, both as individuals and as a society.

The Lighthouse, the Shore, and the Sea:
A Coastal Perspective

She Was Built to Last

Hatteras Light was first lit in 1870 (table 1.1), replacing a smaller lighthouse dating from 1803 whose ruined base was also a landmark for many years. At 208 feet in height, this tallest brick lighthouse in the United States weighs 2,800 tons. Hatteras Light rests on a relatively small foundation: two layers of yellow pine timbers support a foundation base of granite rubble and masonry about 3 feet thick. Because its base is above sea level, the lighthouse could be undercut by storm waves or by storm-surge current scour in a large hurricane or northeaster.

The lighthouse's thick masonry walls were designed to withstand hurricane-strength winds and waves, but the history of lighthouses tells us that even massive storm-resistant buildings can fall victim to the sea. The shal-

Figure 1.1 The beautiful Cape Hatteras Lighthouse has warned mariners of the treacherous waters of Diamond Shoals since 1870. Three groins (the southernmost is shown here) and the sandbag revetment are part of a several-decades-long fight to hold back the sea. The "right" storm will remove the lighthouse overnight. Constructed on a site set well back from the beach, the light today sits at the ocean's edge.

low above-sea-level foundation is the Achilles heel of the lighthouse, and neither seawalls nor groins are long-term deterrents to its collapse.

Reference Point to Measure Shoreline Retreat

The lighthouse, originally located inland more than 1,500 feet from the shore, is a static structure. It remained in one spot while the shoreline moved relentlessly toward it, changing position in response to changes in sea level, wave energy, and sediment supply. By 1919 the beach was within 300 feet of the lighthouse, and by 1935 within 100 feet, leading to its abandonment. This shoreline retreat continues to the present day (fig. 1.2). For a brief period after World War II the shoreline actually built seaward, but it soon reversed course and moved landward again.

Hatteras Light teaches us that setting construction back from the sea only delays the day when the shoreline catches up with static structures, and that the beach does not disappear during its migration. The latter point may seem obvious, but it is significant in that the term *beach erosion* is sometimes used to describe the shoreline retreat. Erosion implies loss, but the beach is still there. On the other hand, when a resistant barrier is placed in the path of beach retreat, the beach *does* erode, as reflected by its narrowing and eventual disappearance in front of seawall barriers.

Figure 1.2 The saga of the Cape Hatteras Lighthouse.

A. Comparison of 1872 and present shorelines

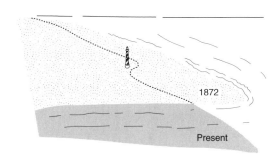

B. What will happen if lighthouse stays in place

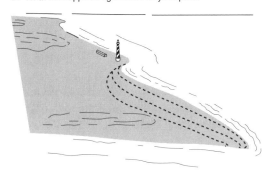

C. What will happen if lighthouse is moved

Shoreline changes are not confined to the open-ocean shores of the North Carolina coast. The barrier islands are truly restless ribbons of sand in their entirety. Inlets between islands are particularly subject to rapid change, as measured by the location of the Bodie Island Lighthouse, not far north of Cape Hatteras. The present lighthouse was built in 1872 north of Oregon Inlet to replace its predecessor south of the inlet. Bodie Island Light today is a significant distance from Oregon Inlet, which has migrated to the south. The southerly shift of the inlet eroded away the site of the former lighthouse, which waves would have eventually claimed had not Confederate troops destroyed it during the Civil War.

The lessons taught by the Hatteras Island coast are these: shorelines change, inlets migrate, and barrier islands may be built in part by natural processes that humans regard as destructive and attempt to block or retard through coastal engineering. The history of the Cape Lookout Lighthouse reiterates these lessons. The first lighthouse was threatened by drifting sand before it, too, was abandoned. The present structure, built in 1859, is now threatened by the migration of the shore on the back side of the island.

Responses to Shoreline Retreat

The state's response to the shoreline retreat affecting much of the Outer Banks, including the Hatteras Lighthouse, in the 1930s was an attempt to engineer nature by lending a helpful hand. Unfortunately, the nature of barrier islands was poorly understood at the time. The Civilian Conservation Corps (CCC) built artificial dunes along the length of the Outer Banks, effectively creating a dune dike meant to hold the islands in place (table 1.1). At that time no one knew that islands migrate. When the sea level is rising, as it is today, barrier islands do not stay in one place; they migrate landward in order to survive. The CCC's dune dike blocked the natural cross-island processes by which the islands move landward and upward.

The early stabilization effort was on the right track, however, in that by building dunes, humans were mimicking the natural system. The 1966 beach nourishment project in front of Hatteras Light was a harbinger of the "soft" engineering approach that would come to characterize coastal engineering by the end of the century.

Unfortunately, the concern for preserving the lighthouse also led to several attempts at shore hardening, including the construction of groins and seawalls. Between 1978 and 1980, the ocean reached the ruins of the old lighthouse base, covered them, and moved closer to the present lighthouse.

Builders of lighthouses have developed three strategies in response to the threat of the sea. First, shoreline retreat is sometimes factored into the site planning so the sea will not arrive at the doorstep until the light is past its useful life. George Washington is supposed to have ordered that the lighthouse at Montauk Point, New York, be built far enough back from the bluff edge to survive bluff erosion (retreat) for 200 years. He made a good call.

The implied expectation was that in 200 years the light would be abandoned and allowed to fall into the sea, the second strategy. Lighthouses, however, are designed and built to survive punishment by great storms, and sometimes abandoned lighthouses persist and become of historic and touristic interest. Local residents and tourists view them with nostalgia and may go to extreme lengths to preserve them. Once again, there are lessons to be learned from this. South Carolina's most famous lighthouse is the Morris Island Light (fig. 1.3). The lighthouse was built in 1874, 1,300 feet inland, but Morris Island migrated out from under the structure and today it stands 2,000 feet out to sea. The tower's feet went into the water sometime in the

Figure 1.3   The Morris Island Lighthouse now stands hundreds of yards out to sea, a victim of shoreline retreat that was hastened when the sand flow was halted by the Charleston, South Carolina, harbor jetties. The lighthouse passed across the shoreline in the mid-1940s. It has survived because its foundation is more than 30 feet deep. The foundation of the Cape Hatteras Lighthouse is only 6 feet deep, and the bottom of the foundation is actually above sea level. Thus, the Cape Hatteras Lighthouse will not survive if the shoreline erodes past it.

late 1940s to 1950s, and its use was discontinued in 1962. When this light-house was threatened by the sea, the Coast Guard provided minimum protection (a sheet-pile wall and concrete cap were installed in 1938) and decided to let nature take its course, rather than spend taxpayers' dollars in an attempt to hold back the Atlantic Ocean. The lighthouse was sold in the 1960s and is now privately owned.

The third strategy, moving a lighthouse threatened by shoreline retreat, might be viewed as modern, but in fact it is quite an old solution to shoreline retreat. Again, the classic example comes from neighboring South Carolina. The Hunting Island Lighthouse, built in 1875, was constructed of metal sections that could be disassembled when it became necessary to move the lighthouse. Fourteen years later, the need arose, and the lighthouse was moved!

Move It or Lose It!

Between the 1930s, when the present Cape Hatteras Lighthouse was first seriously threatened by shoreline erosion, and 1981, the National Park Service (NPS) spent about $15 million on interim protection methods, many designed primarily to protect a U.S. Navy facility located just to the north of the lighthouse. These shoreline projects, which included groins, beach nourishment, and sandbagging, cost ever-increasing amounts and did nothing to stop the shoreline retreat. In the 1960s and 1970s, three groins were built, destroyed by a storm, and rebuilt. Nylon sandbags were placed in front of the lighthouse. Three unsuccessful beach replenishment projects were also undertaken during this time. In 1980 the light was almost lost to a winter storm, and the NPS began investigating methods of long-term protection in order to find a "solution" to the erosion problem.

The National Park Service was directed by the Department of the Interior to find a protection method that would meet three criteria: (1) the lighthouse would be saved, (2) the solution would be permanent, and (3) there would be no major recurring costs. Although a great deal of controversy accompanied the Park Service's efforts to find a way to save the lighthouse, an examination of all the facts clearly showed that *only* moving the lighthouse would satisfy all three criteria. That conclusion was reached by the Move the Lighthouse Committee and the Committee on Options for Preserving the Cape Hatteras Lighthouse, formed jointly by the National Academy of Sciences and the National Academy of Engineering in July 1987 at the request of the Park Service. In 1997, a committee of North Carolina state scientists reached the same conclusion. The chronology taken from the Park Service's Environmental Assessment for the Lighthouse Protection Plan (1982) is presented in table 1.1.

Table 1.1   History of the Cape Hatteras lighthouse

1870	Existing lighthouse first lit. Original distance from the sea: 1,500 feet (450 meters).
1919	Shoreline within 300 feet (90 meters) of lighthouse.
1935	Shoreline migration brings the sea to within 100 feet (30 meters).
1936	Coast Guard abandons lighthouse. Light is moved to steel skeleton tower in Buxton Woods, one mile west. Erosion control attempted with construction of sheet-steel piling.
Late 1930s	Civilian Conservation Corps begins dune-building project to prevent overwash and allow future development behind it.
1950	Shoreline stabilized (naturally and temporarily) and Cape Hatteras Lighthouse reactivated by Coast Guard. Ownership of the structure had been transferred to the National Park Service (NPS).
1966	312,000 cubic yards of sand pumped from Pamlico Sound to stabilize the shoreline.
1967	Nylon sand-filled bags emplaced in front of lighthouse to stabilize the shoreline. Some still remained in 1995.
1969	U.S. Navy builds three groins to protect naval facility and lighthouse. They were destroyed by storms and rebuilt in 1975.
1971–1973	Two replenishment projects emplace 1.5 million cubic yards of sand from Cape Hatteras Point to the lighthouse area. September 1973 finds the sea 175 feet (50 meters) from the old lighthouse ruins and 600 feet (180 meters) south of the present lighthouse.
1978	Water reaches old lighthouse ruins.
1980	March storm washes away remaining ruins of the original lighthouse and water comes within 70 feet (20 meters) of present lighthouse.
1980	During the summer, NPS receives results of study of Cape Hatteras erosion problem and asks the U.S. Army Corps of Engineers to begin evaluation for methods to preserve the light.
1982	Public workshop held April 1–2 in Manteo, N.C., to discuss alternatives for protecting the lighthouse. Options include a seawall revetment, offshore breakwaters, beach nourishment, additional groin, relocation, and no action.
1985	NPS selects seawall revetment as best option.
1986	Move the Lighthouse Committee organizes.
1987	NPS decides to review options, asks the National Research Council (NRC) for help.
1988	NRC final report unanimously selects relocation as the best option.
1989	NPS announces in early summer that relocation is the preferred alternative, and again asks for public input. In December, NPS announces relocation of the lighthouse is the best way to preserve it.
1991	NPS seeks bids for moving designs.
1994	Construction of a fourth groin to protect the southern exposure of the base of the lighthouse proposed.
1997	Fourth groin still being debated. Lighthouse still waiting to be moved . . .

If the lighthouse is not moved, the shoreline will continue to erode past it, and the curvature in the shoreline south of the lighthouse will become more and more pronounced. The costs of maintaining the shoreline at the lighthouse and to the north will continue to increase. Eventually, the lighthouse will be destroyed in a storm and all the money and effort spent to stabilize the shore will have been wasted.

In contrast, if the lighthouse is moved back, it will be in the same position relative to the shoreline as when it was first constructed, and there will no longer be a need to stabilize the shore. The groins and sandbags will either be removed or destroyed by storms, at which time the shoreline will straighten and quickly assume its normal equilibrium profile and shape. Other nearby structures threatened by the shoreline adjustment and migration can be moved along with the lighthouse or later, as they become threatened. Moving the Cape Hatteras Light is the only way to save this state and national treasure.

The main lesson learned from the efforts to save the Cape Hatteras Lighthouse is that Americans cannot afford to stand and fight the sea on all of our coasts. There are dozens of lighthouses that need "saving." We must either plan an organized retreat from the encroaching sea or face the prospect of spending vast amounts of money and other resources, only to fail and be forced to retreat grudgingly in a disorganized fashion. Moving the Cape Hatteras Lighthouse will set a bold example for all coastal zone managers to follow. If a lighthouse can be moved, then other large buildings can be moved as well.

Some people argue that no public money should be spent on the Hatteras Light. They say it should be allowed to go the way of the Morris Island Lighthouse. And why, they ask, should taxpayers in Dallas or Des Moines pay to protect private buildings in Ocean City, Maryland, or Ocean Isle, North Carolina?

Lessons from the Shore: The Need for a View into the Past

The lighthouse keepers of old lived on the coast by necessity. Most of today's residents are there by choice. "We knew we'd get a storm eventually, but we had no idea it would be this bad," was a sentiment heard up and down the North Carolina coast following the hurricane season of 1996. Coastal residents were battered by two hurricanes, Bertha and Fran, within eight weeks (fig. 1.4). Many people were still trying to repair the damage done to their homes by Bertha when Fran ripped through the same stretch of coastline, leaving people dazed and sometimes even homeless. Together, the two storms caused more than $5 billion in damage.

Figure 1.4 Hurricane Fran left its mark on Topsail Island, a spot too low in elevation, too narrow, with too few frontal dunes and too little maritime forest for safe development.

Bertha and Fran occurred in an area where similar storms have struck in the past. Thus, one might have expected the hurricane victims to admit defeat and leave the area after Fran. Instead, many of them rebuilt their homes again in harm's way! Some call them foolhardy, some credit them with showing "the human spirit," and some see them exerting their "God-given right."

Regardless of the risks involved in living there, the allure of the coast will continue to attract and hold people, even in the face of repeated losses. Some go there in search of the relaxing sound of the ocean lapping against the beach, ocean breezes, a sense of remoteness (even on islands populated beyond their carrying capacity), or the solace of a walk on the beach. Recreational swimming, fishing, boating, and shelling bring thousands to the beach. Others are drawn by the summer scenes of miniature golf, ferris wheels, and the night life.

For more than 150 years vacationers have basked in the sun and bathed in the waters along the beaches of North Carolina. During this time the push for more and larger developments with better beach access and better views has boldly marched residents and visitors alike to the very brink of the sea. At the same time, the North Carolina barrier islands have migrated steadily landward. Dynamic barrier islands and static buildings are a poor combination.

Development has reached almost every stretch of coast in the state, from Corolla in the north to Sunset Beach in the south (fig. 1.5); but like the Hatteras Lighthouse, our cottages and coastal castles are built on thin, ephemeral ribbons of sand. Coastal communities such as North Topsail Beach (which we believe to be North Carolina's most hazardous island community) that once stood as monuments of arrogance in the face of nature became ruins in the wake of Hurricane Fran.

Currently six of the eight North Carolina coastal counties are growing faster than the state average; two are growing at well over twice the state average. Nor will the growth along our coasts diminish anytime soon. Estimates indicate that by 2010, more than 125 million Americans will be living near the coast, a 60 percent increase from 1960.

Figure 1.5   The North Carolina coast. (A) The northern coast (*below*).
(B) The southern coast (*right*).

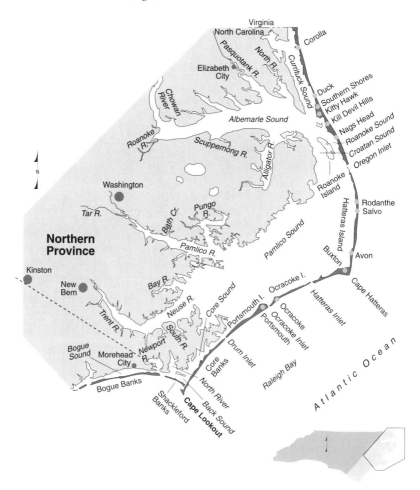

The beaches of North Carolina are now entering a critical period. The state's coastal protection laws will face tough challenges over the next few years. The rebuilding and replacement patterns after future storms in the post-Fran era will be especially good indications of the future of our coast. Will communities choose to protect beaches or buildings?

North Carolina's beaches are in remarkably good shape in spite of the development pressure on the coast. Just compare them with the beaches of

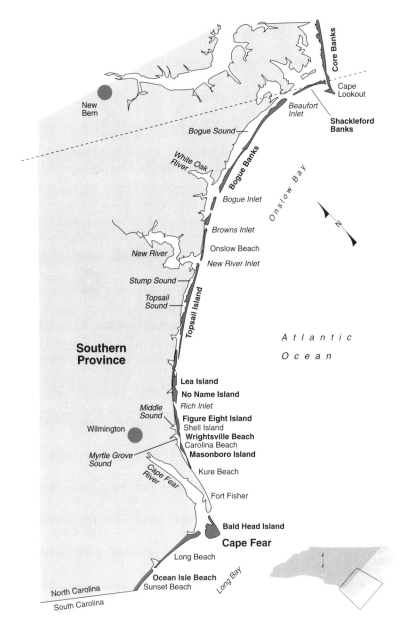

New Jersey, where unchecked growth and lack of legislative foresight have left many areas completely seawalled in, with no beach whatsoever. To protect our coast for this generation and generations to come, however, every citizen must be vigilant, especially during poststorm rebuilding processes.

Lessons from Development History: The Good, the Bad, and the Ugly

Olden Times

The first Europeans to visit the Cape Fear region were the Spanish, in the 1520s. In 1584 Sir Walter Raleigh began his efforts to explore and colonize the Outer Banks. The failure of Raleigh's "Lost Colony" is a familiar story (appendix C, ref. 2). Roanoke was only the first of several settlement efforts on the islands to be abandoned.

The early Outer Banks dwellers survived through the 1700s by assuming a variety of occupations, including raising stock, scavenging shipwrecks, processing beached whales, and fishing. Some lived on the islands to escape the laws, taxes, and other requirements of society, and may have been considered unsavory by today's standards. Nevertheless, the early islanders were skilled in survival and lived in harmony with their environment. Until the late 1700s the islanders built their homes on the sound side of the islands, in wooded hammocks that provided some protection against wind and flood. The persistence of such Outer Banks settlements as Hatteras, Ocracoke, and Portsmouth attests to the wisdom of that building strategy.

Also around this time, however, dangerous development began to occur. In 1787, for example, plans were made to dig a new inlet on Beacon Island, a marsh island inside Ocracoke Inlet. Beginning in 1790, buildings that ultimately included wharves, residences, a gristmill, windmill, store, fishery, and tavern were built on the 60-foot-wide, half-mile-long Beacon Island, said to be dry at low tide (appendix C, ref. 3). Hurricanes and unstable inlets brought an end to that enterprise and removed all traces of its existence in the early 1800s.

The First Resort

The early development of the barrier islands was slow by today's standards. Access to the islands was limited, and social and political pressures to build bridges to them were not strong. Although summer vacationers visited Portsmouth, Ocracoke, and Beaufort as early as the mid-1700s, Nags Head became the first important seaside resort in North Carolina. The community grew rapidly in the 1830s and was flourishing by the beginning of the Civil War. In consideration of hurricanes, most of the buildings were built on the sound side rather than the ocean side of the island. After the Civil War, however, residents began to build on the beachfront.

Morehead City, which originated in the late 1850s as a resort to rival Nags Head, was built on the mainland to increase accessibility and to better withstand the elements. In the late 1800s, the Ocean View Railroad was built from Wilmington to Wrightsville Beach, and another shoreline resort boomed. Atlantic Beach on Bogue Banks began its development with the construction of several dance pavilions in the early 1900s. Construction in 1928 of the first bridge to Bogue Banks hastened that resort's growth.

Not all of the towns born on the islands flourished or survived. Diamond City at Cape Lookout was abandoned in 1899 by its 500 inhabitants, who were discouraged over continual hurricane damage. The townspeople of Rice Path on Bogue Banks moved because of encroaching sand dunes, and Portsmouth on Portsmouth Island suffered gradual economic death when the adjacent Ocracoke Inlet, the source of its economic growth, was abandoned as a North Carolina port of entry.

It isn't necessary to delve into the last century for examples of disappearing coastal towns. Holden Beach in Brunswick County was completely wiped out in 1954 by Hurricane Hazel, the most devastating storm of this century in North Carolina. Hazel should not have been a surprise; it was one of nine destructive storms that had struck the Brunswick County coast since 1740. A U.S. Army Corps of Engineers report noted that "hardly a vestige of human habitation [remained] on the Brunswick County shore following Hurricane Hazel." The report also noted the "absolute totality of the damage" and the increased potential for storm damage to areas under heavy development. Unfortunately, the history lesson has gone unheeded; the development at Holden Beach and other coastal communities in Brunswick County is presently much more extensive than it was before Hazel.

World War II brought military bases to several islands, including Onslow Beach and Topsail Island. Temporary bridges were made permanent and roads were built. When the army moved out of Topsail Island in the late 1940s, the roads and buildings it left behind became the seeds of the island's present-day development.

Before 1941 and the advent of the bulldozer, however, most of the Outer Banks islands were either untouched or hardly touched by humans. The New Jerseyization of the North Carolina shore began immediately after World War II.

The New Jerseyization Phase

Even the most casual observer can see the results of unimpeded development along the New Jersey coast. A trip there would be worthwhile for every North Carolinian, for the sight of the New Jersey shore conveys a more dramatic message than the pages of any book can deliver. In part, New Jerseyization is the destruction of natural beauty. But beauty is in the eyes of the beholder; some prefer to see a hot dog stand on the beach rather than an untouched dune covered with sea oats. There are, however, nonaesthetic problems as well that stem from New Jerseyization, and these pose a more serious threat to coastal residents:

1. *Hurricanes and winter storms.* These storms are a constant threat to shore residents, and lives are endangered by unsafe construction and hazardous building sites. Unfortunately, modern development on the North Carolina islands has not proceeded from the safest areas to the least safe ones; historically, the most eager builders have often owned the most dangerous stretches of land. When it comes to safety, construction quality is independent of building site quality. On North Topsail Beach, for example, some very well built houses were situated on dangerous sites with low elevation, no protective dunes, and a history of frequent storm overwash. It was no surprise that Fran was so thorough in its destruction there (fig. 1.6)! On Bogue Banks, on the other hand, there are mobile homes that, although situated at high elevations with good dune protection, are poorly secured to the ground. A single poorly secured mobile home detached from its foundation in a storm creates a significant hazard to the surrounding area.

2. *Pollution.* Improper waste disposal threatens to destroy the health of coastal citizens and the natural resources that support the local marine fishing industry. Several of North Carolina's estuarine fishing grounds for

Figure 1.6 Most of the buildings on North Topsail Beach were moved off their foundations by Fran. This scene is typical of the beachfront damage that occurred in both North Topsail Beach and Surf City.

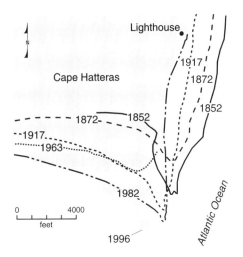

Figure 1.7 Historic shoreline changes at Cape Hatteras. The east-facing shoreline has eroded, and the south-facing shoreline has accreted, or built up.

crabs, oysters, shrimp, and fish have been closed because of pollution. Some of North Carolina's more crowded islands have already reached the point at which development had to be halted because there was no place to put sewage. Freshwater pollution is a particular problem after storms. During floods, raw sewage mixes with drinking water, making the water unsafe to drink.

3. *Environmental destruction.* The beach, the very environment we rush to the island to enjoy, is ultimately destroyed when the shoreline is overdeveloped. Scenic dunes, maritime forests, and marshes disappear. This alteration of the environment is the most striking aspect of New Jerseyization. Beach-saving devices work only temporarily at best. Where seawalls are built, the beach is eventually lost. Old beach resorts in Florida, South Carolina, and New Jersey would have no beaches at all if sand were not pumped in to maintain them. Such beach repairs are done at great and recurring cost to the taxpayers as well as the community.

4. *Reduced public access.* Private development inevitably reduces beach access to the public that foots the bills for beach repairs. In North Carolina, free access to the beach often is prohibited to all but adjacent property owners; others must pay access charges. Entire islands have been "gated," cutting off land routes to the public domain of the beach.

These New Jerseyization problems can occur in almost any developing area. Shoreline development is occurring extremely rapidly in North Carolina, for the most part on ephemeral, delicate islands that are subject to severe natural forces (fig. 1.7). Very little accessible shoreline remains in the state. The situation is aggravated by a unique political framework on the islands whereby only a few landowners—the year-round residents—have a local vote. Finally, the coastal zone of North Carolina historically has been an economically poor area so that development of almost any kind tends to be welcomed because of its presumed positive economic effect.

Lessons from the Sea: Rules for Management

Living by the Rules of the Sea (appendix C, ref. 45), a companion primer for the Living with the Shore books, is the culmination of years of work dedicated to helping people make informed choices about where or whether to live along our nation's coastlines. Based on more than 20 years of study and mapping of barrier islands, *Living by the Rules of the Sea* outlines coastal physical processes, describes risk assessment of potential property damage from coastal natural hazards, and provides a guide to property damage mitigation. Poststorm observations of the impacts of Hurricanes Gilbert (1988), Hugo (1989), Bob (1991), Andrew (1992), Emily (1993), Bertha (1996), and Fran (1996) and several winter storms helped define several key principles set forth in *Living by the Rules of the Sea*. We conclude chapter 1 and set the stage for the chapters that follow by restating these "lessons learned."

1. *Wide beaches protect property.* The more beach available to absorb and dissipate storm-wave energy, the greater the protection for developed areas.

2. *Dunes protect property.* Sand dunes are often referred to as the "barrier" in barrier island; they are nature's shock absorbers. The mass of dune sand may absorb and dissipate storm-wave energy, thus protecting buildings located behind them.

3. *Vegetation protects property.* Overwash penetration and storm damage are noticeably greater in areas where vegetation, especially maritime forest, has been removed for development. A stabilizing cover of dune grass, marsh grass, maritime forest, or even lawn and landscaping is important to each respective environment.

4. *Shore-perpendicular roads act as overwash and storm-surge ebb conduits.* Roads that are elevated and curved so they approach the beach at an oblique angle reduce the extent and amount of overwash and damage from ebb flow.

5. *Notches in dunes create overwash passes.* Notches cut in dunes for beach access, views, or construction sites are naturally exploited by waves and storm surge, and by storm-surge ebb flows. Notching can be avoided by constructing walkovers, elevating structures, and generally protecting frontal dunes. Existing notches can be filled or fitted with flood protection gates to restore the dune line.

6. *Overwash and storm-surge ebb are intensified when funneled by structures.* Storm surge that has overwashed an island and is returning to the sea is intensified when it is constricted to run between structures. The greater the density of buildings, the worse the problem. Extensive open space along the island front should be a community priority.
7. *Seawalls can protect buildings, but they also can cause narrowing of the beach in both a recreational and a protective sense.* Large seawalls do protect shorefront buildings from wave attack. But as a rule, seawalls also cause degradation and eventual loss of beaches.
8. *Setbacks protect.* Choosing a building site well back from the sea is the easiest and least costly method of protecting development.
9. *Elevation protects.* Elevation, whether achieved by natural land elevation, by infilling of a construction site, or by building on pilings, may be the single most important site-specific factor in reducing property damage.
10. *Proper development offers a degree of self-protection.* Development in areas where building codes are enforced and barrier island processes are allowed to operate is less susceptible to property damage.

These principles must be applied everywhere on the island and all together; they are inadequate if applied singly, only at one site or in one subenvironment. All is not lost in areas of dense or preexisting dangerous development, however. Mitigation plans can be put into effect to repair natural features such as dunes and vegetative cover as well as to upgrade buildings to code or better. Storms provide opportunities for mitigation improvements when old structures are destroyed, and you can count on nature to provide the storms!

2 Storms!

For many residents and visitors on the North Carolina coast, the passage of Hurricanes Bertha and Fran within a few weeks in 1996 was an unbelievable nightmare. For the real old-timers, however, it was nothing new. They had only to think back to 1954 when Hurricanes Carol and Edna brushed the North Carolina coast 11 days apart (fig. 2.1), and just five weeks before the great Hurricane Hazel struck! Or to 1955, when Hurricanes Connie and Diane crossed the coast only 5 days apart, and less than five weeks before Ione. In fact, hurricanes are an integral part of the North Carolina coastal experience—a truth unknown by some and long forgotten by most, and a vital lesson relearned during the fall of 1996. Bertha and Fran should do more than just shake our memories, however; they should provide us with a glimpse of the future.

Second to hurricanes in concentrated energy are winter storms, the so-called northeasters. The northeasters of 1988, 1991 (the Halloween Storm), and 1993 (the Storm of the Century) are still fresh in the minds of year-around coastal residents. Northeasters are associated with large, intense low-pressure systems that move offshore along the coast and are accompanied by winds and waves out of the northeast. Perhaps 50 such storms severe enough to cause coastal damage occurred along the North Carolina shoreline in the first 80 years of this century. Rarely does a year go by without a hurricane or northeaster eroding some part of the state's shores.

Hurricanes

The Physical Nature of Hurricanes

Hurricanes are responsible for most of the storm-related coastal property damage in the United States, although other types of storms, particularly northeasters along the East Coast and southwesters on the Gulf Coast, are important as well. The actual processes that affect the coastal zone are similar in all these storms, but they are most intense in hurricanes. During the relatively hurricane-free period from the 1960s until 1989, when Hurricane Hugo struck, most Atlantic coast residents and property owners had never experienced the full force of a severe storm. This lack of experience led to an apathetic disregard of the hurricane menace and increased development in high-hazard zones. Then, in rapid succession, Hurricanes Hugo, Bob, Andrew, Emily, Opal, Fran, and their smaller cousins arrived and blew away the apathy (fig. 2.2). The odds are evening out; time is not on the side of coastal development.

Each year on June 1 the official hurricane season begins. For the next five or six months conditions favorable to hurricane formation can develop over the tropical and subtropical waters of the Western Hemisphere. Early-season tropical cyclones form mostly in the Gulf of Mexico or the Carib-

Figure 2.1 Tracks of significant hurricanes of the 1950s that approached the vicinity of the North Carolina coast. The five numbered hurricane probability segments of North Carolina's coastline are keyed to table 2.1.

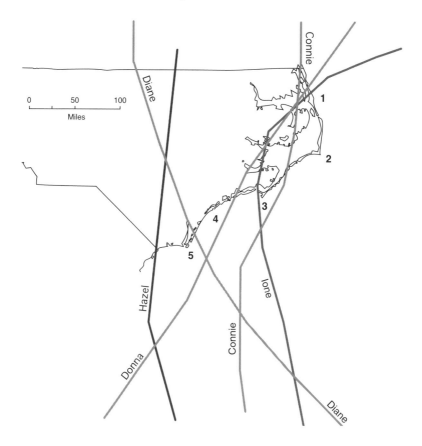

bean Sea, whose waters heat up faster than the Atlantic Ocean does. The monster hurricanes that strike the East and Gulf Coasts usually originate later in the season (August, September, and October) in the eastern Atlantic near the coast of Africa, and grow in size and intensity on their long, slow westward trek across the ocean. Once formed, the hurricane mass tracks into higher latitudes and may continue to grow in size and strength. The velocity of this northwestward movement can vary from nearly zero to greater than 60 miles per hour.

When a hurricane makes landfall, the destructive forces are at their maximum in the area to the right of the forward motion of the eye; but the entire landfall area will experience the high winds and storm surge generated by the storm. Even storms that pass by offshore can cause significant damage. A hurricane that tracks north to south along the shoreline, as Emily did in 1993, may create serious flooding and wave conditions along the shores of

Figure 2.2 Tracks of significant hurricanes that approached the North Carolina coast from 1970 through 1996.

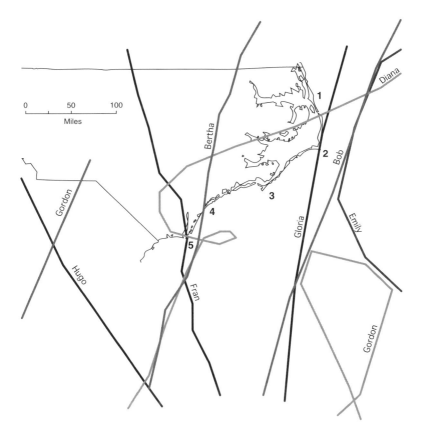

the sounds (appendix C, ref. 12). Do not allow the knowledge that you are to the left of the eye or that the eye is passing offshore to generate a false sense of security. Even in areas where the tidal range is small the damage can be severe, and if the hurricane comes at high tide, especially on a spring tide (the highest high tide), the effects of storm-surge flooding, waves, and overwash will be magnified.

Hurricane Probability and Rank

The probability that a hurricane will make landfall at any given point along the coast in any one year is low, and the probability of a great hurricane is even lower (table 2.1). Such low probabilities impart a false sense of security. Hurricane history tells us that such storms are almost a certainty during the lifetime of a coastal structure. For example, the National Hurricane Center's summary for North Carolina shows 25 hurricanes between 1900 and 1996, 11 of which were classified as "major" hurricanes! Furthermore, the occurrence of a great hurricane one year does not reduce the likelihood that a similar storm will strike the next year.

Death tolls from modern hurricanes have been greatly reduced thanks to National Weather Service warnings, radio and television communications, and evacuation plans. Nevertheless, we must not become complacent; our storm response can be improved. The hurricane watchers of the National Oceanic and Atmospheric Administration (NOAA) track hurricanes and provide advance warning that allows the evacuation of threatened coastal areas. Yet, as little as 9 to 12 hours of advance warning may be all that is possible, given the unpredictable turns a hurricane can take. Individuals need to be prepared, to know their community's storm-response plan, and to take appropriate action when the warning comes. Unsafe development and population growth that exceeds the capacity for safe evacuation must not be allowed.

Table 2.1 Probability of Hurricanes along the North Carolina Coast

Sector	% Probability of a Great Hurricane	% Probability of a Tropical Storm	% Probability of a Hurricane
1	4	9	8
2	8	18	11
3	–	14	5
4	2	7	6
5	2	13	6

Notes: Percentage probability indicates the number expected to occur over a 100-year period. Sectors 1–5 are shown on figure 2.1
Source: Ecological Determinants of Coastal Area Management, by F. Parker et al., 1976, Center for Urban and Regional Studies, University of North Carolina, Chapel Hill (p.16, table 2).

Portions of the North Carolina coast are now at population densities that stretch the system's capacity for storm evacuation. We must avoid exceeding that critical limit, as has happened in other coastal zones. A hurricane approaching the South Florida coast, for example, triggers the evacuation of tens of thousands of residents and visitors from the Florida Keys into the Miami metropolitan area. This influx adds to the metropolitan area population that must be evacuated or sheltered. Add to this the large number of retired, elderly, and special needs people living in the area, and the emergency preparedness and response teams will certainly be taxed to the limit. The situation is similar for the New Jersey shore, part of the South Carolina coastal zone, New England's urban corridor, and even the metropolitan New York City area.

One thing is certain from a review of storm history: storms do not occur in a regular pattern or with regular spacing. One big storm can follow on the heels of another, or several years may go by without a storm. The certainty is that several storms will affect a house or other coastal structure during its lifetime. If we are to prepare for such storms and reduce their impacts in terms of property losses and potential loss of life, we must first understand how barrier islands and storms interact and the potential for conflict between nature and development.

Table 2.2 The Saffir/Simpson Scale of Hurricane Intensity

| | Scale Number (Category) | | | | |
	1	2	3	4	5
Central pressure:					
millibars	980	979–965	964–945	944–920	919
inches of mercury	28.94	28.91–28.50	28.47–27.91	27.88–27.17	27.16
Winds:					
mph	74–95	96–110	111–130	131–155	>155
kph	119–153	154–177	179–209	211–249	>249
meters/ sec	32–42	42–49	50–57	58–68	>69
Surge:					
feet	4–5	6–8	9–12	13–18	>18
meters	1.2–1.5	1.8–2.4	2.7–3.7	4.0–5.5	>5.5
Damage	Minimal	Moderate	Extensive	Extreme	Catastrophic

Source: Developed by H. Saffir and R. H. Simpson (Simpson, 1974).

Ranking Hurricane Intensities

The National Weather Service has adopted the Saffir/Simpson scale (table 2.2) for communicating the strength of a hurricane to public safety officials of communities potentially in the storm's path. The scale ranks a storm on three variables: wind velocity, storm surge, and barometric pressure. Although hurricane paths are still unpredictable, the scale communicates quickly the nature of the storm and what to expect in terms of wind, waves, and flooding.

Do not be misled by the scale, however. Any hurricane is an awesome force of nature; the scale simply defines how bad is "bad." When the word comes to evacuate, *do it*. Wind velocities are subject to change, and the configuration of the coast may amplify the storm surge, so the storm's category rank can change. Don't gamble with your life or the lives of others.

We use the category 3 storm here to define the upper-level conditions to guide property damage mitigation. Category 4 and 5 storms will cause massive property damage or destruction in spite of mitigation efforts.

Hurricane History: A Stormy Past

In June 1586, Sir Francis Drake arrived off Roanoke Inlet with a shipload of supplies for the Roanoke Island colony. A violent storm—possibly a hurricane—arrived at the same time, and the supply ship was blown out to sea, forcing the colonists to abandon the settlement. This event marked the beginning of a lively record of hurricane history for North Carolina. Perhaps because of the way the coast protrudes into the hurricane alley of the Atlantic, this state has received more than its share of hurricane winds, waves, and floods—and considerably more than the neighboring states of Virginia and South Carolina (figs. 2.1, 2.2; tables 2.1, 2.3).

Historical records indicate that North Carolina has a major hurricane on an average of every two to three years (appendix C, ref. 9). Hurricane occurrence, however, is irregular. The 1950s brought considerable destruction by hurricanes, whereas the 1960s, 1970s, and 1980s were relatively quiet. The 1990s seem to have reversed the trend and gone back to a more active hurricane period. No one knows what is in store for the twenty-first century, but more Hazels and Andrews will certainly occur. It doesn't take a great hurricane to destroy property, however. Your house may be destroyed by a category 1 storm if it is poorly sited or poorly built, or if your neighbor's house is poorly built and the wreckage smashes into your house.

In the past, there was little advance warning of storms, and people were not always able to flee before a hurricane struck. That lack of warning time made the need for safe development imperative. Today, anyone on a North Carolina barrier island during a hurricane is almost certainly there by choice, but the need for safe development has not changed since the *Raleigh Observer* noted after the August 19, 1879, hurricane: "Men cannot build houses upon sand and expect to see them stand now any more than they could in the olden times. . . . Summer seaside resorts must be built high enough above the tide line to insure safety as well as patronage. People are wary of making hairbreadth escapes in seeking health and rest" (August 20, 1879).

Early Hurricanes
The effects of seventeenth-, eighteenth-, and even nineteenth-century storms on North Carolina islands are generally not well documented because so few people lived on the islands then. We do know that Diamond City at Cape Lookout was abandoned because of an 1899 hurricane that followed a path similar to the one taken by Hurricane Hazel in 1954 (fig. 2.1). The 1879 hurricane referred to in the *Raleigh Observer* quotation above also did great damage to Diamond City. Many accounts of early North Carolina

Table 2.3 Post-1950 Hurricanes That Affected the North Carolina Coast

Hurricane	Year	Saffir/Simpson Category	Landfall or closest passage
Barbara	1953	2	Cape Lookout Area
Carol	1954	2	Cape Hatteras area
Edna	1954	3	Off Cape Hatteras
Hazel	1954	4	N.C./S.C. border
Connie	1955	1	Outer Banks
Diane	1955	1	Carolina Beach
Ione	1955	2	Bogue Banks
Helene	1958	4	Off Cape Fear/Cape Lookout
Donna	1960	2	Topsail Island area
Ginger	1971	1	Bogue Banks
Diana	1984	2	Cape Fear area
Gloria	1985	2	Skirted Outer Banks
Charley	1986	1	Ocracoke
Hugo	1989	4	Charleston, S.C.
Bob	1991	2	Off Cape Hatteras
Emily	1993	3	Off Cape Hatteras
Gordon	1994	1	Off Cape Lookout
Felix	1995	1	Off Outer Banks
Bertha	1996	2	Topsail Island
Fran	1996	3	Cape Fear area

Notes: The Saffir/Simpson scale rank shown is for North Carolina, but some of these storms had a higher rank when they approached. Some of these storms passed offshore without making landfall. Hugo's rank of 4 was for its South Carolina landfall, but its circle of influence extended into southeastern North Carolina.
Source: Derived from the National Hurricane Center, NOAA, Internet World Wide Web site.

hurricanes are based on observations made by ship masters at sea. The severity of a hurricane was often judged by the number of vessels demasted or lost. Ocracoke accounts typically expressed storm severity in terms of the number of ships sunk or blown aground.

The year 1827, when at least 11 hurricanes came up "Hurricane Alley," may have been the most active hurricane season ever. The fourth storm of that series was named Calypso, after a sailing vessel that was miraculously saved by its desperate crew. Blown over on its side by the hurricane's winds, the ship righted itself and made landfall in the Cape Fear River. The "great" North Carolina hurricane of 1827 drove the two-year-old Cape Hatteras lightship ashore on Ocracoke Island. The captain, his wife, and their three daughters were rescued.

The July 12, 1842, hurricane, which apparently passed off the Outer Banks, was among the worst in Carolina history. Only one building in Portsmouth was undamaged, 28 vessels were blown aground near Ocracoke, 2 were sunk on Diamond Shoals with all hands lost, and many livestock were killed. Three months later, a bottle washed ashore in Bermuda with a note dated July 15, 1842, detailing the struggle of the schooner *Lexington* off Cape Hatteras. This scrap of paper was the last trace of the *Lexington* and her crew, victims of the full fury of the storm.

The origin of storms so terrifying and destructive has understandably puzzled many people over the centuries. In 1769 Governor William Tryon of North Carolina wrote a letter in which he attributed the hurricane of that year to "the effect of a blazing planet or star that was seen from both Newborn [*sic*] and here [Brunswick] rising in the east for several nights between the 26th and 31st of August." One hundred years later the problem of hurricane genesis was apparently still unsolved. The "Terrible Storm" of August 19, 1879, was regarded by some Beaufort residents as the wrathful judgment of God on the people of Beaufort for dancing on Sunday night.

Hurricane chroniclers note that old-timers always consider the most recent major storm "the worst ever." It's doubtful that storms really are increasing in intensity, but it is certain that as development increases, storm damage increases in proportion. For example, the hurricane that sank the passenger ship SS *Central America* in September 1857, taking more than 400 lives, swept ashore on Wrightsville Beach to destroy only large stands of oak trees. The hurricane that struck the beach in October 1899—of apparently less intensity—washed away 16 cottages and damaged all the others.

Recent Hurricanes

By the 1950s the stage had been set for even greater destruction. Following close on the heels of Hurricanes Carol and Edna, Hurricane Hazel (October 15, 1954), the most damaging hurricane ever to strike Wrightsville Beach, destroyed 89 buildings and damaged 530; only 20 buildings escaped intact. In August 1955 Hurricane Diane became the country's first "billion-dollar hurricane."

After suffering through nine hurricanes between 1953 and 1960, the waters off North Carolina remained relatively quiet through the early 1990s, with a few exceptions. Diana (1984) approached the coast as a category 4 hurricane, but stalled and weakened (fig. 2.2, table 2.3). Eventually, after sitting off Cape Fear for a full day, Diana made landfall as a category 1 hurricane. In 1985 another strong storm approached and threatened the coast. Fortunately for Carolina coastal residents, Hurricane Gloria's full wrath was saved for New England; the storm veered off to the north after only a glancing blow to North Carolina (fig. 2.2). Gloria made landfall over Cape Hatteras and continued north along the Outer Banks, keeping its strongest winds offshore.

One of the twentieth century's most powerful storms appeared on the horizon in 1989: Hurricane Hugo. Despite making its landfall to the south, near Charleston, South Carolina, Hugo's long arms gave a one-two punch of destruction to North Carolina, with waves eroding the beaches of southern Brunswick County and wind damage as far inland as Charlotte and on into the Appalachian Mountains. Approximately 120 homes were destroyed on the Brunswick County beaches, and an estimated $75 million in damage occurred throughout the county—this from a storm that made landfall some 115 miles to the southwest (appendix C, ref. 9). Perhaps the hardest hit area in North Carolina was Charlotte. Winds in excess of 85 miles per hour blew through the Queen City, bringing down 80,000 trees and leaving some residents without power for more than two weeks. All told, Hugo cost the Tar Heel State $1 billion. And Hugo was only a warm-up!

The first real scare for the North Carolina coast in the 1990s was Hurricane Bob in 1991, but Bob followed the offshore storm track. Two years later, Hurricane Emily stayed offshore, too, although not without strong effect. Packing winds of nearly 115 miles per hour, Emily charged toward the Outer Banks. When its center was only 24 miles off Cape Hatteras, Emily veered to the north and then northeast and drifted out into the Atlantic Ocean, the eye having never crossed land. As a result, the highest recorded wind gust at Buxton Weather Station was 98 miles per hour; the highest sustained wind recorded at the station was 62 miles per hour.

Although the Outer Banks were spared the worst of Hurricane Emily, close to $13 million in damages was reported along the coast, and an estimated $10 million in tourist revenue was lost as a result of the storm's approach just before the Labor Day weekend. Of particular interest was the large amount of flooding from Pamlico Sound. Approximately 10 feet of surge covered the Buxton area as water piled up in the "elbow" of Cape

Hatteras (appendix C, ref. 12). There were reports that small harbors and marinas from Avon to Rodanthe were dry because Emily's winds had forced the water south to Buxton. In some places N.C. Highway 12 was covered with as much as 6 feet of water, nearly breaching the dunes from the sound side! Parts of Highway 12 north of Rodanthe were flooded after Atlantic floodwaters breached the dunes.

With recent images of the destruction caused by Hurricane Andrew in South Florida fresh in their minds, almost everyone evacuated the Outer Banks as Emily approached. The estimated 1,000 people who stayed on Hatteras Island during the storm (appendix C, ref. 9) emerged with a sense of victory, and "I survived Hurricane Emily" T-shirts and bumper stickers became hot items. In fact, those who stayed did *not* survive the strong category 3 Hurricane Emily; they witnessed only the fringe of Emily's tame side. Had a cold front from the west arrived a few hours later, Emily would have struck the Outer Banks in full force, and the shrouds for those who stayed could have read "I was an idiot."

A rare late November hurricane, Gordon, teased the residents of Bogue Banks in 1994. Gordon danced in circles off Cape Lookout for a day as a category 1 hurricane, causing minor erosion along Bogue Banks before heading back out to sea. Although Gordon did little more than remind North Carolina residents how fickle and unpredictable hurricanes can be, it did claim an estimated 1,000 lives a week before in Haiti from mudslides generated by its rains.

One of the most active hurricane seasons on record followed in 1995. Nineteen named storms formed; 11 of them reached hurricane stage. Once again, however, North Carolina was spared. The most significant threat came in mid-August when Felix, charging toward Bermuda, suddenly veered to the west and zeroed in on the Outer Banks. But just 190 miles off the coast Felix turned north, then showed its unpredictable nature again by stalling off Nags Head before tearing off to the northeast.

A meteorologist will tell you that the 1996 hurricane season was less active than the 1995 season. There were only 12 named storms, 8 of which became hurricanes. But as far as the coastal residents in North Carolina are concerned, 22 years worth of hurricanes were packed into only 2 hurricanes in 1996, Bertha and Fran!

Hurricane Bertha. Hurricane Bertha struck the southern North Carolina coast on July 12, 1996, as a category 2 storm. It was an early-season storm, but that was not unusual in the state's history. The hurricane had sustained winds of approximately 105 miles per hour, and gusts up to 144 miles per hour. Significant wind and water damage was reported from Wrightsville Beach to Topsail Island, and the early assessment indicated $60 million in damage to houses and other structures, and $150 million in agricultural

Figure 2.3 Aerial view of North Topsail Beach showing one of the new inlets formed during Hurricane Fran. Notice how narrow, low, and lightly vegetated the island is. These characteristics make Topsail Island one of the least desirable places in North Carolina for coastal development. Fran confirmed this evaluation.

losses. Crop loss was severe because of the high winds and heavy rainfall. The loss or narrowing of dunes (e.g., on Figure Eight Island and Topsail Island) caused by Bertha set the stage for increased overwash, flooding, and associated destruction from Hurricane Fran.

Bertha shocked coastal residents unaware of the real power of a hurricane. It was the first direct hit on North Carolina in quite some time (table 2.3), and the first for Topsail Island since Hurricane Donna in 1960 (figs. 2.1, 2.2). Most buildings escaped with damaged roofs and water damage. A few houses were lost, many beach access walkways were destroyed, and roads on North Topsail Beach were overwashed and destroyed.

Hurricane Fran. Hurricane Fran, a category 3 hurricane, struck the same area hit by Bertha with sustained winds of about 115 miles per hour and gusts to at least 125 miles per hour. The hurricane made landfall over Cape Fear at approximately 9:00 P.M. on September 5, 1996, expending its greatest energy in the northeast quadrant of the storm. The greatest property loss in the coastal zone occurred from Cape Fear northward to Topsail Island. The storm surge reached a maximum of 12 to 14 feet, and there was extensive overwash and flooding on the shore. Dunes were destroyed, seawalls overtopped, and swash channels cut, while waves and currents smashed and undercut buildings. The wind damage was extensive—far greater than Bertha's, even though Fran's wind speeds were not much higher.

Loss of its beach sand increases a community's vulnerability to storms. Because their dune defenses had been weakened by Bertha only a few weeks before, parts of Topsail Island and Carolina Beach were literally leveled by Fran. Hardest hit were the low-lying communities of Surf City and North Topsail Beach. Along some stretches in this area houses were completely missing; the returning storm surge scoured through houses and pavement, forming inlets (fig. 2.3), and some houses were pushed into the marsh. Overwash sand covered the islands—up to mailbox height in some locations. Kure Beach and Carolina Beach also lost buildings, particularly those not built on pilings.

The protective role of the heavily nourished beach at Wrightsville Beach during Fran is unclear. Wrightsville Beach sustained less damage than neighboring islands, but that may have been attributable more to storm wind-field variability than to the mitigating effects of beach replenishment.

Fran finished off the dune removal begun by Bertha on Figure Eight Island, with resulting undermining of buildings by waves and extensive overwashing of the island. Again, one result of this damage is the island's increased vulnerability to future storms.

Like Hugo in 1989, Fran's fury was felt far inland as well. Its winds struck hard in the Raleigh-Durham area and then continued northward. As a tropical storm Fran generated flooding in Virginia, West Virginia, Maryland, and Pennsylvania. Early estimates of property damage were more than $4.1 billion in North Carolina alone, and there was an associated death toll of 23. Consider these figures, and then consider that Fran, the most powerful storm to strike the North Carolina coast directly since Hurricane Hazel in 1954, was only a category 3 hurricane. Hazel was a major category 4 hurricane, much more powerful than Fran. The message to those who rebuild and expand development on barrier islands seems obvious. Is the high value of coastal property real or artificial?

Northeasters and Winter Storms

Northeasters occur far more frequently than hurricanes. On average, there are about 30 such storms each year, although only a few affect North Carolina. Northeasters are much larger and longer lasting than hurricanes. A typical hurricane is 300 to 400 miles in diameter, with the greatest winds concentrated around an eye wall 50 to 60 miles in diameter. A hurricane's exposure to any given area of the coast is usually measured in hours. Winter storms are not so concentrated. A northeaster is commonly spread over a thousand miles and usually hugs the Atlantic seaboard for days.

Northeasters typically form as low-pressure cells over coastal areas where there is a large difference between air temperatures—cold over the land and relatively warm over the water (appendix C, refs. 14, 15). The waters off the

Carolinas are one of the major breeding grounds for big northeasters because this area lies close to the winter track of the polar jet stream. The influence of fast, high-level winds on the formation of northeasters helps distinguish these storms from hurricanes.

Northeasters develop a counterclockwise rotating air circulation resulting in winds that blow onto the east coast from out of the northeast when the storm center is out over the Atlantic, hence the name. Most often these cells track north up the Atlantic seaboard, gaining strength from the relatively warm ocean waters. The development of a destructive winter storm requires the presence of a strong, stable high-pressure system over eastern Canada. The high pressure prevents the storm from moving quickly to the north or northeast, and holds it off the Atlantic coast for a long period, often several days. The longer the storm remains offshore, the more powerful it can become. Storm surge and waves are the most destructive forces generated by northeasters.

Ranking Northeasters

The Dolan/Davis scale, an intensity scale for U.S. Atlantic coast northeasters similar to the Saffir/Simpson scale for hurricanes, is based not on wind velocity but on the size of the waves and the duration of the storm, and is expressed in terms of intensity of property damage (appendix C, ref. 14; see table 2.4). Since the early 1980s, an average of about two dozen northeasters have occurred each year along the U.S. Atlantic coast. Since 1960, there have been eight class 5 northeasters.

Northeasters in North Carolina

Perhaps we remember events, happy or sad, better if they are associated with a celebration, religious holiday, or anniversary. Thus, many coastal residents remember the 1987 New Year's Day Storm, just as many recall the Thanksgiving Day Storm and the Halloween northeaster of 1991. A large storm during December 1992 that didn't fall on a day of particular note was designated "the No-Name Storm."

The most destructive coastal northeaster of the twentieth century in the United States was the 1962 Ash Wednesday Storm, a class 5 storm. It struck during spring tides, resulting in extreme storm surge, and persisted over five high tides. From the Carolinas to New York, hundreds of houses were damaged or destroyed, new inlets breached, seawalls and groins destroyed, and ships run aground (fig. 2.4). Some damage occurred to every beachfront community between southern Massachusetts and northern Florida. The beach loss caused by the 1962 storm was so severe that the U.S. Army Corps of Engineers entered the arena of beach replenishment.

Here in North Carolina, the northern Outer Banks were subjected to high winds and waves for nearly two days. Large sections of Nags Head, Kitty Hawk, and Kill Devil Hills were flooded and overwashed. Many residents had been unaware of the impending storm and had to make heroic escapes from the oncoming water. To make matters worse, Jigsaw Road formed a breach across the island, cutting off escape for many residents. David Stick's book, *Ash Wednesday Storm, March 1962* (appendix C, ref. 16), provides an excellent description of the storm's havoc on our shores.

The northeaster/southwester of March 1993 known as the Storm of the Century was not a record-breaking coastal storm, but its damage was widespread: there was storm surge and wave erosion in the Florida Panhandle, record-breaking snow cover inland along the East Coast, and cosmetic but costly wind damage to coastal buildings. Communities such as Sunset Beach and Topsail Beach were littered with the shingles from stripped roofs, and property owners scrambled to get tarpaulins over their bare roofs to

Table 2.4 The Dolan/Davis Northeaster Intensity Scale

	Storm Class		
Damage	1 (weak)	2 (moderate)	3 (significant)
Beach erosion	Minor changes	Modest: confined to lower beach	Erosion extends across entire beach
Beach recovery	Full and usually immediate	Full	Usually recovery is over a considerable time (months)
Dune erosion	None	None	Can be significant
Dune breaching	No	No	No
Overwash	No	No	On low-profile beaches
Inlet formation	No	No	No
Property damage	No	Minor, local	Loss of many structures at local scale

Source: Davis and Dolan, 1993

prevent water damage from the storm's rains. The storm also tore fiberglass insulation out from underneath elevated homes, covering parts of some islands with a snowlike blanket of fluff.

Coastal Storm Processes

Storms are natural forces that include wind, waves, coastal and inlet currents, storm-surge flooding, and storm-surge flood and ebb currents. They often result in environmental impact and property damage. Wind, waves, and rising water (storm surge) account for most of the damage. Currents are responsible for moving vast amounts of sediment during storms.

Storm surge, the onshore movement of water, causes flooding and may induce scouring currents around and behind structures. The rising water level allows the zone of wave attack to move inland, washing sediments onto the land. Storm-surge ebb, or the seaward return of storm surge, is a less familiar storm process that may erode new inlets and contribute to the overall erosional damage.

4 (severe)	5 (extreme)
Severe beach erosion and recession	Extreme beach erosion (up to 50 m in places)
Recovery seldom total	Permanent and clearly noticeable changes
Severe dune erosion or destruction	Dunes destroyed over extensive areas
Where beach is narrow	Widespread
On low-profile beaches	Massive in sheets and channels
Occasionally	Common
Loss of structures at community level	Extensive regional scale: millions of dollars

Figure 2.4 Buxton Inlet was opened by the Ash Wednesday, 1962, northeaster just north of the Cape Hatteras Lighthouse, which is visible in the distance. The inlet was briefly bridged before being filled in by the N.C. Department of Transportation.

Natural Processes: Energy in Motion

Storm processes rarely act separately. That is, wind, waves, and currents are all active at the same time and combine to form secondary processes. For example, storm surge is formed by several processes acting together, any one of which may be dominant during any given storm or for a given period during a storm: wind pushes water toward shore, waves push water toward shore, low pressure allows the sea surface to dome, and the rotating winds of a hurricane actually cause the shallow water near shore to spiral higher.

Wind
The most common of the storm processes that damage buildings is wind, either through its direct impact on structures or through missiling—wind transport of debris. Strong winds can uproot and knock over trees, defoliate vegetation, blow down shrubs and grasses, and damage leaves directly either by blasting them with airborne sand or by carrying damaging salt spray inland. The same salt-spray pruning effect that produces the nearshore sloping profile of maritime vegetation will kill or damage inland vegetation that is not salt tolerant. Strong winds are also responsible for transporting sediment on and off islands.

Storm Waves

Property can be damaged by direct wave attack on structures or by ramrodding, the pummeling of structures with floating debris (fig. 2.5). Probably the only type of buildings capable of surviving direct wave assault unscathed are concrete pillboxes. Even lighthouses have been known to topple under wave attack. Waves are also responsible for shoreline erosion (on both lagoon shores and ocean shores), dune erosion, overwash, and destruction of vegetation.

Storm Surge

The local rise in sea level caused directly by storms extends the zone of wave impact inland and causes flooding. Storm surge is technically defined as "the superelevation of the still-water surface that results from the transport and circulation of water induced by wind stresses and pressure gradients in an atmospheric storm" (appendix C, ref. 8). "Pressure gradient" refers to the lowered atmospheric pressure in storms which by itself can cause a rise in sea level. Storm-surge impacts include flooding, floating structures off their foundations, and floating debris inland, sometimes with ramrod force (fig. 2.5). The initial water flow over and around obstructions (e.g., pilings) may cause scouring and sediment transport. The rising water also elevates waves and increases their landward incursion, resulting in a wider zone of destructive impact. Waves combined with storm surge wash beach sand onto islands, forming "overwash" deposits. Saltwater flooding kills or damages inland plants.

Figure 2.5 Houses on Topsail Island were carried off their foundations (pilings) and ramrodded into adjacent residences during Hurricane Fran in 1996. A barrier island dweller must be concerned with the construction quality of *adjacent* buildings, too!

Figure 2.6 One of several breaches formed by Hurricane Fran across North Topsail Beach. Such channels or temporary inlets sever escape routes and make post-storm access difficult.

Currents

Storm-generated currents transport water, sediment, and storm debris both parallel with and perpendicular to the coast. Waves usually approach the coast at an angle; on breaking, they create a current moving parallel to the shore called the *longshore current.* Currents can move sediment (and storm debris such as trees, sand fencing, and dune crossovers) long distances. The loss may be temporary or permanent, depending on many other factors. In some cases storms can intensify *rip currents,* making conditions even more dangerous for those foolhardy enough to surf or swim during storms.

Changes in channel positions during storms may cause erosion of, or deposition on, adjacent islands. Mason Inlet, for example, has historically migrated to the south, with periodic updrift relocation during storms. Other inlets, such as Bogue Inlet, demonstrate relocation of the main inlet channel position within the tidal delta rather than relocation of the entire inlet.

Storm-Surge Ebb

The storm-surge water that "piles up" on land eventually flows back to sea, either by the force of gravity alone or driven by offshore-blowing winds, generating an erosive ebb current. This type of current occurs while the storm is moving out of the area or diminishing. Storm-surge ebb can cause an existing inlet to change shape, create a new inlet, scour shallow cross-island channels (breaches), transport storm debris (including houses) off-shore, and cause permanent removal of sand from the beach-dune system to deeper offshore waters (figs. 2.6, 2.7). After Fran, seaward-directed sediment lobes were present offshore of Topsail Island, a clear indication of seaward-flowing storm currents.

Human Modification of the Coast

Construction in the coastal zone may enhance or otherwise alter natural processes and their resulting impacts. Roads and beach access paths perpendicular to the shore that penetrate the dune line may become overwash passes or focal points for storm-surge flood or ebb currents. Seawalls may redistribute wave energy or obstruct sediment movement. Jetties may block great volumes of sand from being transported along the coast, resulting in deposition of sand and beach widening on their updrift side and a long-term sand deficit and erosion on their downdrift side. Ground-level houses and closed-in ground floors of houses on stilts may obstruct the passage of

Figure 2.7 Wind and storm surge from a coast-parallel hurricane. (A) The hurricane arrives and storm surge is the dominant process. (B) The hurricane moves past, the winds reverse, and storm-surge ebb becomes dominant. Modified from "Geomorphic Expression of Former Inlets along the Outer Banks of North Carolina," by J. J. Fisher (master's thesis, University of North Carolina at Chapel Hill, 1962).

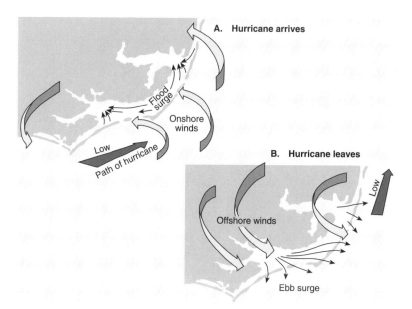

overwash sand, which is then lost to front-side erosion. If the vegetation cover has been removed, erosion by wind or water may occur.

In order to avoid bumping heads with nature it is important that we understand both natural processes and the overall dynamics of barrier islands.

3 Barrier Islands: Fast-Moving Property

Ringing almost every gently sloping coast in the world are narrow strips of sand called barrier islands. These fascinating islands, capable of actually migrating landward when the sea level rises, are both the most dynamic and the most sought-after real estate in the world. North Carolina is blessed with a beautiful, extensive set of barrier islands protecting its mainland shore.

By definition, barrier islands are elongate bodies of sand bounded on either end by inlets that allow salt and fresh water to flow into and out of the estuary behind the island. In front of, or seaward, of the island is the shoreface, which dips steeply out to a depth of 30 or 40 feet, at which point the slope of the continental shelf becomes more gentle.

Barrier islands exist on many coasts. Barrier island chains (three or more islands) are found in such diverse locations as the North Sea coast of Holland, Germany, and southern Denmark; Colombia's Pacific coast; the Alaskan and Siberian Arctic coast; the east coast of Australia; the southern coast of China; and locally along the Portuguese, Brazilian, and African coasts. But the grandest chain of all is the one along the eastern and southern coasts of North America. It extends almost without interruption from the South Shore of Long Island, New York, to South Florida, and from western Florida to northern Mexico.

Most barrier islands are open-ocean features, although in rare instances they can form in large, "protected" bodies of water. One such barrier island in North Carolina is Cedar Island, which faces a wide expanse of Pamlico Sound. When northeast winds blow, the island is buffeted by large waves capable of moving sand and constructing an island.

All barrier islands form in response to four common factors: a rising sea level, a large sand supply, a gently sloping coastal plain, and sufficient wave energy to move sand. All four requirements must be met before islands will form. The Big Bend coast of Florida known as Apalachee Bay, along the

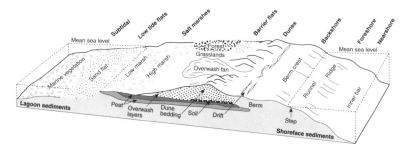

Figure 3.1 Typical barrier island cross section. Environments change quickly both laterally and across the island, and storm impacts vary between environments. Adapted from work by Paul Godfrey.

northeastern corner of the Gulf of Mexico, has no barrier islands. This shoreline reach has a gentle mainland coast, plenty of sand, and a rising sea level, but because it is missing the wave energy component it has no barrier islands. The continental shelf is so broad and slopes so gently here that wave energy is dampened and the shoreline receives only small waves.

As soon as an island forms, it immediately begins to migrate and change its shape, vegetation, and landforms (fig. 3.1). Different islands evolve in different ways and at different rates. No two islands are the same. Understanding island evolution mechanisms is particularly important for those interested in living in harmony with these ephemeral, dynamic features. We must understand island processes if we are to prevent damage to the structures we build there.

The Origin of Barrier Islands

In order to understand how North Carolina's barrier islands formed, it is first necessary to review the recent history of sea level changes caused by the ice ages. Because large amounts of water have been alternately tied up in and released from the massive glacial icecaps (e.g., Greenland and Antarctica), the sea level has gone up and down at an amazing rate since the ice ages began about 2 million years ago. The last such rise in sea level, which is known as the Holocene transgression, began about 10,000 years ago (fig. 3.2) and until 5,000 years ago probably averaged a rise of 3 to 4 feet per century. At the beginning of the sea level rise, the sea level was 300 to 400 feet below its present level, and the shoreline was out beyond the continental shelf edge, lapping onto the continental slope.

When ice age glaciers covered large areas of land in the higher latitudes, the land area of North Carolina was much larger than it is at present. A vast forest with marshes and river valleys stretched across what is now the submerged continental shelf (fig. 3.3). As the sea level rose, the shoreline retreated inland, gradually flooding and removing the forest.

When the sea first began to rise, seawater flooded the river valleys, and a formerly straight shoreline (fig. 3.4A) became a very sinuous one (fig. 3.4B). The indentations thus formed are today's estuaries, and their formation is the *raison d'être* for barrier islands. Nature abhors a crooked ocean shoreline, and barrier islands are the ocean's way of straightening out the shore.

The straightening begins to occur as waves attack the upland divides between the now-flooded river valleys. The waves' attack on these protruding headlands (fig. 3.4B, C) produces sand, which forms into spits that extend into and across the mouths of the former river valleys. These spits gain in elevation as dunes are formed from sand blown in from the beach or washed in by storm waves. Along comes a big storm, the spit is breached, new inlets form, and a chain of three or more islands has been formed between the ocean and the sound (fig. 3.4D).

Barrier Island Evolution

Once a barrier island chain is formed, a new set of natural processes takes over, and the islands begin to move landward in response to the rising sea level. This process, called *island migration,* is a remarkable mechanism by which the islands avoid being drowned by the encroaching sea. Needless to say, if the barrier islands are to remain islands, the mainland shoreline they are approaching must move back too, a process achieved through flooding and shoreline erosion. Viewed in this context, the narrow sand islands on which we build our beach cottages are indeed transitory and ephemeral features.

After their initial formation at the edge of the continental shelf during the low stand of sea level, the barrier islands began to migrate across the continental shelf toward their present locations. The rate of sea level rise

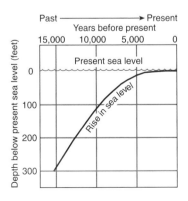

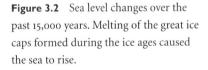

Figure 3.2 Sea level changes over the past 15,000 years. Melting of the great ice caps formed during the ice ages caused the sea to rise.

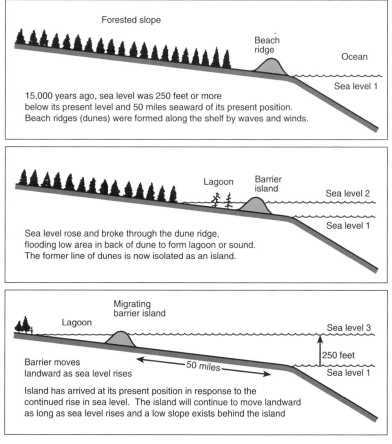

Figure 3.3 Barrier island formation and migration across the continental shelf in response to a rising sea level.

varied significantly over time, as did the nature of the islands. When the sea level was rising rapidly, the islands may have been only small spits; indeed, they may have been missing altogether for some periods. Off Georgia, for example, where the sand supply is relatively large, the islands may have been present throughout the sea level rise. Off Onslow Bay, between Cape Lookout and Cape Fear, the sand supply is relatively small and the islands probably were absent at times during the sea level rise.

The rate of island migration during the last 10,000 years has been a function of the slope of the inundated land and the rate of sea level rise. Typically the lower Coastal Plain of North Carolina has a slope in the neighborhood of 1 to 2,000 (expressed as vertical change over horizontal distance). This means that for every foot of sea level rise, the amount of shoreline retreat theoretically should be about 2,000 feet (fig. 3.5)!

Do you want to prove to yourself that North Carolina's barrier islands are migrating? The next time you visit one, go to the ocean-side beach and look at the seashells. On most North Carolina beaches you will find the shells of oysters, clams, or snails that once lived in the estuary behind the barrier island. How did shells from the estuary get to the ocean side of the island? The answer is quite simple: the island migrated across the estuary, and open-ocean waves attacking and breaking up the old estuary sands and muds, now exposed on the shoreface, threw the shells up onto the beach. Estuarine oyster shells found on Shackleford Banks beach have been radio-carbon-dated at 7,000 years old. Occasionally, salt marsh peats that formed in back of the islands at some earlier time are exposed on their ocean-side beaches (e.g., on Topsail Island) after storms. Tree stumps exposed on beaches (e.g., on Topsail Island, Caswell Beach, the Outer Banks) are the remains of forests that once grew well inland from the beach (fig 3.6).

Every barrier island is unique. Each island responds in a different fashion and at a different rate to its surrounding oceanic environment. The reasons for this variability include differences in the amount or type of sand on the island's surface, the island's orientation, the type and size of the waves that strike the beach, and the nature of the rocks underlying the barrier island. This uniqueness is a particularly important consideration for those who choose to live on these dynamic ribbons of sand. Unfortunately, those who

Figure 3.4 Barrier island formation during a rising sea level. (A) Straight coast forms during lower sea level. (B) Sea level rises and floods valleys on land, transforming a straight coast into a sinuous coast. (C) Sand eroded from preexisting ridges forms spits. (D) The spits are breached by storms, making them into islands.

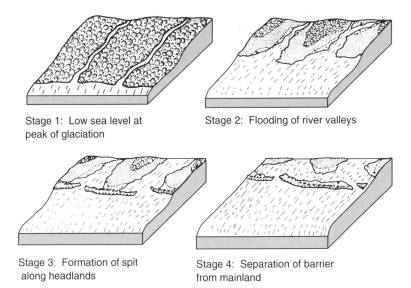

Stage 1: Low sea level at peak of glaciation

Stage 2: Flooding of river valleys

Stage 3: Formation of spit along headlands

Stage 4: Separation of barrier from mainland

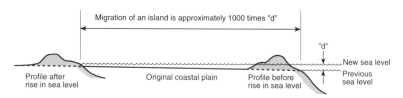

Figure 3.5 Ratio of horizontal barrier island migration to the vertical sea level rise. A very small vertical increase in sea level will lead to a much larger horizontal island migration because the slope of the land surface is very gentle.

set the price of real estate on barrier islands do not recognize these differences.

Even adjacent barrier islands can be enormously different. A striking example in North Carolina is the contrast between Core Banks and Shackleford Banks, two adjacent islands that form the Cape Lookout National Seashore. Shackleford, west of Cape Lookout, is a high, forested island with extensive dune formation. Core Banks, north of and contiguous with Cape Lookout, is a low, narrow island with almost no dunes that is overwashed by even minor storms. Both are healthy islands, but each exists under different conditions. The dominant wind directions on both Shackleford and Core Banks are approximately north or south. Because Core Banks is oriented north and south, the wind usually blows sand brought to the beach by fair-weather waves up or down the length of the island. Shackleford Banks, in contrast, is oriented east and west. The dominant winds at least part of the year blow beach sand into the island, building up dunes and increasing the height and width of the island.

On Masonboro Island south of Wrightsville Beach, shrubs take years to become established on overwash fans created by storms. Plants grow slowly there because the sand washed across Masonboro Island by storms has a coarse grain size and doesn't hold water well. On nearby Figure Eight Island, in contrast, the sand is finer grained and retains water better, and vegetation grows much faster. Even the parts of a single island may differ in their origins and dynamics. For example, the Oak Island complex consists of a remnant of an earlier barrier island that is now heavily forested, and a more recently formed island front that is more lightly vegetated.

Rolling Sandbars: How Islands Migrate

In order for an island to migrate, four things must happen:

1. The front (ocean) side must move landward via shoreline retreat.
2. The back (sound) side must move landward by landward growth (island widening).

3. The island must continually build up in order to maintain its elevation above a rising sea level.
4. The mainland shoreline must retreat to keep pace with the island's migration.

The best place in North Carolina to see all of these things happening—and thus true island migration—is Masonboro Island. Assateague Island, Maryland, and Capers Island, South Carolina, also are migrating at present.

Island Migration Step 1: Retreat of the Front Side

The beach moves back for a number of reasons, one of them being the current sea level rise of about 1 foot per century. This sea level rise is a principal worldwide cause of beach erosion, although other local factors such as lack of sand supply from rivers may also be responsible. Along specific shoreline segments, humans are to blame for a great deal of the shoreline retreat in recent decades. The shoreline of the Nile Delta in Egypt, for example, is eroding at an unprecedented rate because the Aswan Dam on the Nile River cuts off the supply of new beach sand. Similarly, dams on the Rio Grande and the Brazos River are cutting off the sand supply to the barrier islands off the coast of Texas and causing them to rapidly erode. Loss of Columbia River sands for the same reason is causing the barrier spits of Oregon and Washington to retreat. Construction of seawalls, groins, and offshore breakwaters, and deepening of channels within inlets are all significant worldwide

Figure 3.6 A 1987 photo of Long Beach showing a large outcrop of salt marsh mud and, in the background, tree stumps. These features are strong indicators of very rapid erosion.

contributors to sand supply reduction leading to shoreline erosion (see chapter 5).

Island Migration Step 2: Sound-Side Widening

The back, or sound, sides of North Carolina's islands widen by two mechanisms: tidal delta incorporation and overwash.

Tidal deltas are the bodies of sand that form outside (seaward) and inside (landward) an inlet. The open-ocean tidal delta is called the *ebb delta*; the tidal delta inside the sound is the *flood delta* (fig. 3.7). When a new inlet forms, usually by water pouring from the estuary into the ocean in response to a major storm surge, these tidal sand bodies build up (the sand is moved primarily by tidal currents). If the inlet closes or migrates away, the flood-tidal delta eventually becomes part of the island (fig. 3.7). As the inlet mi-

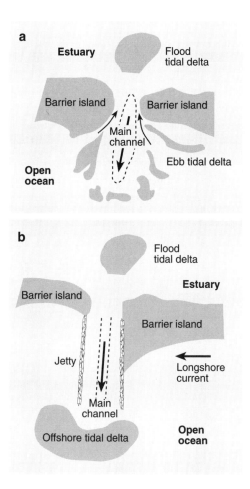

Figure 3.7 Flood-tidal and ebb-tidal deltas are found at all barrier island inlets. These are bodies of sand forced into and out of the inlet by tidal currents. Flood-tidal deltas, the bodies of sand formed in the estuary side of the inlet, are often incorporated into the island once the inlet closes. (A) Natural ebb-tidal deltas are capable of transporting sand across the inlet from one island to the next. (B) The ebb-tidal delta moves offshore when jetties are built to improve navigation, and its sand is lost forever to the island.

grates, sand continues to pour into the estuary, and a series of new flood-tidal deltas form along the entire zone of inlet migration. In this way the island is widened over the full distance the inlet shifted. The migration of Oregon Inlet has created just such a situation. At least a three-mile section of the island to the north has been widened by tidal delta incorporation since the inlet opened in 1846.

Tidal delta incorporation widens only a portion of an island. Other portions migrate landward via storm overwash, a mechanism at work today on Masonboro Island. Overwash sand widens an island when it is carried completely across the island and deposited in the sound, an event that occurs several times a year on Masonboro, which no longer has dunes to block the overwash. The island is only a few tens of yards wide, so sand is easily carried across it and into the sound. Core Banks is another narrow, overwash-dominated island.

Most North Carolina islands are too wide for the overwash migration mechanism to work as it does on Masonboro. These islands are currently eroding rather than widening on the sound side. Some geologists believe such island narrowing is a precursor to renewed migration. Is your island getting ready to migrate?

Island Migration Step 3: The Island Maintains Its Elevation during Migration

How does a migrating island retain its elevation as the sea level rises and the island moves toward the mainland? Two processes are involved: dune formation and overwash fan deposition. Both processes obtain their sand from the beach. In fact, every grain of sand on an island was on the beach at some point in its history.

Dunes are formed by the wind. If a sufficiently large supply of sand comes to the beach, pushed up by the waves from the continental shelf, a high-elevation island may form. Good examples are Bogue Banks and the Nags Head–Kill Devil Hills area. Unfortunately, islands are sometimes "scalped" when developers remove dunes or reduce their elevation.

The reason why dunes do not form on islands with low elevation is the poor sand supply from the adjacent shoreface. Topsail Island is a good example of this type of barrier island (see below).

Island Migration Step 4: Mainland Shoreline also Retreats

The water level of back-barrier sounds and estuary mouths is essentially that of sea level. As sea level rises, the level of the sound rises, flooding the mainland shore. The low slope of the North Carolina Coastal Plain allows a significant landward retreat of the mainland shore for even a slight rise in sea level (fig. 3.5). Comparison of historic maps of the land areas behind Albemarle and Pamlico Sounds shows land loss that can be accounted for by the sea level rise since the time of English colonization. Under natural conditions the fringing marsh or swamp forest will shift landward, but where the mainland coast is developed, the width of the marsh will be reduced, and erosion problems similar to the open-ocean shore develop. The typical response is to bulkhead the shoreline. Although this mainland shore retreat receives less attention, the results of human activities are the same: loss of habitat and more property at risk.

The Role of the Shoreface in Barrier Island Evolution

The shoreface plays a major role in determining barrier island behavior. The North Carolina shoreface (fig. 3.1) is a relatively steep surface extending from the shoreline to the innermost continental shelf at a depth of 30 to 40 feet. In effect, the shoreface is the active beach. The portion of the beach we walk on is really only the tip of the zone of active sand movement. Among other things, the rate of shoreline retreat, the way an island responds and recovers from a storm, the size of the dunes, and even the size of the island are all greatly affected by the nature of the shoreface.

The nature of the shoreface is a central element in the models engineers use to predict beach behavior. Most coastal engineers assume that all shorefaces are composed of a loose pile of sand that forms a predictable "profile of equilibrium." In this view, the shoreface has a profile produced entirely by ocean waves; the shape of the shoreface is determined by the grain size of the sand. This simplistic concept is the basis for the design of most coastal engineering projects (such as beach nourishment)—and the

	Holocene	
Quaternary		0.01 Ma
	Pleistocene	
		2 Ma
	Pliocene	
		5 Ma
	Miocene	
		25 Ma
Tertiary	Oligocene	
		38 Ma
	Eocene	
		55 Ma
	Paleocene	
		65 Ma
Cretaceous		
		140 Ma
Jurassic		

Ma: Million years before present

Figure 3.8 The geologic time scale from the Jurassic to the present day.

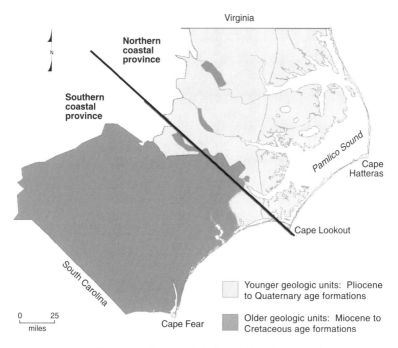

Figure 3.9 Generalized geologic map of the North Carolina coastal plain showing the relationship of the coastal systems in the northern and southern provinces to the underlying geologic framework. See figure 3.8.

reason why coastal engineers generally have a poor record in predicting beach behavior, particularly the behavior (i.e., the life span) of nourished beaches. In fact, because storms are usually responsible for the demise of nourished beaches, no one can accurately predict how long such beaches will last. The shoreface is much more than a loose pile of sand.

Geologic Framework of the North Carolina Coast

The underlying geologic framework of North Carolina's barrier islands consists of sediment and rock units that range in age from just formed to 90 million years old (fig. 3.8). The older geologic units that dominate the southern coastal province (fig. 3.9) include rock formations that range in age from 5 to 90 million years old (fig. 3.8). Younger geologic units dominate the northern coastal province (fig. 3.9), and include sediment formations of Pliocene and Quaternary ages (5 million years or less). The earth is still in the Quaternary period, and has recently experienced a major rise in sea level and change in climate. The present coastal features of North Carolina were formed during this period.

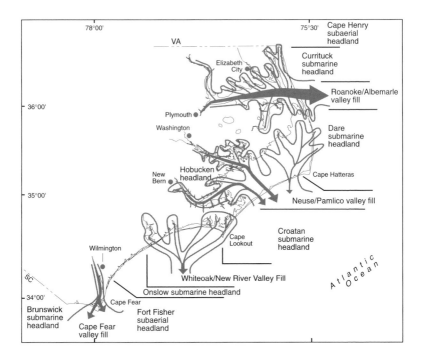

Figure 3.10 Map of the North Carolina coastal zone showing the ancient river drainages and the associated interriverine divides (ridges) that now form major headlands at the coast. Adapted from Riggs et al. "Influence of Inherited Geological Framework on Barrier Shoreface Morphology and Dynamics," *Marine Geology,* 126 (1995), pp. 213–234.

The coast of North Carolina is considered a sand-poor coast. That is, the sand supply is low, in part because most of the sand coming down the rivers at the present time is trapped in the upper estuaries and does not make it to the beaches. As a result of these limited sand supplies, North Carolina (and the entire East Coast) has thin barrier islands that are "perched" on top of older geologic units.

Perched barriers rarely develop a profile of equilibrium because they consist of a thin layer of modern beach sand sitting on top of a shoreface composed of older, eroding geologic units. Depending on the composition and shape of these older units, the underlying platform may act as an erosion-resistant, protruding submarine headland or an easily eroded, soft shoreface. A shoreface composed of hard mudstone, sandstone, or limestone will be affected differently by shoreline processes than a shoreface composed of soft sand or mud. Along many parts of the coast, the same rocks that crop out on the shoreface also form shoals or shallow areas on the adjacent inner continental shelf (e.g., Wimble Shoals off Pea Island).

Such shoals greatly modify incoming wave and current energy, and affect the patterns of erosion and deposition on adjacent beaches.

Thus, rather than being infinitely thick piles of sand, the barrier islands along most of the U.S. Atlantic coast are thin accumulations of sand perched on a preexisting and highly dissected surface previously eroded by rivers, tidal channels, and old inlets. Putting it another way, the recent postglacial rise in sea level has produced the modern barrier island and estuarine coastal sediments deposited over irregularly preserved remnants of preexisting sediment and rock units of variable ages, origins, and compositions. The complexity of this underlying geologic framework, in consort with the physical dynamics of the specific barrier island, ultimately determines the island's three-dimensional shoreface shape, the composition of beach sediments, and the shoreline erosion rate.

The old drainage system that formed on the continental shelf when it was left high and dry by the lowered ice age sea level controls today's large-scale topography (fig. 3.10). When the sea level last rose, beginning 10,000 years ago, the inundated river valleys filled with mud and sand. Coastal reaches dominated by these former river valleys form the nonheadland segments of the coast. Such coastal segments are often characterized by rapid rates of shoreline recession. The nonheadland segments are separated by interriver divides (former ridges), composed of older and harder geologic units, that form the headland segments of the coast. These coastal segments are often characterized by seaward protrusions (e.g., the capes) along the barrier islands.

Headland-Dominated Shorefaces

Headland-dominated shorefaces occur on the high interriver features or ridges composed of harder sediments and rocks of older geologic units (figs. 3.9, 3.10). These rocks sometimes crop out on the beach, as do the Quaternary coquina rocks found on the beach between Kure Beach and Fort Fisher. More commonly, however, the rocks crop out on the underwater shoreface below sea level. Examples of such submarine headlands can be found on northern Topsail Island and southern Onslow Beach, where Oligocene limestones form high-relief hardbottoms immediately in front of the beach. In both cases the rocks extend beneath the barrier island, affecting both its shape and erosion rate, and crop out at sea level in the estuary behind the island. Similarly, along the shoreline reach between Oregon Inlet and Cape Hatteras, Quaternary (fig. 3.8) submarine rock headlands affect the shape of the Outer Banks and Pamlico Sound. These rock units crop out in Pamlico Sound, on the eroding barrier island shoreface, and on the inner continental shelf as a series of rock shoals (fig. 3.11). These shoals, which rise

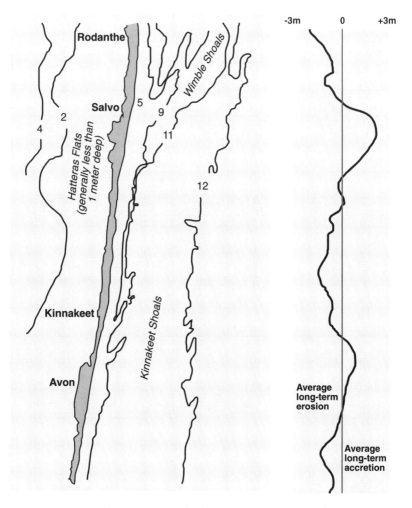

Figure 3.11 Map of the Outer Banks from Rodanthe to Avon showing (1) the shape of the sea floor (bathymetry, in meters below mean sea level [MSL]) for the inner shelf and eastern portion of Pamlico Sound; (2) inner-shelf shoal structures that occur between Rodanthe and Salvo and between Kinnakeet and Avon; (3) minor cape features landward of the shoals with broad beaches and narrow recessional beaches between the minor capes; and (4) plot of the average long-term erosion and accretion rates along this stretch of the barrier. The point illustrated here is that offshore bathymetry influences shoreline erosion rates. Figure adapted from Riggs et al. "Influence of Inherited Geological Framework on Barrier Shoreface Morphology and Dynamics," *Marine Geology* 126 (1995), pp. 213–234.

as much as 20 feet above the shelf floor, modify incoming waves and affect the rates of shoreline erosion on the adjacent beaches.

Nonheadland-Dominated Shorefaces

Nonheadland-dominated shorefaces are common along the North Carolina coast (fig. 3.10). The material that crops out on these shorefaces and affects barrier island behavior is generally composed of four different kinds of sediment, described below.

Valley-Fill Shorefaces

Some barrier islands overlie prehistoric river valleys that were filled as the sea level rose to its present height. Beneath these barriers lie thick accumulations of soft river and estuary channel-fill sediments. Barrier islands migrate faster across such soft valley-fill complexes in response to rising sea level, which creates indentations in the coastline because these sediments exhibit higher erosion rates than the surrounding sediments. Examples occur in the Outer Banks where the former Roanoke River valley passes beneath the barrier in the shoreline reach between Kitty Hawk and Kill Devil Hills, and where the former Neuse and Tar River valleys lie beneath Ocracoke Island (fig. 3.10).

Inlet-Fill Shorefaces

Barrier island segments underlain by the fill of either historic or prehistoric barrier island inlets have a shoreface composed of the unconsolidated sand and gravel that back-filled the inlets as they migrated. One example is the migration path of modern Oregon Inlet, which extends along the barrier island for about 3 miles southward from the point where the inlet originated in 1846. On the southern portion of the North Carolina coast, the shorefaces of Wrightsville Beach and Figure Eight Island are dominated by inlet fill.

Migrating or Retreating Shorefaces

In areas where narrow and low barrier islands are actively migrating up and over the back-barrier estuary (e.g., Masonboro Island), the shoreface is composed of peat and mud sediments. These young sediment units extend from the estuaries, under the barrier, and crop out within the surf zone and shoreface. Tree stumps and peat blocks, commonly seen during the winter months and after storms, are telltale indicators of this type of erosive shoreface (fig. 3.6).

Seaward-Building Shorefaces

In a few places where there is an adequate sediment supply, the shoreface temporarily builds, or progrades, seaward with sand similar to the composition of the barrier island. These shoreline segments occur only immediately adjacent to some of the capes and inlets and are often short-lived phenomena. Examples are the eastern tip of Shackleford Banks and Sunset Beach.

Know Your Shoreface

It is a very good idea for anyone locating on a North Carolina barrier island to know the type of shoreface, because it is a predictor of future island changes. When the island does change, as in a hurricane, the appropriate "solution" you apply to mitigate the impact of the changes should also be based on the type of shoreface. For example, the north end of Topsail Island is a very sand-poor, headland-dominated shoreface, and the likelihood of substantial natural beach recovery is slim—a good reason to build well back from the beach or to move buildings back after storms. The "one solution" or "one size fits all" approach to barrier islands is inappropriate because each island is different.

Shoreline Erosion and the Acquisition of New Beach Sand

During storms, ancient strata that crop out on the shoreface are eroded, providing an immediate source of "new" sediment to the modern beach. The composition of most beaches reflects the composition of ancient sediments eroded from the shoreface through this process, as the following examples demonstrate.

Sections of beach between Nags Head and the Virginia line contain high concentrations of nonshell gravel, which was once mined for construction aggregate. These beach gravels occur in locations where gravel-bearing prehistoric river channels underlie the barrier.

Shells of an extinct fossil oyster and associated limestone gravels occur in great abundance on Onslow Beach and Topsail Island. These gravels are derived from the erosion of Oligocene (fig. 3.8) hardbottom scarps that crop out on the inner continental shelf and are subsequently transported to the beach during storms. The extinct oysters found on the beach at North Topsail are gigantic, often more than a foot long. If they were alive today to be served in seafood restaurants, a single oyster would make a meal!

Overwash fans on Masonboro Island contain abundant cobble-sized pieces of coquina (a shelly rock) as well as shells derived from rock outcrops exposed on the adjacent inner continental shelf.

Black-stained oyster shells and brown or orange-stained clamshells are the dominant shells on many North Carolina beaches. These shells are fossils that usually date to the age of the ancient underlying rock units.

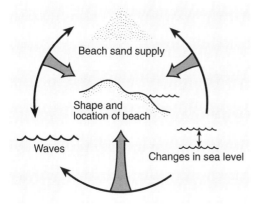

Figure 3.12 Dynamic equilibrium of beaches. When one factor changes, all the others adjust accordingly.

Beaches: The Shock Absorbers

The Dynamic Equilibrium

The beach is one of the earth's most dynamic environments. On barrier islands the beach is the source of sand for the entire island. Defined as the zone of active sand movement, and extending from the toe of the dune to an offshore depth of 30 to 40 feet, the beach is always changing. Most beaches are retreating gradually in a landward direction. As this process goes on, the beach changes its shape on almost a daily basis.

The natural laws that govern the beach control a beautiful, logical environment that builds up when the weather is good and strategically (but only temporarily) retreats when confronted by big storm waves. Beaches do such logical and predictable things that they almost seem to be alive. Beach behavior depends on four factors:

1. Wave energy (proportional to wave height)
2. The quality and quantity of beach sand
3. The shape and location of the beach
4. The rate of sea level change

The beach maintains a natural balance referred to as a "dynamic equilibrium" (fig. 3.12) of the above four factors. When one of the four factors changes, the others all adjust accordingly to maintain the balance. When humans enter the system and oppose the status quo of natural processes, the dynamic equilibrium continues to function predictably, but in a way that damages or destroys buildings and infrastructure.

Keep in mind that the part of the beach on which we walk is only the upper beach. Also remember that, like barrier islands, every beach is different.

Answers to the following often-asked questions may clarify the nature of the dynamic equilibrium.

How Does the Beach Respond to a Storm?

Old-timers and storm survivors on North Carolina's islands have frequently commented on how beautiful, flat, and broad the beach is after a storm. The flat beach can be explained in terms of the dynamic equilibrium: as wave energy increases and sea level rises (as part of the storm surge), sand is moved about, changing the shape of the beach. Most North Carolina beaches respond to storms by flattening, which causes storm waves to expend their energy over a broader and more level surface. On a steeper surface, storm-wave energy would be expended on a smaller area, causing greater change.

Figure 3.13 illustrates the way the beach flattens in response to a storm. Departing waves take sand from the upper beach or from the first dune and transport it to the lower beach. If a hot dog stand or beach cottage happens to be located on the first dune, it may disappear along with the dune sands.

Figure 3.13 Beach flattening in response to a storm. The "goal" of beach flattening during a storm is to dissipate the wave energy over a wider surface and thereby reduce the impact of the waves.

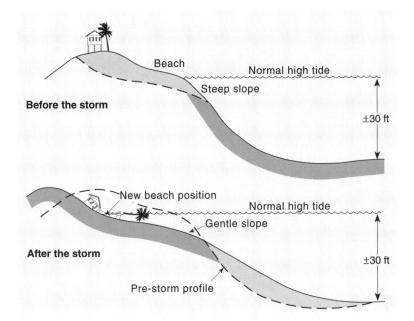

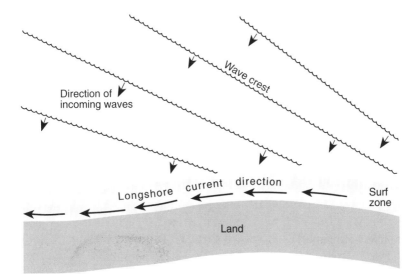

Figure 3.14 Longshore currents, sometimes referred to as "the longshore drift," are formed by waves approaching the shoreline at an angle. The longshore current transports sand parallel to the shore.

In major storms the surf-zone sand is sometimes transported beyond the base of the shoreface and is lost from the beach forever.

An island can lose a great deal of sand during a storm. The sand that remains in the shoreface system, however, may return, gradually pushed shoreward by fair-weather waves. This process is known as *beach recovery*. Beaches with coastal engineering structures (such as seawalls) and nourished beaches generally recover much less sand after a storm than natural beaches do.

How Does the Beach Widen?

Beaches grow seaward principally by the addition of new sand carried laterally by longshore (surf-zone) currents (fig. 3.14), or by the addition of new sand from the shoreface brought by the shoreward movement of sandbars. Actually, these two methods of beach widening often occur simultaneously.

Longshore currents are familiar to anyone who has swum in the ocean; they are the reason you sometimes come out of the water far down the beach from your towel. Such currents are produced by waves that approach the shore at an angle; the angle causes a portion of the breaking waves' energy to be directed along the beach rather than directly onto it. When combined with breaking waves that put sand into suspension, the current is capable of carrying large amounts of sediment for miles along a beach. Sand can move in either direction on beaches, depending on the direction of the wind that produces the waves. Most beaches have a dominant, or net, direction of sand transport, called "downdrift" or "updrift" (analogous to downstream and upstream in rivers) depending on the dominant wind direction.

During the summer it is common to see a sandbar within a few tens of yards of the shore on many (but not all) North Carolina beaches. This *offshore bar* or *ridge* is usually where the better swimmers and surfers congregate to catch the big wave (fig. 3.15). The trough between the beach and the ridge or sandbar is called the *runnel.*

Ridges and runnels are typically formed during small summer storms. In the quiet weather between storms, the ridges virtually march onto the shore and are "welded" to the beach. During the summer, the beach between low and high tide frequently has a runnel filled or partly filled with water. This trough is formed by a ridge that is in the final stages of filling the runnel and welding onto the beach.

The next time you are at the beach, observe the offshore ridge for a period of a few days and verify this for yourself. You will find that each day you have to swim out a slightly shorter distance to stand on the sandbar. As in all beach processes, there are exceptions to this type of beach behavior. For example, the offshore bar off Core Banks is almost always present but never seems to move ashore.

Figure 3.15 Ridge and runnel system off North Myrtle Beach, South Carolina. Two ridges (sandbars) and two runnels (troughs) are shown here. The ridges are actually bodies of sand that will move ashore and widen the beach.

Where Does Beach Sand Come From?

North Carolina's beaches receive a constant supply of sand from the adjacent shoreface and from inlets, deltas, and capes. The shoreface is the most important source of sand for most islands. Fair-weather waves gradually push the sand shoreward, and storm waves tend to carry it rapidly seaward. Additional sand is carried parallel to the beach by longshore currents. These currents move sand into and across inlets, which is why sand removal during the dredging of navigation channels often leads to sand starvation and increased erosion rates on the downdrift islands.

At the present time, rivers do not contribute material directly to North Carolina beaches. The sand carried by rivers is stored in the river channels and upper estuaries, miles from the beach. As a barrier island migrates landward, the former river-channel sand deposits are overrun by the shoreface, and erosion releases sand to the barrier island and the beaches. Thus the river sand does not come to the island directly; instead, the barrier island comes to the river sand.

Why Are Our Shorelines Retreating?

The causes of shoreline erosion are many. Anything that affects the sand supply to the beaches will cause a change in the rate of erosion. Human activities are often responsible for changes in the sand supply. Add the rising sea level and the previously discussed differences in the erodibility of shorefaces, and you have all the factors acting in shoreline retreat. Shoreline erosion is here to stay, and in fact is likely to increase as more navigation channels are dredged and as the sea level rise accelerates. It is important, however, to distinguish shoreline erosion from a shoreline erosion "problem." No erosion problem exists until buildings and roads are built close to the beach.

Where Do Seashells Come From?

Surprisingly, perhaps, most of the shells on North Carolina beaches are fossils. Many of the North Carolina beach shells dated by radiocarbon dating techniques are between 7,000 and 9,000 years old. Even some of the shiny lettered olive and pretty lightning whelk conch shells are very old.

If you use a shell guide (appendix C, ref. 29) to identify specimens from a North Carolina beach, you will find that estuarine shells are very common on the ocean-side beach. The easiest of these shells to spot are the oysters. As the island migrated landward, it "ran over" the shells that once lived in the back-island environment. After a few hundred or thousand years, the lagoon shells cropped out on the shoreface and were carried by waves onto the ocean-side beach.

But as any beach buff knows, not all of North Carolina's beach seashells are fossils. For example, coquina clams still live in the upper beach and hasten to rebury themselves when exposed by sand castle builders. Other modern shells are carried onshore by waves, particularly during storms.

If the Ocean Shorelines of North Carolina Are Eroding, What Is the Long-Range Future of Beach Development?

Most of the North Carolina coast is eroding, although sand does accumulate locally and temporary beach growth may occur in some spots (e.g., on Sunset Beach). As storm frequencies and storm tracks vary through time, so do the local patterns of erosion, often depending on the type of shoreface, as described above. Erosion rates should definitely be expected to increase, for three reasons:

1. Impacts of humans on barrier island sand supplies are increasing, leading to increasing shoreline retreat rates.
2. The rate of sea level rise will likely increase due to the greenhouse effect, leading to increasing shoreline retreat rates.
3. Storminess is also expected to increase due to the greenhouse effect.

The future does not bode well for responsible North Carolina beachfront property owners. The current state setback regulations mandating the distance buildings must be set back from the beach simply put the long-term erosion problem off for the next generation to deal with. But they can't put off the major damage and erosion caused by individual hurricanes.

And the same three factors—human impacts, sea level rise, and increased storminess—also affect the back shores of the islands and their associated estuaries.

4   North Carolina Estuaries

A look at a map of the North Carolina coastal plain will show major variations in the underlying geology (see figs. 1.5, 3.9). There are dramatic differences in the character of the state's coastal systems that reflect the direct influence of this geological heritage. A line drawn from Raleigh through
Kinston and Cape Lookout separates the coastal system into the northern
and southern coastal provinces (see fig. 3.9). Each province has a unique
geologic framework that results in distinctive types of barrier islands, inlets,
and estuaries with particular wave and tidal energies and processes. These
in turn result in distinct types of coastal habitats with different water salinities, plant and animal communities, and problems resulting from human
intervention. To understand our coastal systems we must first understand
the basic features of the two coastal provinces.

The Geologic Framework

The coastal system in the southern province, from Cape Lookout south to
the South Carolina border, is underlain primarily by relatively old rock
units dating from the Upper Cretaceous (about 90 million years ago)
through Pliocene (about 1.6 million years ago) periods (see figs. 3.8, 3.9). In
this region only a thin and highly variable skin of Quaternary age surficial
sands and muds were deposited during the last 1.6 million years. The older
units are generally composed of harder rocks such as mudstones, sand-
stones, and limestones. These older rock units are associated with a large
geologic structure called the Carolina Platform, which underlies the region
between Myrtle Beach, South Carolina, and Cape Fear, North Carolina.
During the geologic past, this platform rose slightly, and the rocks dipped
toward the north and east, causing them to be eroded and truncated by the
shoreline. As erosion cut deeper along the more uplifted southern coast, the
older rock units were exposed.

Figure 4.1 Aerial view across the central portion of Bogue Banks. Bogue Sound, in the background, is the largest back-barrier estuary within the southern province. Bogue Sound at this location is an open-water body dominated by high-brackish water. Water movement is due to regular astronomical tides.

In contrast, the coastal system in the northern province, from Cape Lookout north to the Virginia border, is underlain primarily by sediments of Quaternary age that were deposited during the many sea level fluctuations that occurred during the ice ages of the past 1.6 million years (see fig. 3.8). These units generally consist of unconsolidated muds, muddy sands, sands, and peat sediments that thicken northward to fill the slightly subsiding Albemarle Embayment with up to 230 feet of sediments. Consequently, a gentle depositional topography is common along the present northern coastal system, and the older rock units are buried deep beneath the surface sediments.

These two very different geologic frameworks produce two different land slopes in the coastal zone. The southern province is characterized by an average slope of 3 feet per mile; the northern province has an average slope of only 0.2 feet per mile. The ocean surface intersects these differently sloping land surfaces in two distinct ways. Thus, the rising sea level floods the disparate slopes to form our present coastal system with two kinds of barrier island–inlet systems and associated estuaries (see fig. 1.5). The steeper slopes of the southern province have produced short, stubby barrier islands and narrow back-barrier estuaries. There are more than 18 inlets along this stretch of coast. The gentle slopes of the northern province have produced long barrier islands with an extensive system of drowned-river estuaries and only 4 inlets. The long northern islands project seaward, forming Cape Hatteras and the famous Outer Banks, which act as a sand dam isolating the vast Albemarle-Pamlico estuarine system from the ocean.

North Carolina's estuaries are drowned lowlands that lie behind the barrier islands. In places where these lowlands are drowned river valleys, the ocean has flooded up the rivers' channels to the point where the valley bottom rises above sea level. The resulting shore-perpendicular estuaries have two sources of water: fresh water flows down the rivers to the ocean, and ocean water is pushed through the inlets by astronomical and storm tides. Consequently, these estuaries are great mixing basins where the two water masses interact to form the following salinity gradients: (1) fresh water in the upstream portions, (2) low-brackish water in the central regions, (3) high-brackish water in the outer estuaries and inlets, and (4) normal seawater salinities in the offshore regions. The estuarine mixing basins of the southern and northern coastal provinces have dramatically distinct geometries, physical processes, and biological communities.

Estuaries of the Southern Province

Back-Barrier Sounds

The narrow, coast-parallel estuaries that back the barrier islands of the southern province range from open water to areas dominated by salt marshes and tidal creeks, depending on the width of the estuarine system (see figs. 1.5, 3.9). The widest systems contain small bodies of open water and include Back and Bogue Sounds south of Cape Lookout (fig. 4.1). These estuarine systems are narrower toward the southern end of the province, and the size of the open-water bodies diminishes significantly, forming Stump and Topsail Sounds behind Topsail Island and the very small Middle and Myrtle Grove Sounds behind Wrightsville Beach and Masonboro Island, respectively. In the latter regions and in the area from Caswell Beach to Sunset Beach, south of Cape Fear, the very narrow back-barrier estuaries are dominated by salt marshes that are highly dissected by tidal creeks. In the coastal segment stretching from the southern portion of Carolina Beach to Fort Fisher (see fig. 1.5), the coast has no natural estuaries or barrier islands. Here the mainland forms the shoreline, and the Intracoastal Waterway is a ditch cut through the upland.

The southern province is characterized by 18 or so inlets through the barrier islands. The combination of abundant inlets and few small Coastal Plain rivers draining into the coastal zone results in an estuarine system dominated by ocean water and ocean processes. The mixing within these estuaries is driven from the ocean by the highly regular astronomical tides (with amplitudes of 3 to 5 feet, increasing southward) and their associated tidal currents, which rapidly mix the estuaries to form high-brackish waters.

Because of their relatively small surface area, the water in the southern province estuaries experiences minimal effects from waves and wind-driven tides. Consequently, the perimeters and interiors of the estuaries are dominated by sloped mudflats that are riddled with tidal channels and feature extensive *Spartina* salt marshes (fig. 4.2). These narrow estuaries are regularly flooded, tidal-current-dominated coastal systems that have been highly modified by human activity, including an extensive network of dredged channels and associated spoil islands.

Trunk Estuaries

Most rivers draining to the coast in the southern province are small "blackwater" streams that discharge low volumes of fresh water into the estuarine systems. These rivers carry relatively low sediment loads but contain large quantities of organic components, giving the water the color of overbrewed tea. The river valleys form a series of coast-perpendicular, drowned-river estuaries (trunk estuaries) that include the North, Newport, White Oak, and New River estuaries (see fig. 1.5). The estuaries of the southern prov-

Figure 4.2 Aerial view of a southern province back-barrier estuary at low tide showing the extensive distribution of salt marshes cut by navigation channels. This photo is of the western portion of Bogue Sound with Bogue Banks in the background.

ince, with its steeper slope, are generally much smaller than those of the northern province. The one major exception to this rule is the Cape Fear River, which drains the North Carolina Piedmont. The Cape Fear River not only has a larger river valley and a greater water discharge, it is also a red-water river. The red color comes from the presence of a significant sediment load derived from the erosion of the red clay soils of the Piedmont.

Many of the trunk estuaries are partially cut off from the back-barrier estuaries as a result of human activities. Development along the Intracoastal Waterway and its associated navigational channels have created an extensive network of dredge-spoil piles that have greatly modified the water flow. In addition, bridges built across some estuaries act as partial dams, further restricting current flow. Such changes have dampened the ocean's influence, resulting in estuaries that are not as well mixed as the back-barrier estuaries and are significantly less affected by regular astronomical tides. Consequently, the estuarine waters generally grade over short distances from high-brackish salinities at the estuary's mouth into low-brackish and fresh water landward from the mouth.

Unlike back-barrier estuaries, the open waters within the drowned-river trunk estuaries are generally not broken by salt marshes and are often deeper, causing wind-driven waves and irregular wind tides to be important processes. Thus, the trunk estuaries tend to be irregularly flooded, wave-dominated coastal systems with shorelines characterized by eroding sediment banks. Protected segments of the shoreline often contain small fringes of *Juncus* salt marsh (fig. 4.3), which give way upstream to extensive riverine swamp-forest shorelines (fig. 4.4).

Smaller drowned-river tributary streams flow into each main trunk estuary. These shallow estuaries are commonly filled with *Juncus* salt marsh (fig. 4.3) for some distance upstream until they grade into the riverine swamp forests.

Estuaries of the Northern Province

Back-Barrier Sounds

The back-barrier sounds of the northern province are medium to large, coast-parallel estuaries that include Core Sound to the south; Pamlico Sound, the largest of all the North Carolina estuaries; and Roanoke, Croatan, and Currituck Sounds in the north (see fig. 1.5). The presence of only four inlets in more than 190 miles of barrier islands, plus a major input of fresh water from rivers draining the Piedmont and the Coastal Plain, result in estuaries with low-amplitude, regular astronomical tides and highly variable salinities that range from fresh to medium brackish throughout extensive portions of these large bodies. Only in the regions around the inlets

Figure 4.3 A tributary estuary that contains a salt marsh dominated by black needlerush (*Juncus*). This type of salt marsh, characterized by irregular flooding and low- to middle-brackish waters, occurs throughout the trunk and tributary estuaries of the North Carolina coast.

subject to direct oceanic influence do the waters exhibit regular astronomical tides and develop high-brackish salinities.

Core Sound has the highest salinities, due to the presence of inlets at both ends and in the middle in combination with a minimum of freshwater input from rivers. Pamlico Sound ranges from high-brackish salinities around its three major inlets, to medium- to low-brackish salinities along its western shores, which receive a high volume of freshwater river discharge. Currituck Sound is totally fresh today because it has no inlets; historically, however, there have been abundant inlets into Currituck Sound. Roanoke and Croatan Sounds tend to have highly variable salinities that range from fresh to medium brackish depending on the variable freshwater discharge and wind patterns.

Because these sounds have relatively large surface areas with moderately uniform depths and no interior salt marshes, they respond maximally to waves and wind tides. The water is generally well mixed by wind waves and currents as the water sloshes back and forth in response to irregular and rapidly changing weather events. Normal wind tides are minor (less than 1 foot), with storm tide amplitudes commonly up to 3 to 5 feet, and, rarely, up to 10 feet in response to major hurricanes. The currents and tide levels are determined by the direction, intensity, and duration of the wind. For example, a northeaster that blows strongly for several days will produce strong south-flowing currents and blow much of the water out of Curr-ituck, Roanoke, and Croatan Sounds (creating water levels 3 to 5 feet lower than normal), and produce flood conditions in southern Pamlico and Core Sounds (with water levels 3 to 5 feet higher than normal). This sloped water surface will hold its shape as long as the wind continues to blow. If the wind relaxes in intensity or shifts direction, the water flow responds immediately.

On the other hand, considerably less mixing occurs during low-energy periods or seasons, resulting in much longer residence times for the estua-rine water. Consequently, the back-barrier sounds of the northern province tend to be irregularly flooded, wind-tide-dominated coastal systems sur-rounded by scarped and rapidly eroding marsh and sediment bank shore-lines.

Trunk Estuaries

Four major Piedmont-draining rivers flow into the northern portion of the coastal zone (see fig. 1.5). The Chowan and Roanoke Rivers become the Albemarle Sound estuary, the Tar River becomes the Pamlico River estuary, and the Neuse River becomes the Neuse River estuary. These four red-water

Figure 4.4 Swamp-forest shoreline characterizes the upstream portions of all trunk and tributary estuaries throughout the North Carolina coastal zone. The ris-ing sea level permanently floods the river floodplain vegetation, which is character-ized by cypress, tupelo, and swamp maple trees that can tolerate only temporary flooding by fresh water.

rivers form the major coast-perpendicular, or trunk, estuaries in the north. They drain the Piedmont and Appalachian regions, and the large volumes of fresh water they discharge into their estuaries carry a significant load of sediment derived from the weathering and erosion of the upland red clay soils.

The transition zone where each river becomes an estuary (fig. 4.5) occurs at the point where the river valley becomes flooded as it reaches sea level and riverine processes give way to estuarine processes. Because of the low slope of the land in this region, flooding occurs far upstream, producing a deeply embayed estuarine system with several thousand miles of shoreline.

The northern trunk estuaries have low salinities because the total volume of ocean flow through the four inlets is small and the freshwater discharge is high. The Neuse and Pamlico River estuaries range from medium- to low-brackish salinities on the seaward side, and grade into low-brackish to fresh water landward. Albemarle Sound, which experiences almost no oceanic influence, is almost totally fresh water. The lack of oceanic influence also means that regular astronomical tides and associated tidal currents are absent.

The large expanse of open waters in the trunk estuaries of the northern province makes wind and storm tides among the most important physical processes responsible for irregular mixing of the water column and setting up the current patterns. Because these fluctuations in water level are driven by the major weather patterns and individual storms, the large, embayed estuaries of the north are irregularly flooded, wave-dominated coastal systems that are well mixed only during storms and the stormy seasons. During the hot, calm summer months, the northern trunk estuaries are generally unmixed, which can have significant chemical and biological consequences, including massive fish and shellfish kills.

Tributary Estuaries

Flowing into the trunk estuaries is a network of tributary streams that resemble the capillaries that flow into the arteries of the human circulation system. These myriad black-water tributary streams drain the sandy Coastal Plain. The lower portion of each tributary valley is drowned when it reaches sea level, forming a generally coast-parallel estuary. Tributary estuaries consist primarily of fresh water whose black color derives from the decomposition of organic matter in the upland swamps and pocosins their tributaries drain. Small tributary estuaries tend to have irregular riverine geometries and are characterized by low wind and wave energy.

The tributary estuaries are smallest on the western, inner portions of the trunk estuaries (e.g., the Trent River, Bath Creek, and Scuppernong River estuaries) and become generally larger to the east as the slope of the land approaches sea level (e.g., the South, Bay, Pungo, Alligator, Pasquotank, and North River estuaries). Finally, on the eastern trunk estuarine mouths, where much of the land is now below sea level, the former tributaries have flooded completely to form the very large back-barrier estuaries that include Core, Pamlico, Roanoke, Croatan, and Currituck Sounds.

The Estuarine Basins

Basin Morphology

Most North Carolina estuaries have a cross-section that resembles a shallow, flat-bottomed dish with a small lip around the perimeter (fig. 4.6). The shoreline is a cut bank incised into older sediments with a narrow and shallow perimeter platform that slopes gradually away from the shoreline to depths of 3 to 7 feet below mean sea level (MSL) and then slopes more abruptly to the broad, flat floor of the central basin, which lies at depths between 12 and 24 feet below MSL.

Figure 4.5   The transition zone between the Roanoke River and its swamp-forest floodplain (*top*) to the drowned-river trunk estuary of Albemarle Sound (*bottom*). In this zone, the sea level intersects the slope of the river valley, permanently flooding the river valley and producing a swamp-forest shoreline. The trees are drowned as the swamp-forest shoreline recedes, eventually intersecting the adjacent upland to form a sediment bank shoreline like the one seen on the lower right side of Albemarle Sound.

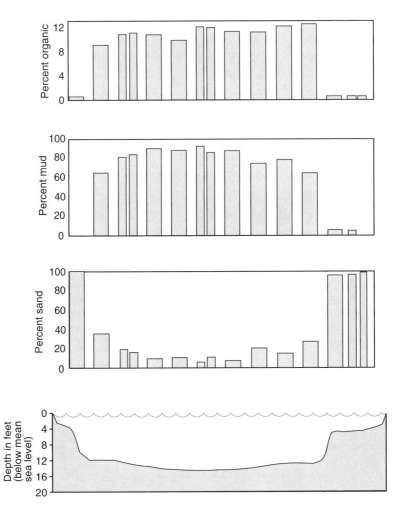

Figure 4.6 Cross-sectional profile of the Neuse River trunk estuary showing the shape of the basin and the distribution and composition of bottom sediments. Note that sands are almost totally limited to the shallow perimeter platforms (*lowest bar graph*) and that organic-rich muds (*top bar graph*) fill the extensive central basin habitats, which constitute about 70 percent of the estuarine habitats in North Carolina.

Within the trunk estuaries, the flat central basin floor gradually deepens from the inner estuary seaward to the outer estuary. Tributary estuaries have smaller-scale, dish-shaped cross-sectional profiles with extensive fine-sand shoals across the central basin where they flow into the trunk estuary. These shoals form in response to increased wave energy from sand eroded out of the rapidly receding shorelines of the trunk estuary. In addition, each estuary is characterized by a downstream transition from the riverine zone, to the drowned-river estuary, to either the barrier islands or the trunk estuary. Within the back-barrier estuaries, the central basin shallows eastward onto extensive fine-sand flats behind the barrier islands. The sand flats form as the estuary fills with sand from barrier island processes that include wind, storm overwash, and formation of flood-tide deltas associated with both modern and ancient inlets.

Sediments

Estuarine basins generally act as repositories that trap and accumulate sediments. Thus, most estuarine basins are shallow (less than 24 feet deep). The sediments that form the floor of the estuarine system interact with waves and currents and play integral roles in the life and health of the system. Sediments provide substrate for the bottom community of plants and animals, and also interact with the water column, serving as a sink and a source for nutrients, gases, and contaminants. As the sediment type varies, so do the bottom communities and the water column interactions in the estuaries.

Estuarine sediments generally consist of three types—sand, peat, and organic-rich mud (fig. 4.6)—derived from four sources. (1) Peat and organic-rich sediments accumulate in response to vegetation in riverine swamp forests and estuarine brackish and salt marshes. (2) Suspended sediment (mud) is delivered by the major rivers, primarily during flood stage, that drain the Piedmont and Appalachian regions. (3) Sand, mud, and organic matter are supplied to the estuaries through the erosion of sediment bank and marsh shorelines that surround the estuaries. (4) Fine sands are transported from the oceans into the estuaries by wind and water currents either through inlets or over the tops of barrier islands during storms. The input of new sediment into the estuarine system from the latter three sources is largely storm dependent and is associated with high-energy winters or individual hurricanes or northeasters. Thus, the distribution pattern of each sediment type is related to basin morphology (fig. 4.6), sediment source, and estuarine processes.

Chemically inert quartz is the main mineral in the sands. Medium- to coarse-quartz sand is the dominant sediment on the shallow perimeter platforms and in the channels in the riverine zones of all trunk and tributary rivers. The back-barrier estuaries contain abundant fine sand derived from the oceans and intervening barrier islands.

The concentration of organic matter in the sediments is highly variable throughout the estuaries, ranging from 0 to 86 percent of the total sediment. Sediments comprising 50 percent or more organic matter are called peats. Fine-grained organic detritus in concentrations of less than 50 per-

Figure 4.7 High sediment bank shorelines are common in the western portions of trunk and tributary estuaries in the northern province of North Carolina. The wave-cut scarp shown here is eroding the bank of Quaternary-age sediments, which have slumped and are being reworked by the waves to form the sand beach. Note the vegetative debris in the background that helps to buffer wave energy and slow the rate of shoreline erosion. When such shorelines are "cleaned up," erosion rates immediately increase.

cent mixes with inorganic clay to form the extensive deposits of organic-rich muds. Organic-rich muds are the most pervasive sediment, forming the benthic habitat for about 70 percent of the estuarine systems and generally filling the central basins. The fine-grained organic detritus is flushed by storms from swamp forests and marshes or eroded from the associated peat shorelines. The interface between the organic-rich mud and the water contains a large and diverse population of microorganisms as well as a large community of marine invertebrates such as worms, clams, shrimp, and crabs, many of which are filter or detritus feeders that concentrate, pelletize, and redeposit the organic-rich mud.

Peats comprise more than 50 percent organic matter and form in one of two ways. First, peats may represent in-place growth of vegetation in swamp forests or grass marshes. The peat formed in this way contains a framework of plant roots and stems in growth position mixed with organic detritus and inorganic mud from sediment-laden storm waters. Swamp-forest peats form in floodplains of the trunk and tributary rivers. Marsh peats form around low-energy shorelines in the outer portions of the trunk and tributary estuaries and contain much finer-grained organic matter than swamp-forest peats. Second, detrital or reworked peats form as organic detritus derived from the erosion of swamp forest and marsh peats that is transported and redeposited as secondary accumulations of organic matter. All of these sediment types—sand, mud, and peat—are highly erodible.

Shorelines

Sediment Bank Shorelines
About one-third of North Carolina's estuarine shoreline is dominated by sediment banks consisting of sediment beds of Quaternary age or older. Sediment bank shorelines consist of a wave-cut platform and an associated wave-cut scarp that are eroding back into older sediments. The sand that forms the beach along the shoreline is derived from the erosion of the sediment bank. These eroding sediment bank shorelines border the land that is in greatest demand for homesites. Sediment bank shorelines with the highest relief include bluffs (above 20 feet) and high banks (5 to 20 feet). These are the least abundant shorelines, and they occur primarily in the westernmost portion of the estuarine system (fig. 4.7). Low sediment bank

Figure 4.8 The low sediment bank shoreline is the most common shoreline type throughout the North Carolina estuarine system. The wave-cut scarp shown here is eroding the bank of Quaternary-age sediments to produce a very small sand beach. Note that the rapidly receding shoreline has intersected the rows of the crop since it was planted.

shorelines (less than 5 feet), the most common type of sediment bank, occur throughout the estuarine system (fig. 4.8).

Organic Shorelines
Approximately two-thirds of North Carolina's estuarine shoreline is dominated by the vegetative growth of swamp forests (figs. 4.4, 4.9) and marsh grasses (figs. 4.3, 4.10). Organic shorelines are characterized by peat sediment composed of organic matter with varying amounts of fine sand and mud. The types of plants that dominate organic shorelines and their zonation patterns change laterally as the water salinity and tidal processes change.

Swamp forests dominated by cypress (*Taxodium*), tupelo (*Nyssa*), and swamp maple (*Acer*) trees occur in the riverine floodplains and uppermost portions of the trunk and tributary estuaries that were flooded by the rising sea level (fig. 4.5). As the sea level rises, the riverine floodplain is permanently flooded and the trees drown. As the receding shoreline advances into the floodplain, a fringe of dead and dying trees is left behind in the water, producing one of the most characteristic and beautiful sights within the North Carolina estuarine system (figs. 4.4, 4.9).

Marsh shorelines occur throughout the estuaries and are dominated by emergent grasses with a transition zone to the adjacent upland composed of shrubs that include wax myrtle (*Myrica*), marsh elder (*Iva*), and sil-

Figure 4.9   Remnants of a receding swamp-forest shoreline left behind as the rising sea level permanently floods the river floodplain. Cypress is the most tolerant of the floodplain vegetation to permanent flooding and is left standing alone offshore as the vegetative shoreline rapidly recedes.

Figure 4.10 An eroding salt marsh shoreline characteristic of the northern province and the trunk estuaries in the southern province of North Carolina. Note the highly irregular shape of the shoreline and the exposed edge of fresh peat, reflecting the rapid erosion of this smooth-cordgrass (*Spartina alternaflora*) marsh. Below the water, the marsh peat will be scarped and severely undercut, with pieces of the root mass breaking off and lying in 3 to 8 feet of water. The shrubby vegetation in the background represents the transition zone to the upland vegetation.

verling (*Baccharis*). Within the inner estuarine system, freshwater and brackish marshes may either occur as narrow fringing zones in front of wave-protected segments of sediment bank shorelines (fig. 4.11) or may completely fill small tributary estuaries (fig. 4.3). Freshwater marshes occur in the innermost riverine and estuarine regions and are dominated by cattails (*Typha*), bullrush (*Scirpus*), reed (*Phragmites*), and black needlerush (*Juncus*). These marshes grade seaward into the brackish marshes that occur throughout most of the estuaries. In the outer estuarine regions of the Pamlico and Neuse River estuaries, where the land slope is minimal and approaches sea level, the brackish marshes form vast and spectacular wetland habitats. The irregularly flooded brackish marshes—large, flat areas with few tidal channels—are dominated by black needlerush with fringes of saltmeadow cordgrass (*Spartina patens*) and giant cordgrass (*Spartina cynosuroides*).

Organic shorelines of brackish marshes are characterized by thick beds of fairly pure peat abruptly truncated by vertical and undercut scarps around the estuarine edge of the marsh (fig. 4.10). Brackish marsh environments are generally wave dominated and are characterized by irregular storm-tide

Figure 4.11 A fringing-marsh shoreline in front of an upland area covered with young pines. Note the dead trees along the shoreline in the background. This was a rapidly eroding, low sediment bank shoreline until the fringing marsh was established and trapped sand to form a small accretionary beach. The fringing marsh and associated beach now buffer wave energy and have slowed the shoreline erosion.

flooding. This situation generally causes the organic shorelines to be in an erosional mode (fig. 4.10). The outer marsh perimeter is often exposed to large stretches of open water (e.g., the outer Neuse and Pamlico Rivers and Pamlico Sound). High wave energy causes the peat shorelines to be actively eroded along the outer marsh edge, producing scarps that drop abruptly into 3 to 8 feet of water on the estuarine side. The soft organic matter below the live root mass is readily eroded, causing large blocks of root-bound peat to flop wildly in the waves until they break off. This erosion leaves a trail of peat blocks on the estuarine floor in front of the rapidly receding shoreline.

The landward side of these marshes is usually in a constructive mode. The marsh laps onto and migrates across the adjacent upland areas as the sea level rises. Thus, as the marshes are eroding on the estuarine side, they are generally expanding on the landward side. This process continues until the upland slope becomes too steep or the upland is bulkheaded for development; then marsh expansion is terminated and habitat loss occurs.

The waters of the back-barrier estuaries of the southern province and the areas around the inlets in the northern province have high-brackish salinities and are regularly flooded by astronomical tidal currents. The organic shorelines in these areas are characterized by sandy peats of the salt marsh that grows above mean-tide level. Smooth cordgrass (*Spartina alternaflora*) and saltmeadow cordgrass, with varying amounts of glasswort (*Salicornia*) and saltgrass (*Distichlis*), are the dominant grasses in these salt marshes. Extensive low-sloping mudflats and sandflats extend below mean-tide level and into the adjacent channels. The marsh vegetation grows on the upper portions of these low-sloping ramps, where it actively traps sediment. This situation represents a constructive mode in which the salt marsh and associated shorelines are actively accumulating sediment and building the shoreline out into the estuary.

Estuaries and Development

Shoreline Erosion

Most estuarine shorelines are actively eroding, although the erosion rates are extremely variable, ranging from a few feet per decade in the innermost trunk estuaries and small tributary estuaries up to an average of 3 feet per year in exposed low sediment banks and marsh peats in the outer estuaries. Local rates may exceed 15 feet per year in some of the most exposed marsh shorelines surrounding Pamlico Sound. The actual rate of recession of any specific segment of estuarine shoreline is highly variable and depends on many factors. Among the more important factors determining the rate of recession are the following:

> *Fetch:* the average distance of open water across which the wind can blow in front of the shoreline (a large open sound versus a narrow tributary; see fig. 1.5).
>
> *Water depth, bottom slope, and beach:* bottom characteristics of the nearshore area (width and depth of the shallow versus deep water in the nearshore area) and the presence and width of a sand beach between the eroding sediment bank and the shoreline.
>
> *Bank height and composition:* height of the sediment bank at or immediately behind the shoreline and the hardness of the sediments or rocks that compose the bank (high bank of loose sand versus high bank of tight mud versus low bank of soft peat; see figs. 4.7, 4.8).
>
> *Vegetation:* type and abundance of vegetation occurring on the sediment bank and shoreline, and in the offshore area (presence or absence of submerged grass beds, marsh grass, shrubs, or trees; see figs. 4.7, 4.11).
>
> *Shoreline geometry, orientation, and geographic location:* general shape of the shoreline, direction the shoreline faces, and geographic location within the estuarine system (straight versus highly irregular, a point ver-

sus an embayment, northeast-facing versus southwest-facing, inner estuary tributary versus Pamlico Sound; see fig. 1.5).

Boat wakes: proximity to and type and amount of use of boat channels. This is particularly important on major boating channels and the Intracoastal Waterway (fig. 4.12).

Most shoreline erosion takes place in direct response to high-energy storms. Thus, the amount of recession at any location is quite variable from year to year and depends on the frequency of storms; the type and direction of approach of any given storm; the intensity and duration of each storm; and the resulting wind tides, currents, and waves produced by that storm. In specific locations, boat wakes are a serious cause of shoreline erosion, especially along the Intracoastal Waterway where the channel was dug through upland areas (fig. 4.12) or through very narrow and shallow estuarine bodies.

Energy levels along the estuarine shoreline are significantly less than they are on the ocean shoreline. Thus, the estuarine shoreline can be successfully engineered to temporarily retard shoreline recession (fig. 4.13), although at a significant cost. Bulkheads work in some settings, but they have a limited

Figure 4.12 A high sediment bank shoreline along the Intracoastal Waterway where the navigational channel was dug through upland topography. The shoreline was originally at the edge of the channel, which still contains water in this low-tide picture. The significant shoreline recession was caused directly by erosion resulting from boat wakes along the waterway. Note the unsuccessful attempt to stop the erosion with a bulkhead.

Figure 4.13 A failed bulkhead built to stabilize an eroding low sediment bank shoreline.

life expectancy and definite impacts on the estuarine system (fig. 4.13). For example, a bulkhead built to protect an eroding sediment bank shoreline severs a critical supply of sand for the local beaches. A landowner who bulkheads a shoreline may luck out if the neighbors' shorelines continue to erode. However, as more of the adjacent shorelines are bulkheaded, the sand beach will rapidly disappear.

Natural vegetation is often the most effective protection from erosion (figs. 4.14, 4.15). The vegetation may be a zone of trees and shrubs, a fringe of marsh grass, a tangle of dead brush and logs, or, if the landowner is lucky, a line of live cypress trees and stumps. A vegetation buffer effectively absorbs wave energy during high-water events, slowing down rates of shoreline recession, and also acts as a natural trap for sand. Unfortunately, most landowners immediately attack shoreline vegetation—particularly if it is dead—cutting, clearing, and removing the trees, shrubs, stumps, logs, and snags to improve both the view and swimming and to eliminate "snake-infested" habitats. Such clearing dramatically changes the shallow-water habitats and always increases the rate of shoreline erosion, ensuring

Figure 4.14 A stable high sediment bank shoreline that has been left vegetated. The tree debris acts as a groin, trapping sand to produce a beach.

the future need for bulkheads. A large proportion of the estuarine shoreline that has been or is being developed is now bulkheaded. This represents a massive change in critical shallow-water habitats.

Storms, Storm Tides, and Coastal Flooding

Estuaries in the northern province tend to be large, open bodies of water dominated by wind-tide processes. These characteristics in combination with their shallow basin geometries lead to serious problems resulting from storm tides and coastal flooding. The location and magnitude of the storm tides depend directly on the direction, duration, force, and type of storm.

Storm winds readily push water around, blowing it out of upwind areas and piling it up against the opposite, downwind shoreline, forming water ramps. When there is no wind, the estuary is a flat, smooth surface without waves or slope. When the wind begins to blow, waves form, and the wave size increases over time. As the wind intensity builds, the water currents begin to move in the direction of the wind flow, lowering the water surface in the upwind direction, raising the water surface in the downwind direction, and flooding the adjacent lowlands. The wind waves that form on top of this sloping ramp erode the shoreline and damage marinas and inland structures. The sloped water ramp will be maintained as long as there is a wind to hold it up. When the wind diminishes, the water will flow back down the ramp to its original flat surface.

Sloped-ramp storm tides occur whenever a northeaster blows or a hurricane strikes the North Carolina coast. The nature of the estuarine storm tides depends on the intensity, duration, and direction of movement of the storm. Even if a hurricane moves offshore of the barrier islands in a generally coast-parallel fashion without making direct landfall, its winds can create major estuarine storm tides. In 1993, for example, Hurricane Emily grazed Cape Hatteras with sustained winds of 92 miles per hour as it traveled northward. The counterclockwise winds of this storm blew the waters from the northern sounds southward across Pamlico Sound and piled them up in the bend behind Cape Hatteras (see fig. 1.5). The storm tide reached its maximum, 10.5 feet above normal, between Buxton and Avon, decreasing gradually to the north and south. The resultant flooding caused severe damage, and the storm's winds destroyed the Buxton maritime forest.

Hurricanes that make landfall across the coast in the southern province have a significant impact on the estuarine waters throughout North Carolina. In 1996, Hurricanes Bertha and Fran made direct landfall between Wrightsville Beach and Onslow Beach (see fig. 1.5). The ocean-side storm

Figure 4.15 A bulkheaded, low sediment bank shoreline with a fringing marsh of smooth cordgrass (*Spartina alternaflora*). The cordgrass was planted here. Such fringing marshes not only buffer the wave action and help protect the bulkhead, they also contribute additional marsh habitat to the coastal ecosystem. Note that the bulkhead has prevented the marsh from gradually expanding upslope in response to the rising sea level on this lowland coast. Photo from the North Carolina Sea Grant Program.

tide readily spilled over the barrier islands and poured through the numerous inlets. Storm tides in the back-barrier estuaries were up to 14 feet above mean sea level. The energy of these floodwaters was significantly diminished from that experienced on the ocean side, however, because of the buffering effect of the barrier islands, the relatively small size of the estuaries, and the abundance of vegetation. Bertha and Fran also had significant impacts on the trunk estuaries in the northern province. The counterclockwise winds along the north side of the storms blew the water westward in the trunk estuaries, resulting in storm tides up to 10 feet above mean sea level, with significant waves superimposed on top of the water ramp that seriously flooded and battered the upper reaches of the Neuse and Pamlico River estuaries.

Hurricanes that cross the coast in the northern province produce storm tides that slosh back and forth in the estuaries, impacting both the inner and outer portions. The initial winds blow the waters up the estuaries, producing low wind-driven tides along the barrier islands and high wind-driven tides in the upper reaches of the trunk estuaries. After the storm passes and storm winds come from the opposite direction, there is a rapid backflow of high water resulting in catastrophic consequences for the barrier islands. Historically, walls of water 10 feet or higher have roared back on the Outer Banks as hurricanes passed, wreaking havoc on the sound side and often blowing open new inlets through the islands. In fact, this is the probable origin of many major inlets.

Coastal flooding by salt water has numerous consequences. Salt water is toxic to all freshwater plants; consequently, storm winds containing salt spray and salty floodwaters may either kill the vegetation directly or stress it to the point that it becomes vulnerable to poststorm diseases. This happened to much of the vegetation in the Buxton maritime forest after Hurricane Emily. The pine trees that were not broken off by the wind were subsequently killed by pine-bark beetle infestations.

The salinity of the floodwaters is determined by where the flooding occurs—in the outer or inner estuary. The saltier the water, the greater the impact of the flood. The shallow groundwater aquifer becomes contaminated with salt water that takes weeks or months to dilute and flush out. This groundwater impact is the main reason why older homes in the outer coastal region once had individual cisterns. Septic systems, fuel tanks, parking lots, chemical loading docks, industrial complexes, old dump sites, and marinas and their many boats are also flooded and damaged by storms, leading to the discharge of oil, fuel, chemicals, and other contaminants into the estuarine system.

Coastal development has resulted in the modification and loss of critical shallow-water habitats in the estuarine system. In spite of laws that protect wetlands from being drained and filled, a major annual loss directly attributable to the rapid rate of population growth and development within our coastal system continues at an alarming rate. A report of the Albemarle-Pamlico Estuarine Study indicates that between 1980 and 1985, four of the five counties with the greatest population growth rates in North Carolina were coastal counties: Dare, 28.9 percent; Brunswick, 27.3 percent; Currituck, 16.1 percent; and Carteret, 14.7 percent.

This population growth has caused an explosion of the urbanization process throughout the coastal zone. New four-lane bridges are being constructed at unprecedented rates, new water supplies are being developed, and the pressures on already burgeoning sewage disposal systems are increasing. This growth, intimately intertwined with a booming tourist industry, is causing major habitat modifications. In the name of coastal development maritime forests are cleared, shorelines are bulkheaded, shallow waters are dredged, wetlands are channelized, dune fields are bulldozed, and the ground is paved for parking lots. All of these activities modify the land surface, alter the drainage, and result in increased contaminants moving into the adjacent coastal waters.

The booming boating industry parallels the growth in development and tourism. Everyone wants a dock or a marina with their boat close at hand; it's one of the prime reasons for having a place at the coast. Boats in shallow coastal waters generally require a system of navigational channels, which means dredging initial channels followed by regular maintenance dredging. Channel dredging and spoils disposal significantly alter the morphology of the shallow-water habitats, which in turn affects the water circulation system, benthic habitats, and marsh hydrology. Despite the damage it causes to local ecosystems, however, dredging is a sacred cow that is exempt from many regulations and is rarely allowed to be put on the agenda for discussion at any level of government.

Shallow-water habitats are particularly susceptible to urban growth and development. Everyone wants instant access to the water, so more and more houses are being built along the shoreline. More and more water-related businesses are being opened as well, all resulting in long-term cumulative impacts on the estuarine ecosystem.

Fortunately, some of our attitudes are changing, if ever so slightly. For example, we generally no longer use wholesale ditching and draining of the coastal marshes as a means of mosquito control. But mosquitoes still thrive along the coast, and tourism and development demand that they be controlled or eliminated. So instead of draining the marshes we spray them with insecticides. In any case, most of our marshes have already been altered by past ditching and draining projects.

Estuarine Pollution

Population and pollution are wed in an intimate relationship. When the number of people in an area increases, so does human-produced waste. Unfortunately, much of this waste is discharged into our rivers. Today there are thousands of National Pollution Discharge Elimination System (NPDES) point sources discharging industrial and municipal waste into North Carolina's rivers and estuaries. In theory, these point sources represent known volumes and compositions of waste material. In reality, the composition is poorly known for anything other than a handful of components that are regulated and monitored, including oxygen, chloride, nutrients such as phosphorus and nitrogen, and organic components such as fecal coliform along with temperature, pH, turbidity, and a few other factors. Occasionally, an individual discharger is required to monitor the discharge for known contaminants such as dioxin, mercury, lead, zinc, or copper; only rarely are such waste materials actually regulated. In fact, almost every chemical and compound used in our homes and industries has the potential to be discharged into our sewers—the rivers and estuaries of North Carolina. This approach is considered acceptable because our society believes that "dilution is the solution to pollution." Toxic materials are diluted to small enough concentrations to make particular components "harmless." But is this really the case? If enough polluters are discharging toxic materials in "harmless" amounts, the cumulative result is inevitably harmful amounts.

Point source discharges are only a part of the pollution problem, however. Such discharges (67 percent from municipal and other domestic point sources, 33 percent from industrial point sources) represent approximately one-third of the total pollution load dumped into the estuarine system. The other two-thirds of the estuarine contaminants come from nonpoint sources, about which little is known. Sources of nonpoint discharges are extremely varied in space, time, volume, and chemical composition and include agricultural and urban runoff, peat mining and timbering, groundwater discharge associated with historic waste dump sites and landfills, land and shoreline erosion, and atmospheric fallout. In addition, much of the Coastal Plain farmland is dissected by drainage ditches, swamp forests have been drained or bypassed, and associated streams have been channelized. Such major drainage modifications represent standard land-use practice, but they have devastating effects on both the nearby rivers and on downstream estuarine water bodies. Storm waters, their associated sediments, and the chemical pesticides, herbicides, and fertilizers applied to farmlands are shunted directly off the fields through ditches and into the streams and estuaries with minimum natural filtration.

The rapid growth of the hog industry in the North Carolina Coastal Plain during the 1980s and 1990s exemplifies nonpoint pollution sources that affect the estuarine system. Innumerable hog lagoons have been built in the lowlands adjacent to, and sometimes within, the swamp forests. Improper construction and weak regulations governing their use have led to lagoon leaks and spills. Increasingly, poorly managed field applications of lagoonal wastes have led to sharp increases in downstream impacts, the most obvious being the extensive algal blooms and associated fish kills that occur during the warm summer months.

Approximately 70 percent of our estuarine system is floored by organic-rich mud. The main ingredients in this mud, organic matter and clay minerals, are chemically reactive and play important and varied roles in the chemical and physical dynamics of the estuaries. The chemically reactive muds move into and out of the water column in response to storms, biological processes, and human activities, causing turbidity and interacting with chemicals and waste material in the water column. The muds continuously strip toxic materials from the water column, and thus the long-term discharge of large volumes of wastewater and runoff with low concentrations of contaminants leads to substantial pollutant enrichment within the estuarine sediments. The contaminants are then available to be further concentrated in the detritus- and filter-feeding organisms that live on or near the bottom, and may move up through the food chain, becoming more concentrated at each step.

Chemically reactive muds are important sinks and sources for many substances, including oxygen, nutrients, and contaminants. As bottom conditions change, these muds affect the chemical conditions of associated waters and the health of the entire biological community living at the sediment-water interface.

Analyses of chemicals in bottom sediments done for the Albemarle-Pamlico Estuarine Study between 1989 and 1993 identified 18 contaminated areas of concern in the Albemarle Sound, 10 areas in the Pamlico River, and 6 areas in the Neuse River estuarine systems. The most severely contaminated areas included the Elizabeth City, Washington, and New Bern waterfront areas; Welches, Tranters, and Slocum Creeks, with their major industrial facilities; and numerous wastewater treatment facilities. In addition, the western portions of the Albemarle, Pamlico, and Neuse River trunk estuaries were severely contaminated by riverine input draining the large agricultural, industrial, and urban regions within the drainage basins.

In sum, North Carolina's estuaries are settling basins that receive the riverine sediments, organic matter, and human waste and chemicals produced by agriculture, urbanization, and industrialization throughout the associated drainage basins. All of these materials accumulate within the settling basin, although with different residence times and pathways through the system. Some waste material remains and becomes part of the estuarine dynamics, affecting the sediment and water qualities and ultimately stressing the organisms living within the ecosystem. Some of the waste is ephemeral and eventually passes on through the estuaries and into the oceanic system, as it is intended to do. The rates, pathways, and effects of these contaminants are different in the northern and southern provinces and in each type of estuarine system within each province.

Booming coastal growth and development results in ever-increasing amounts of waste discharged into the coastal system. So far, North Carolinians have not been willing to confront the issue of the waste and its cumulative ecosystem impacts. Until we change our attitudes and approach toward waste, however, the quality of our estuarine systems will continue to decline, and the estuarine waters that move around our barrier islands will continue to bathe the islands in this unhealthy soup.

Living on the Estuary

Hazards—both natural and human induced—abound in the estuarine setting. Property losses from natural hazards—flooding, shoreline erosion, and storm winds—are as likely to occur in back-barrier settings as on an ocean beach. Pollution, the most insidious of the human-produced hazards, threatens both our health and the natural habitats we come to the coast to enjoy.

The actions of individual neighbors or communities can cause rapid changes that will have negative impacts on your property. Bulkheads may rob your beach of sand. A channel project may alter the currents affecting your shoreline. Changes on a nearby barrier island may affect your estuarine homesite. Like residents of barrier islands, residents of estuarine shorelines must expect to deal with the forces of nature and the depredations of human developers.

5   Shoreline Engineering: Stabilizing the Unstable

Between 80 and 90 percent of the open-ocean shoreline of the United States, including the coast of North Carolina, is retreating in a landward direction. Since more and more immovable buildings are being placed right next to this moving line in the sand, it follows that our society is facing a major problem. How do we keep our buildings from falling into the ocean?

Actually the problem is more complex than that. More than a century of experience with seawalls and other engineering structures in the state of New Jersey has taught that the process of holding the shoreline in place leads inevitably to the loss of the beach. So the real issue is how to save both buildings *and* beaches—a very difficult task.

A solution to this problem can take one of four approaches. First, we can *zone* the coastal area to keep people from building in harm's way. But there are few areas "safe" for development on most barrier islands. In addition, as islands change in size and shape over the coming decades—as they certainly will—areas that were once relatively suitable for development will become unsuitable. A second approach is to *engineer the shoreline* in an attempt to stabilize it or hold it in place. The terms *shoreline armoring* and *hard stabilization* refer to the construction of hard, immovable engineering structures along the shoreline. A third approach is *soft stabilization*—beach replenishment or nourishment—which consists of bringing in new sand to the beach. A fourth approach is to *retreat* or *relocate*—in other words, to move buildings back, demolish them, or let them fall into the sea.

In 1985, North Carolina effectively prohibited the shoreline armoring approach, so only zoning, beach nourishment, and retreat from the shoreline are now viable alternatives for the residents of this state.

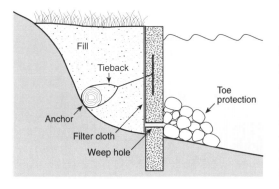

Figure 5.1 A typical bulkhead design. Critical components include anchors, tiebacks, filter cloth (to let water out without soil loss), weep holes, and toe protection in the form of rocks.

Shoreline Armoring

Although shore hardening structures are no longer permitted in this state, a significant number of older structures built before the law came into effect still exist. Their presence continues to negatively affect North Carolina's beaches. Property owners should be aware that continued shoreline retreat and beach loss are associated with seawalls and groins, and that offshore breakwaters have similar potential. In addition, we can expect future attempts by property owners to overturn the state's anti–shoreline armoring regulations. Should they be successful, it would be a huge step backward in the effort to preserve our beaches for future generations. Such a step was taken on Bald Head Island in the mid-1990s.

Seawalls

The term *seawalls* covers a whole family of coastal engineering structures built on land at the back of the beach, parallel to the shoreline. Strictly defined, seawalls are free-standing structures near the surf zone edge. The best examples are the giant walls of the northern New Jersey coast, the end result of more than a century of armoring the shoreline. If such walls are filled in behind with soil or sand, they are called *bulkheads* (fig. 5.1). *Revetments,* commonly made of large rocks, are walls built up against the lower dune face. A special type of revetment is constructed of large plastic sandbags (fig. 5.2). The state of North Carolina allows the use of such sandbags for the purpose of holding back the sea temporarily while a threatened building is moved back from the shoreline (see chapter 8). Unfortunately, some sandbag seawalls have remained in place for years and are causing beach degradation on the Outer Banks, especially in South Nags Head. For our purposes, the distinction between the types of walls is unimportant, and we will use the general term *seawalls* for all structures on the beach that parallel the shoreline.

Seawalls are usually built to protect property behind them, not to protect the beach on which they are built. Sometimes they are intended only to prevent shoreline retreat. Virtually every seawall within the reach of Hurricanes Hugo and Fran was overtopped by waves and storm surge. The walls didn't protect the buildings behind them, but they do prevent the fair-weather shoreline from moving inland. Huge sandbag seawalls were built along the Cape Hatteras National Seashore between Oregon Inlet and Rodanthe as a temporary solution to protect N.C. Highway 12 from storm overwash. The walls were kept in place after the road was moved back from the shoreline, however, and are now an eyesore marring one of North Carolina's most beautiful natural landmarks.

Seawalls are quite successful at preventing property damage if they are built strongly enough. The problem is that such protection comes at a very high price: the eventual loss of the recreational beach. That is why four states—Maine, Rhode Island, North Carolina, and South Carolina—now prohibit shoreline armoring. Former Florida governor, now senator, Bob Graham put it well when he said that "this generation does not have the right to destroy the next generation's beaches." Ironically, Florida has very little control over shoreline armoring on its own coasts, and armoring structures are proliferating at a dramatic rate on Florida's shoreline.

North Carolina is in relatively good shape as far as the extent of armoring on its open-ocean shorelines is concerned. Only 6 percent of our developed

Figure 5.2 Sandbags such as these on a North Carolina beach can do as much damage to the beach as a concrete seawall if they remain for a long period. These sandbags did little to protect the buildings in back of them from Hurricane Fran.

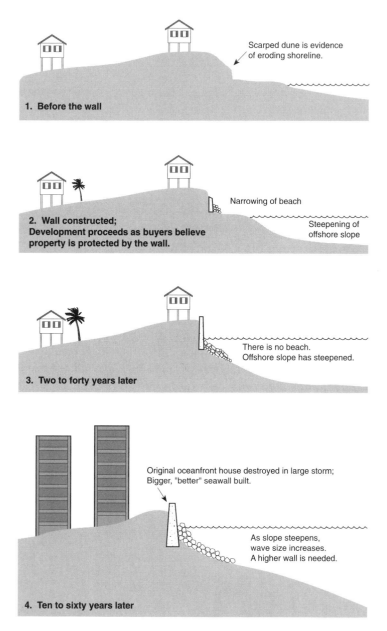

Figure 5.3 The saga of a seawall. This process, which may take several decades, is the very fate that North Carolina's anti-hard-stabilization regulations are designed to prevent. If beaches are to be preserved for future generations, seawalls should not be allowed on our shores.

shoreline is armored, as compared with 27 percent for South Carolina, 45 percent for the east coast of Florida and 50 percent for the west coast, and 50 percent for the New Jersey coast. It is important to emphasize that these figures represent the percentage of developed shoreline and do not include parks and national seashores.

Shoreline stabilization is a difficult political issue because seawalls take a long time to destroy beaches—as long as five or six decades—although the beach may be entirely gone at mid to high tide in only one to three decades. Thus it takes a politician with foresight to vote for prohibition of armoring. Another reason why stabilization is a politically difficult issue is that there is no room for compromise. Once built, seawalls are rarely removed; instead, most walls become higher and longer (fig. 5.3). What politician likes an issue with no place for compromise?

There are three mechanisms by which seawalls degrade beaches: passive loss, placement loss, and active loss (fig. 5.4). *Passive loss* is the most important of the three. Whenever a fixed, immovable object (e.g., a seawall or highway) is built adjacent to an eroding beach, the beach eventually jams up against the wall. Whatever is causing the shoreline retreat is unaffected by the wall, and erosion continues until the beach is gone. *Placement loss* occurs when seawalls are built seaward of the high tide line, thus removing part or all of the beach on the day the wall is constructed. This happened on Miami Beach and led to the need for the largest beach nourishment project in North America, completed in 1981. *Active loss* is the least understood of the three beach degradation mechanisms. It is generally assumed that interaction of the seawall with the surf zone during a storm may enhance the rate of beach loss. This interaction could include a number of factors such as reflection of waves and intensification of surf zone currents.

Groins and Jetties

Groins and jetties are walls or barriers built perpendicular to the shoreline. Groins are small walls built on straight stretches of beach, away from channels and inlets, that are intended to trap sand moving in longshore currents. There are groins present today on many North Carolina beaches, including in front of the Cape Hatteras Lighthouse and on Kure Beach, Bald Head Island, and Yaupon Beach. Groins can be made of wood, stone, concrete, steel, or (increasingly in North Carolina) nylon bags filled with sand. The plastic bag groins on Bald Head Island were emplaced in 1996 and represent the first important exception to North Carolina's anti-armoring laws (fig. 5.5).

Groins are very successful sand traps if a good sand supply exists. If a groin is working correctly, more sand will be piled up on one side of it than

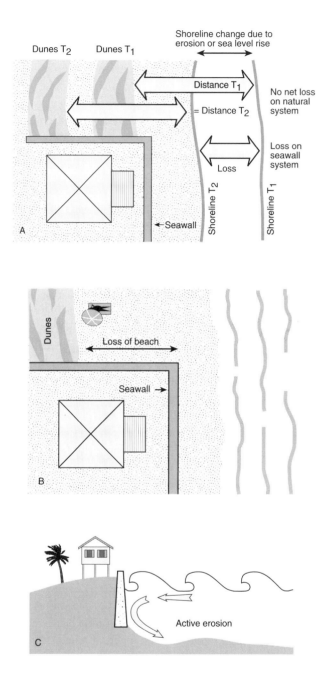

Figure 5.4 Seawalls degrade recreational beaches in three ways: (A) passive loss occurs when the beach and dune line migrate over time (time 1–time 2) but the seawall blocks beach migration; (B) placement loss occurs immediately because the seawall is built seaward of the dune line, narrowing the beach; and (C) active loss occurs when waves reflect off a seawall to scour and erode sediment in front of the wall.

on the other. The problem with groins is that they trap sand that is flowing to a neighboring beach. Thus, if a groin on one beach is functioning well, it must be causing erosion elsewhere by starving another beach (fig. 5.6).

Miami Beach and many New Jersey beaches illustrate the end result of groin usage. After one groin or series of groins (a *groin field*) is built, the increased rate of erosion on adjacent beaches has to be addressed. So more groins are constructed to trap sand on those beaches, and then on the beaches adjacent to them, sometimes extending for miles. Before the 1981 beach nourishment project, Miami Beach looked like an army obstacle course; groin after groin obstructed both pedestrian and vehicular traffic.

Jetties are walls built next to inlets (fig. 5.7) to keep sand from filling in shipping channels. They are usually much longer than groins (sometimes miles), and their purpose is to stabilize inlets to make them safer for navigation and cheaper to maintain (less dredging). On the east coast of Florida, where 17 of 18 inlets have jetties, these structures are considered to be the principal cause of beach erosion. In North Carolina, the Masonboro Inlet jetties are a major cause of erosion on Masonboro Island to the south.

Offshore Breakwaters

Offshore breakwaters should be mentioned here, although as yet there are none in North Carolina waters. Breakwaters are walls built parallel to the shoreline but at some distance offshore, usually a few tens of yards seaward of the normal surf zone. The walls dampen the wave energy on the "protected" shoreline and cause sand to be deposited. But as in the case of groins, trapping sand behind breakwaters causes a shortage somewhere else, leading to additional shoreline retreat.

Snake Oil Devices

A new phenomenon has arrived on the American shoreline: engineering structures, technically known as "nontraditional devices," that claim to prevent shoreline retreat. They come with a fascinating variety of names, including Wave Buster, Surge Breaker, Sta-Beach, Seascape, and Speed Bumps.

Although these structures may not have the appearance of seawalls or groins, and thus can sometimes slip under the no-armoring regulations, they are only variations on the same old shoreline-hardening schemes. The problem with these devices is that, as far as we know, they do not work. Some of them may temporarily protect property, but they are no different from traditional seawalls and groins in that they cause downdrift erosion or the eventual loss of the beach in front of them. They usually have one major advantage: they can be removed if the community is unhappy with them.

In 1997 the state of South Carolina allowed the emplacement on Myrtle Beach of Stabler Disks, concrete disks said to cause sand to accumulate on the beach. State bureaucrats claimed (incorrectly) that these devices did not constitute shoreline armoring. Employees of the city manager's office said they had researched the disks and were certain they would solve the local erosion problem. Apparently the employees confined their research to reading the company's literature. Coastal managers in New Jersey, where the device had previously been used, were disappointed when the disks failed, but the word hadn't reached South Carolina.

In almost every case, the inventors of these too-good-to-be-true devices claim their invention has worked somewhere else. It behooves a prudent community to check out "somewhere else" carefully. In Norfolk, Virginia, the inventors of a shoreline stabilization device claimed success in Australia and New Guinea! Another problem is that most claims of success are for the short term—after only a few weeks in some cases—but success must be viewed in a long-term sense. This means evaluation after at least five years, preferably a decade.

Another anecdote illustrates the difficulty of determining the efficacy of a shoreline stabilization device. Using money collected from North Carolina schoolchildren, the Committee to Save the Cape Hatteras Lighthouse

Figure 5.5 The sandbag groin field on Bald Head Island. The emplacement of these groins represents a major variance granted to North Carolina's anti-hard-stabilization regulations. Ironically, while some properties benefit from the groins, others are endangered by them. The system provides little storm protection, and in fact may focus storm-surge currents into some of the "protected" buildings. The aesthetics of one of North Carolina's most beautiful beaches has been destroyed. Note that the houses that "need" protection were constructed in an extreme-hazard zone!

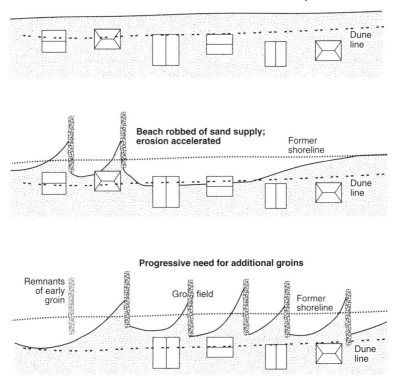

Figure 5.6 Map view diagram of downdrift erosional effect of groins and the typical proliferation of groins into a groin field. Beach retreat typically continues and groins become detached, leading to rapid erosion shoreward of the detached groins.

installed Seascape in front of the lighthouse. Seascape is a form of artificial seaweed consisting of floating plastic fronds, with one end weighted to stay at the sea bottom, that are intended to slow down wave and current activity and cause sand to accumulate. Studies indicated that Seascape didn't work. Undeterred by scientific and engineering criticism, the committee went ahead and put in the plastic seaweed. Lo and behold, a small storm came by within a few weeks and the beach widened. Success! The widened beach was there for all to see. But the same storm widened more than 50 miles of beach to the north. In other words, the wind direction was such as to cause on-shore sand movement and temporary beach widening. It is doubtful that Seascape played any role in the widening at all. In the weeks and months that followed, the plastic seaweed made little difference, and much of it eventually washed ashore, ripped out by high-energy waves.

Beach Nourishment

Beach nourishment consists of pumping or trucking sand onto the beach (fig. 5.8). The goal of most communities who use this method is to improve their recreational beach, halt shoreline erosion, and afford storm protection to beachfront buildings. In order to obtain federal funding for beach nourishment, storm protection is a required justification. A summary of the national beach nourishment experience can be found in *The Corps and the Shore,* by Orrin H. Pilkey and Katherine L. Dixon (appendix C, ref. 37).

Remember that the zone of active sand movement of the beach actually extends out to a water depth of 30 or 40 feet. When a beach is "nourished," only the upper beach is covered with new sand, creating a steeper beach. This new steepened profile often increases the rate of erosion. *In fact, replenished beaches almost always disappear at a faster rate than their natural predecessors.*

There are several possible sources of beach nourishment sand, including the lagoon, the nearby inlet, the nearby tidal delta, the adjacent continental shelf, and mainland sources inland. Lagoon sand is rarely used anymore be-

Figure 5.7   The jetties at the south end of Ocean City, Maryland, were constructed after a hurricane blew open a new inlet in 1933 (arrow). The jetties trapped sand that should have gone to Assateague Island (*bottom left*), causing Assateague to migrate. Today, Assateague's open-ocean shoreline lies landward of its 1933 lagoon shoreline, a spectacular example of island migration.

Figure 5.8   A bulldozer spreading replenishment sand on Atlantic Beach in 1994. In the foreground is the fountain formed by the replenishment sand slurry at the end of the dredge pipe. The seagulls are feeding on displaced marine organisms.

cause of the potential for ecological damage to that very delicately balanced ecosystem, and taking sand from the tidal delta may increase the rate of shoreline retreat on adjacent beaches. In general, it is best to take marine sand from a location as far from the beach as possible in order to reduce the impact of seafloor changes on wave patterns. In a number of locations (e.g., Grand Isle, Louisiana) the hole dug on the continental shelf to obtain the nourishment sand actually brought about the early demise of the beach. The Dutch require that nourishment sand be obtained from more than 15 miles offshore for just this reason!

The most replenished beaches in North Carolina (and among the most frequently replenished in the United States) are Carolina Beach and Wrightsville Beach. Carolina Beach has been nourished and renourished a total of 26 times since 1955. Wrightsville Beach has experienced 20 nourishments since 1939. The total volumes of sand used for Carolina and Wrightsville Beaches, respectively, are 15 million cubic yards and 10 million cubic yards (fig. 5.9). According to ongoing studies by the Duke University Program for the Study of Developed Shorelines, it is difficult to calculate an exact total cost for the nourishment sand. Documented expenditures on Carolina Beach total more $21 million; however, that sum reflects cost information for only one-half of the nourishment episodes. For the rest, no cost information is available.

Figure 5.10 illustrates what happens when a beach is nourished. Immediately after replenishment, there is a protective berm as well as a wider dry beach (the recreational beach at high tide). The beach profile is also steepened, and wave energy begins to redistribute the sand out onto the subaqueous portion of the beach. The sand is moved out beyond the surf zone

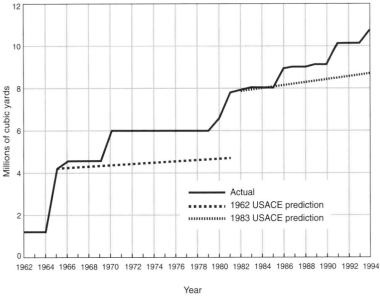

Wrightsville Beach, North Carolina

Figure 5.9   The predicted versus actual sand nourishment volumes needed for Wrightsville Beach. Dashed lines represent predictions, and solid line represents cumulative sand volume through time. Engineers cannot accurately predict the life span of a nourished beach because no one knows when the next storm will occur.

and thus no longer offers much resistance to storm waves, especially if storm surge occurs, as it almost always does. Eventually, the protective storm berm is diminished, and the high-tide dry beach is very narrow or absent. Folly Beach, South Carolina, reached this depleted state approximately two years after the completion of a 1990s replenishment project, and six years before the projected "next needed" nourishment. Underwater sand is an uncomfortable place to play beach volleyball!

Almost every island community in North Carolina considered beach nourishment in the 1990s, mainly because construction of seawalls is discouraged by the state. We recommend that any community in North Carolina considering the nourishment option keep in mind the following generalizations.

1. Beach nourishment is costly.

2. Beach nourishment requires a long-term financial commitment by the community. The beach must be nourished again and again and again. See the example of Wrightsville Beach shown in figure 5.9.

3. The environmental impact of replenished beaches is poorly understood. Certainly some nourished beaches, such as Atlantic Beach, have cre-

ated serious problems for the local fauna and flora (see below).

4. If the nourishment is to be done by the U.S. Army Corps of Engineers with federal funding, it will take 8 to 15 years to come to fruition.

5. A favorable cost-benefit ratio is required for federal participation in beach nourishment. Recreational benefits usually do not count. The principal justification in most cases must be storm protection.

6. The Corps is required to predict long-term (usually 50 years) costs and required sand volumes. You can be certain that the Corps's estimates will be highly optimistic; that is, both costs and required sand volumes will be too low. For example, figure 5.9 shows predicted and actual sand volumes needed for the Wrightsville Beach nourishment project. In this case, the Corps's Wilmington district underestimated the required sand volumes in 1980, even though they had more than a decade of nourishment experience.

7. Much of the design process is useless and wasteful. Each nourishment

Figure 5.10 Replenished beach before sand emplacement (*top*), immediately after emplacement (*middle*), and one to three years after emplacement (*bottom*). Often the sand from the storm berm is removed offshore, where it plays no role in storm protection.

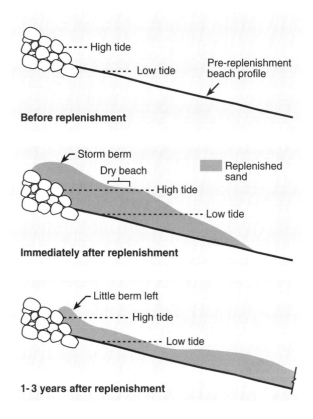

project is different, of course, but in most cases the community or state will pay the lion's share of the beach design costs, which can be millions of dollars. Sophisticated studies that gather wave data and use mathematical models never accurately predict the cost and durability of a nourished beach, in part because no one knows when the next big storm will occur.

8. The 2.7-million-cubic-yard Atlantic Beach nourishment of 1994 used sand from a navigation project (described in item 15 below) and worked just fine even though it was not "designed." The Corps considers such beaches to be dredge spoil disposal, and thus no formal design is required. There is little or no difference between a nourished beach and a dredge spoil disposal beach.

9. The best estimate of the durability, cost, and sand volumes required for a beach project can be obtained by reviewing the experience of neighboring beaches or—especially—of previous nourishments on the same beach. This approach is not precise, but it often proves to be more accurate than a coastal engineering estimate based on unrealistic, oversimplified models. There are strong regional differences in beach durability up and down the East Coast, with South Florida beaches being the longest lived.

10. Nourished beaches usually disappear much more quickly than the original natural beaches.

11. Replenished beaches do not recover as well from storms as natural beaches do. At best perhaps 10 to 20 percent of a nourished beach might come back, but more often there is no storm recovery whatsoever.

12. A lesson based on the experience of Virginia Beach, Virginia, suggests that frequent small nourishments may be more effective in maintaining the beach's width and longevity than less frequent large nourishment projects. In North Carolina, a small beach nourishment would be something like 100,000 or 200,000 cubic yards of sand per mile of beach. A large beach nourishment is of the order of 1 million cubic yards per mile. The Corps does only large beach nourishments.

13. The cost of nourishment sand is highly variable. Sand for Wrightsville Beach from nearby Mason Inlet has cost less than $2 per yard. The sand used in one Carolina Beach nourishment cost more than $10 per yard.

14. Sand is a rare commodity on the continental shelf off North Carolina. A search for sand must be carried out using seismic surveys and coring. This is one aspect of the design process that is essential and cannot be avoided.

15. There *is* such a thing as a free lunch! If the Wilmington district of the Corps can be convinced to pump sand from inlet- or harbor-dredging projects onto adjacent beaches, the cost is essentially zero to the community. Federal taxpayers pay it all. The largest such "free" project ever done in the United States was the 1994 emplacement of 2.5 million cubic yards of

sediment on Bogue Banks (Atlantic Beach). In theory such navigation projects can be done only if beach disposal is the cheapest way to get rid of dredge spoil. In practice this is a highly politicized process.

16. One problem with the "free lunch" is that the "sand" pumped on the beach may be very muddy. Off Atlantic Beach, a widespread layer of mud derived from the nourishment project exists where previously there was sand. The nearshore marine fauna and flora were adversely affected by this mud. In addition, dried mud has made sections of Atlantic Beach as hard as rock.

17. Consider trucking in sand, especially to respond to erosion "hot spots," both before and after nourishment. Every nourished beach has spots where erosion is particularly rapid. Sometimes relatively small amounts of sand (e.g., a few hundred truckloads) can repair a hot spot until the next nourishment project. Virginia Beach successfully used this approach for a number of years, sometimes putting more than 100,000 dump-truck loads of sand on the beach in a single year.

18. It would be to each community's advantage to have its own source of sand. Hire a geologist to find the sand in the lower Coastal Plain. The most likely sand sources are the ice age barrier islands that were stranded on the Coastal Plain when sea levels dropped as a new ice age began.

19. Once a nourished beach is in place it is essential to monitor its progress. This can be done very easily by taking repetitive photos from the same spot, making sure a sunbather or surfer is in the photo for scale. Alternatively, cross-beach profiles can be taken using elementary leveling techniques to provide a more quantitative view of the loss rate (a good community project for high school students).

20. Sand offshore, below the low-tide line, is useless for either recreation or community storm protection. When a replenished beach disappears more quickly than expected (the usual case), the design consultants or the Corps of Engineers may assert that the sand is just offshore providing storm protection, but this is not the case. The portion of the beach most effective for storm protection is the artificial dune (sometimes called a berm in engineering parlance) at the back or landward side of the beach (fig. 5.10).

21. The usual impetus behind beach nourishment is that the first row of buildings is threatened with destruction. That being the case, who should pay for the project?

Retreat

Moving buildings back or letting them fall into the sea has a long tradition in North Carolina. On one shoreline reach in South Nags Head, the houses

Figure 5.11 A post-Fran view of Shell Island Resort on Wrightsville Beach. The building is threatened with undermining by the migrating inlet channel (*right*). State law forbids seawall construction to protect such buildings on the premise that beaches are more important than buildings.

now in row 1 were in row 3 a mere 25 years ago. Unit 3 in a Nags Head motel is next to the beach; seaward units 1 and 2 disappeared in storms long ago. Many houses on the Outer Banks have been moved back over the years. The Outlaw family house in Nags Head has been moved back 600 feet in 100 years in five separate moves. The first of the moves probably involved jacking the house up on logs and rolling it back with mule power. On Hog Island, Virginia, and Edisto Beach, South Carolina, whole communities fell into the ocean; the tombstones of their cemeteries now rest on the continental shelf. In all of the above areas, the shoreline was not armored, and a wide, healthy beach exists.

Retreating from the shoreline is the best way to ensure preservation of beaches for future generations. It is politically difficult, of course, but it is the course of action chosen by North Carolina and other states that prohibit seawalls. State law doesn't allow shoreline armoring, and beach nourishment is extremely expensive; therefore the future of North Carolina's shoreline is bound to involve a lot of moving. Shoreline property owners have exerted pressure on the state government and its agencies to allow armoring in special cases. The controversy over whether or not to let the Shell Island Resort build a seawall in 1997 to keep the building from falling into the inlet is an example and a taste of the future (fig. 5.11).

In the long run, North Carolinians must make a decision. They can have beaches or they can have beachfront buildings; they can't have both. If we opt in favor of buildings, the beaches will be lost—and so, ultimately, will the buildings.

Are Variances Eroding North Carolina's Beach Protection?

The problem of shoreline engineering leading to beach narrowing and degradation is not exclusive to New Jersey or even the east coast of the United States. Thirty percent of the sandy beaches on Oahu, Hawaii, have disappeared because of seawalls. California beaches are starving partly because of dam construction and harbor protection, factors that are also contributing to the erosion of Puerto Rico's coastline. All in all, the Atlantic and Pacific stories are identical; only the place names are different. Shore-hardening structures either directly or indirectly cause loss of beaches.

The coastal states of the United States are finally beginning to view their beaches as national treasures. A time will come when our remaining beaches will be like national parks, protected forever for the benefit of the public at large. Unlike Yellowstone Park, however, where Old Faithful will be in the same location 50 years from now, beach management policy must take into account the facts that sea level is rising and that the beaches are moving. The beaches of the future will be mobile national parks! Already the National Park Service has declared that beach movement will be allowed to occur on national seashores at whatever rate and style nature chooses. Unfortunately, the Park Service doesn't always practice what it preaches. It allowed the North Carolina Department of Transportation to build sandbag seawalls on Pea Island.

Is there a beach degradation problem in North Carolina? The answer is "maybe." Increasing pressure is being put on the Coastal Resources Commission to reverse the state's past philosophy of conservation. Recent years have seen a weakening of North Carolina's forward-looking antihardening laws. The "exceptional case" requiring a variance under the law is becoming less exceptional: the seawall at Fort Fisher, the groins on Bald Head Island, the sandbag wall on Shell Island, and historic lighthouses that apparently are historic only if they remain in place.

Public beaches are arguably far more valuable than a private condo or cottage that only one person or family can enjoy. The state's beaches need the help of the public and of far-sighted planners and developers if they are to be available today and tomorrow. The pressure to "protect" the Cape Hatteras Lighthouse with a seawall (chapter 1) and the effort to stabilize Oregon Inlet clearly illustrate the breadth of the attacks on our shores.

Oregon Inlet: A Pressing Coastal Issue

During the last two centuries more than two dozen inlets have opened and closed along the Outer Banks, a cycle that will continue into the future. Today, Oregon Inlet, which opened in 1846, is the northernmost inlet in North Carolina. Since it opened, Oregon Inlet has migrated steadily and rapidly to the south (fig. 5.12).

In 1970 Congress authorized a dual jetty system to stabilize this dynamic inlet (fig. 5.12). Since then, however, questions about the plans submitted by the Corps of Engineers for jetty construction and maintenance have kept the project in the planning stages. Concerns over whether the Oregon Inlet jetties will be an environmental disaster or an economic boon have created a controversy that has played out on a national level.

Because the jetties will be built on lands managed by the Department of the Interior, the National Park Service impaneled distinguished scientists and engineers from outside North Carolina to review the Corps's plans. The Inman Panel, as it was called, after its first chair, Douglas Inman of Scripps Oceanographic Institution, found numerous shortcomings in the Corps's description of the inlet's dynamics and the project conception. The Corps has never adequately addressed the criticisms made by the Inman Panel or by scientists within North Carolina.

The controversy surrounding the jetty project can be generally divided into three categories: environment, fisheries, and economics.

Environment

A well-known and well-documented effect of jetties is their interruption of sand flow along the coast. As a result, erosion occurs in the downdrift direction, in this case to the south of Oregon Inlet. The Corps proposes to offset the erosion by artificially moving sand across the inlet. But the Corps's reliance on an untested sloping-front floating breakwater for bypassing the sand is questionable. Would such a device function as advertised in the rough waters of Oregon Inlet? In any case, the high cost of bypassing sand *ad infinitum* will be a burden for generations to come.

The Corps assumes that the islands to the north and south of the inlet will essentially stay where they are after the jetties are emplaced. That expectation is unrealistic. Sea level rise scenarios indicate a strong potential for extensive movement of these islands regardless of the presence of jetties. The damage caused by the jetties will affect areas of the Cape Hatteras National Seashore, the Pea Island National Wildlife Refuge, and private property.

The proposed alignment of the jetties is such that waves from the east-northeast may be funneled into the channel, actually *increasing* the hazard to boat traffic within the channel guarded by the jetties.

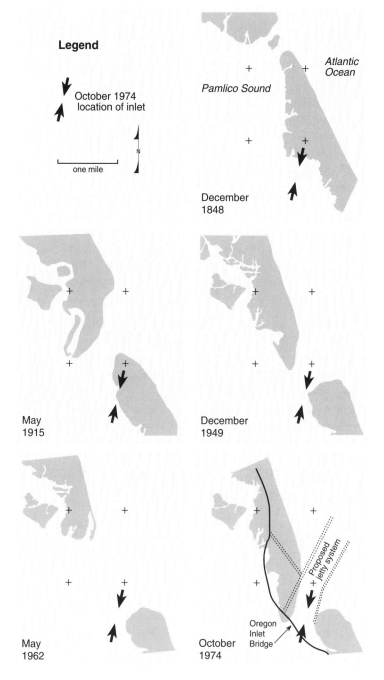

Figure 5.12 Oregon Inlet migration history and proposed jetty system.

Fisheries

The National Marine Fisheries Service (NMFS) has stated that the jetties would significantly reduce the successful passage of fish larvae from the open ocean to the sounds, where they live until reaching maturity. The NMFS has also said that several of the fish species in the North Carolina shelf fishery have been drastically depleted. Increasing the catch through the improved access to the sea, as the Corps proposes, will further damage the fishery. In a letter to the Corps of Engineers released in 1995, the NMFS stated: "The assumption that even a modest increase in landings will be realized as a result of the [Oregon Inlet jetty] project is unrealistic, based on the present condition of fisheries and the need to reduce harvests for a considerable period of time to rebuild depleted fishery stocks."

Costs

The Corps estimates that construction costs for the jetties will be $100 million. Add to this the estimated $5 to $10 million per year for dredging and sand bypassing, and the 50-year project cost becomes $350 to $600 million. It has been estimated that approximately 300 commercial fisherman will benefit from these expenditures. In contrast, in 1995 the NMFS said that "virtually every projected increase in landings attributed to improving the Oregon Inlet harbor facilities will be at the direct expense of other ports, particularly those located in North Carolina, Florida, and the mid-Atlantic."

If the jetties are constructed, the Corps's efforts to mitigate their damage to natural resources will have to be Herculean, driving costs well beyond the current estimates. The actual cost of the Oregon Inlet jetties may be much higher than predicted.

The Corps has stated that dredging alone will not suffice to keep the inlet open. But a dredging panel convened by the National Park Service said that dredging would succeed at a cost comparable with or lower than the jetties.

Truths of the Shoreline

Certain "universal truths" emerge quite clearly from studies of the long-developed shorelines of New Jersey and other areas. These truths are evident to scientists who have studied the shoreline and to old-timers who have lived on the shore all their lives. As aids to safe and aesthetically pleasing shoreline development, they should be the fundamental basis of planning on any barrier island.

1. *Beach erosion is not a natural disaster.* It is an integral and expected part of barrier island evolution (see chapter 2), especially in times, such as these, of rising sea levels.

2. *There is no erosion problem until someone builds a structure along the*

shoreline by which to measure it. No buildings = no problem. The east end of Shackleford Banks in the Cape Lookout National Seashore is retreating at 15 feet per year, but no one cares. On the other hand, a large number of people are concerned about the shoreline retreat problem on Topsail Island, Long Beach, Bogue Banks, and other developed islands!

3. *Shoreline erosion creates no problem for the beach.* As the shoreline retreats, the beach simply changes its position in space. Surfers, swimmers, fishermen, and strolling lovers can't tell the difference.

4. *The activities of humans increase the rate of shoreline retreat.* Most things that people do on barrier islands—including shoreline engineering, dune destruction, building construction, channel dredging, and jetty construction—reduce the beaches' sand supply. Activities on the mainland such as dam building sometimes do the same.

5. *Shoreline engineering protects the interests of a very few people who are responsible for the erosion to begin with, often at a very high cost in federal and state dollars.* On a typical North Carolina island, the shorefront property that is responsible for the erosion problem (truth 2 above) is owned by a few hundred people. In contrast, hundreds of thousands, even millions of people may use the beach over a year's time.

6. *Shoreline stabilization, especially beach nourishment, can lead to intensified development.* The presence of a wide, new nourished beach replacing a narrow, eroded beach where waves once rolled under buildings is a temptation developers cannot resist. After the 1982 nourishment in Carolina Beach, a single-family-home community changed seemingly overnight to a multifamily and high-rise community. The increased population added additional voices in support of the next nourishment and increased the number of people in danger from storms.

7. *Once you begin shoreline engineering, you can't stop it!* Shoreline hardening is rarely removed. Instead, it usually grows larger and longer. Once a beach is nourished, it must be nourished again and again.

8. *You can have buildings or you can have beaches; in the long run you cannot have both.*

The ultimate truth is that we should avoid the hazards, but if we choose to locate on a barrier island, then prudence dictates that we evaluate the level of risk.

6 Assessing Risk Levels for Your Island, Neighborhood, and Site

No locality on a barrier island is safe! Given the right conditions, hurricanes, floods, wind and wave erosion, or inlet formation can attack any part of an island. Furthermore, human activity, particularly construction, almost always reduces the relative stability of the natural environment. Human-built structures are static (immobile); when placed in a dynamic (mobile) system, they disrupt the balance of that system (fig. 6.1). Interference with the sand supply, disruption of vegetative cover, topographic alterations, and similar effects of structures actually create conditions favorable to the damage or loss of those structures.

Although some areas on barrier islands are at less risk from hazards than others, all areas are vulnerable to natural processes. This fact was recognized in the earliest days of settlement. Governor Arthur Dobbs expressed such an awareness in a letter written in July 1756: "Last summer . . . I found a violent storm of about 5 years ago had carried away Beacon Island, which was near 2 miles long, and all of the banks here in time may be lyable to the like fate."

Island Stability: Permanent Paradise or Tempting Trap?

Among the lessons taught by Hurricanes Hugo, Emily, Bertha, and Fran is that each barrier island responds to storms and other coastal processes as a single system. In order to design a way to live with the flexible nature of a barrier island, you must first evaluate the entire island in terms of its physical processes, including the island's response to human activities. The second step is to evaluate the characteristics of the neighborhood; the third step is to focus on an individual building site. Keep in mind that no barrier island is safe from hurricane winds, storm-surge flooding, wave erosion, overwash, or inlet formation and migration. However, a low, bare, rapidly migrating island such as Masonboro Island or Core Banks is more likely to

Figure 6.1 A row of buildings on the beach in South Nags Head. Note the assemblage of black sandbags that has delayed the buildings' fall into the sea. Long-term use of such sandbags is prohibited by North Carolina regulations. Obviously these houses are extremely vulnerable to the next storm.

suffer from these hazards than the inner-island forested beach ridges of Bogue Banks. The latter will be subjected to coastal hazards, but with less frequency and probably less intensity than the former over the short term. An island's elevation and forest cover offer immediate clues to its stability. Other islandwide characteristics should also come into consideration (e.g., inlet formation and migration, overwash, erosion rates); in general, learn how the island has responded to previous storms.

Another important aspect in evaluating overall island stability is to check the island's response to past human activity, particularly construction. An island is not necessarily a low-risk site merely because it has been developed or because there are stabilization structures in place. More likely, the opposite is true. Shoreline stabilization structures are obstacles to the dynamic sediment flow that maintains the island system, disrupting the dynamic equilibrium. They lower the island's natural flexibility, and the system must readjust to the new conditions the structures produce. In other words, structures sometimes create conditions favorable to their own destruction. The presence of groins, seawalls, or revetments on the beach tells you the shoreline is subject to erosion—which is now compounded by the stabilization structures themselves (fig. 6.1). Such a shoreline is definitely to be avoided.

Removal of vegetation for purposes of construction or to improve the view of the sea may increase the potential for storm damage to property or create a blowing sand nuisance. Roads to the beach built through the dune line may act as overwash passes. Removal of dunes invites disaster because the protective buffering action of the dunes has been lost. Hurricanes Fran and Hugo proved the effectiveness of high, wide dunes in preventing or greatly reducing property damage.

The political infrastructure of your prospective island may have a strong bearing on its overall safety. Unchecked growth or unenforced building and dune protection codes are examples of social conditions that may create threats to health or safety. Overloaded sewage treatment systems, inadequate or unsafe escape routes, loss of natural storm protection, unstormworthy buildings, and vulnerable utilities are but a few examples of politically derived development problems. Developers and real estate interests often take a head-in-the-sand attitude and are reluctant to face the reality that the beaches are retreating, that development disrupts the island's dynamics, or that the density of development has exceeded the island's carrying capacity.

The terms *hazard, risk, mitigation,* and *cost* apply islandwide, not just to individual properties. Eroding beaches, leveled dunes, disappearing forest cover, beach nourishment projects, and failing seawalls are examples of community-wide problems that all property owners pay for, whether or not their property is directly involved.

Once you are satisfied with the island's natural stability, its response to past storms as well as to human development activities, and the political setting, the next steps are to select first a general location and then a specific site. The following site selection guide applies to your specific property; remember, however, that property lines are an artificial grid put down over dynamic environments. Look at your site in the context of the developed or developable neighboring properties as well.

Selecting Your Site: Sunny Playground or Watery Tempest?

Human nature is such that we are willing to gamble if we think the potential reward is worth the risk. In the case of a barrier island, the rewards are the amenities of the seashore. Sunny-day decisions may overlook the realities, however, and the wrong choice may place you at risk of losing your property and even your life. Like smart gamblers who know the odds and try to reduce the house advantage, beach house buyers can and should identify the natural odds of coastal hazards and act accordingly. And you don't have to brave a storm to do this!

Structures placed in the least dynamic zones (stable areas subject to less sediment movement or change) are less likely to be damaged. Once you can identify areas, rates, and intensities of natural physical activity, you have the basis for choosing a specific homesite. Consider, for example, an inland river and the flat areas (the *floodplain*) next to it. Even casual observation reveals that rivers flood occasionally. When observed for a long period, the timing and size of the floods can be seen to follow a pattern. Perhaps the area adjacent to the river is flooded every spring, but the entire floodplain is flooded only every 5 to 10 years on average. Once or twice in a person's lifetime the flood is devastating, covering an area greater than the adjacent floodplain (be aware, however, that the "once or twice" may be closely spaced in time). On this basis, it is possible to predict the frequency and size of floods expected in a given area.

Individual floods are classified according to the frequency of a given flood level. For instance, if water has reached a certain level only twice during a 100-year period of record, a flood rising to that level is called a 1-in-50-year flood. Unfortunately, this terminology gives the impression that one does not have to worry about such a flood level for another 50 years. In fact, such flood levels are spaced in time randomly, sometimes occurring in successive years or even the same year! A better way of thinking about such floods is in terms of probability. A 100-year flood is a level of flooding that has a 1 percent probability of occurring in any given year. There could be two such floods in successive years, and it would not preclude the 1 percent probability of another occurring the third year. Like flipping pennies, you don't expect to see three heads in a row when you start with the first flip, but after two in a row, the chance that the third flip will be heads is the same as on the first flip—50:50. And while not worrying about the next 100-year flood, you may experience the 70-year flood, or the 1,000-year flood of which we know nothing because we have no weather records of sufficient length to predict it. Such big events have happened and will again. No one expected the great flood of 1997 in Minnesota and the Dakotas, but its occurrence does not preclude a repeat event very soon.

The same flood possibility is true for the coastal zone and barrier islands. But in this case the flooding usually does not come from rivers. Instead, the flood is storm surge: the rising sea level during a storm, plus winds, waves, and sediments, all mixed in the cauldron of a hurricane or northeaster.

Of course it would be foolish to build a house in a place that is flooded once every year, or even once every 10 years. Far better to build where the likelihood of flooding is 1 percent in any given year (the likelihood of flooding being nearly 100 percent during the lifetime of the building) or a much lower probability. Whether or not to locate in a flood-prone area at all should be determined by how important it is to choose that site, by the level of economic loss you are willing to sustain, and most of all by the level of risk to which you would expose family and friends occupying the site.

The frequency and elevation of storm-surge flooding in coastal areas is somewhat predictable (table 6.1), although no one can predict exactly when a storm that causes flooding to a certain level will occur. Thus, if you expect a 1-in-25-year storm-surge flood level of 8 feet for a particular stretch of coast, the elevation of the house you build or buy should be greater than 8

Table 6.1 Storm Still-Water Surge Levels for 1-in-25-, 50-, and 100-Year Storm Frequencies

	Surge Level(s) (feet above mean sea level)		
	1/25	1/50	1/100
Virginia to Cape Hatteras	7.43	8.20	8.80
Cape Hatteras to Cape Lookout	7.10	7.63	8.00
Cape Lookout to New River Inlet	7.63	9.33	10.95
New River Inlet to Cape Fear	8.80	10.55	12.05
Cape Fear to South Carolina	9.67	11.23	12.45

Note: *"Still-water surge level"* is the level to which the sea rises during a storm; it does not include the height of waves on the sea surface.

feet. Because storm waves will further raise that flood level, you should seek an even higher elevation in addition to using a construction technique that raises the house several feet off the ground (see chapter 9).

The 100-year flood level is a standard used for both inland and coastal regions as the basis for building codes and zoning ordinances adopted by communities that participate in the National Flood Insurance Program (see chapter 8). Flood level data and calculated wave heights are available from the Federal Emergency Management Agency or from community planning and insurance offices (Flood Insurance Rate Maps show these elevations; see appendix B). By comparison, the Dutch use 1-in-500 year, and even 1-in-1,000 year event probabilities in their planning and regulations!

Stability Indicators: Can You Read Nature's Record?

Barrier island processes often leave a record of past events or reflect the dynamic natural history of an area. The natural attributes of a site can guide prospective buyers and builders in evaluating site vulnerability to potentially hazardous processes and events. Natural indicators include terrain (landform types), land elevation, vegetation type and cover, shells, and soil type (table 6.2).

Terrain and Elevation

Terrain and elevation are good measures of an area's safety from adverse natural processes. Low, flat areas are subject to destructive wave attack,

Table 6.2 Parameters for Evaluating Site-Specific Risks from Coastal Hazards. This list is designed specifically for shorelines developed in unconsolidated, potentially erodible materials, such as bluffed shorelines or sandy systems (e.g., barrier islands, barrier beaches).

Parameter	Risk Level		
	High	Moderate	Low
Site elevation	<3 meters	3–6 meters	>6 meters
Beach width, slope, and thickness	Narrow and flat, thin with mud, peat, or stumps exposed	Wide and flat, or narrow and steep	Wide with well-developed berm
Overwash	Overwash apron or terrace (frequent overwash)	Overwash fans (occasional overwash)	No overwash
Site position relative to inlet or river mouth	Very near	Within sight	Distant
Dune configuration	No dunes (see Overwash)	Low, or discontinuous dunes	High, continuous, unbreached ridge, dune field
Coastal shape	Concave or embayed	Straight	Convex
Vegetation on site	Little, toppled, or immature	Well-established shrubs and grasses, none toppled	Mature vegetation, forested, no evidence of erosion
Drainage	Poor	Moderate	Good
Area landward of site	Lagoon, marsh, or river	Floodplain or low-elevation terrace	Upland
Natural offshore protection	None, open water	Frequent bars offshore	Submerged reef, limited fetch
Offshore shelf	Wide and shallow	Moderate	Steep and narrow

Source: Adapted from table 5.1 in *Living with the South Carolina Coast*, by Gered Lennon et al. (appendix C, ref. 20).

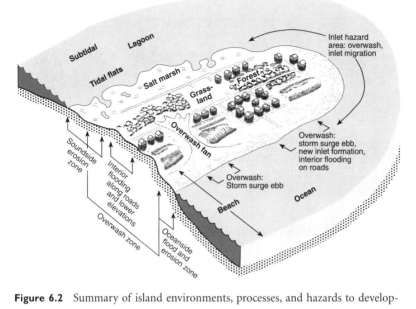

Figure 6.2 Summary of island environments, processes, and hazards to development. The development grid enhances these hazards by removing protective shrub and forest cover, providing avenues for overwash, and building at low elevations too close to the shoreline.

overwash, storm-surge flooding, and blowing sand (fig. 6.2). Quite often, low areas flood from the landward side. Table 6.1 shows expected storm-surge levels for different parts of the North Carolina coast. Most areas under 7 feet in elevation experience relatively frequent, severe flooding. There were five floods along the North Carolina coast in the decade of the 1950s. Even areas of 15-foot elevation incurred water damage from Hurricane Hazel in 1954, and during an 1856 hurricane, breakers are said to have struck areas of 30-foot elevation near Wrightsville Beach! Hurricane Fran flooded Wrightsville Beach with upward of 10.5 feet of water. The streets of North Topsail Beach were 5 feet under water during Fran's 11-foot storm surge. Even Hurricane Emily piled up almost 10 feet of water from sound-side flooding in Buxton.

Vegetation

Vegetation often indicates a site's relative environmental stability, age, and elevation. In general, the taller and thicker the vegetation, the more stable the site and the lower the risk for development (fig. 6.3). Maritime forests grow only at elevations high enough to preclude frequent overwash. In addition, since a mature maritime forest takes at least 100 years to develop, the

Figure 6.3 A dense and beautiful maritime forest such as Buxton Woods, shown here, can provide significant wind protection for buildings if the vegetative cover is maintained.

homeowner can be further assured that the forest areas are generally the most stable and offer the lowest-risk homesites on the island. The exceptions to this rule are areas where rapidly eroding shorelines have advanced into the maritime forest—in Caswell and Yaupon Beaches on Oak Island, for example (fig. 6.4)—and where inlets are cutting into forest beach ridges, usually on the northern ends of islands, such as at Ocean Isle and Holden Beach. A further advantage of building in a maritime forest is the shelter the trees provide from hurricane-force winds.

Trees offer excellent protection from flying debris. Destabilized dunes or an active dune field on the margin of a forest may threaten the stability of forest sites. Examples of forests buried by dunes can be seen at the old town of Rice Path on Bogue Banks and on the west end of Shackleford Banks where a skeleton forest is being exhumed as the dunes continue to move.

Typical maritime forests include live oak, long-needle loblolly pine, red cedar, yaupon, and wax myrtle (the common shrubs found in thickets), cabbage palmetto, dogwood, black cherry, and holly. The forest canopy will be lower at the seaward edge and may be "pruned" by the salt spray (fig. 6.4).

Seashells

Seashells are moved about by both humans and natural processes. A mixture of brown-stained and natural-colored shells is often washed onshore on the ocean beaches of islands during storms. Shells of these colors indicate overwash zones when found inland of the beach. *Don't build in such zones.* If you must build in an overwash zone, elevate the structure enough so as not to interfere with the overwash process.

The presence of mixed black and white shells without brown or natural-colored shells is almost certainly a sign that material has been dredged and pumped from nearby waterways. Such material is used to fill low areas on islands, to fill inlets that break through islands during storms, or to nourish eroding beaches. Thus, such a shell mixture may indicate an unstable area where development should be avoided. The oyster shells now found on Atlantic Beach on Bogue Banks, in front of the Sea Vista Motel on Topsail Island, and on Wrightsville Beach are examples of nourishment sediment taken from the lagoons.

Soil Profiles

A soil profile takes a long time to develop, so a mature soil suggests a stable building site. White-bleached sand overlying yellow sand to a depth of 2 to 3 feet (often found in forest areas) suggests such stability. Determine the soil profile by looking in a road cut or finger canal, or by digging a pit. Keep in mind that even formerly stable areas can be eroded by a migrating barrier island, so you may find a "stable" soil profile in an unstable position, such as

Figure 6.4 This thicket shows the classic shape of a salt-spray-pruned maritime forest on a barrier island. Its presence on the beach indicates rapid erosion because forests prefer the sheltered back sides of islands where salt spray is less common. Erosion is also evidenced by the toppled trees on the beach.

in the wave-cut scarp at the back of a beach (e.g., Caswell Beach). Avoid areas whose profiles show layers of peat or other organic materials. Such layers have a high water content and lack the strength to support an overlying structure. The weight of a house can compress the layers, causing the house to sink. Furthermore, such soil conditions cause septic tank problems.

Island Environments: How Does Your Site Fit into the Bigger Picture?

Inland developments typically occupy a single environment such as a pine forest or former pastureland. In contrast, barrier islands comprise small areas of very different environments (see fig. 3.1), and, typically, developments overlap environmental boundaries without regard to the consequences. By knowing what environment(s) a building site and adjacent properties occupy, you can identify prevailing conditions that may or may not be conducive to development. Typical barrier island environments include primary dunes, dune fields, overwash fans, grasslands, inlets, maritime forests and thickets, and marshes.

Primary Dunes

Primary dunes usually are defined as the row of dunes closest to the ocean, although a distinct line or row may be absent. These dunes serve as a sand reservoir that feeds the beach, the island's interior, and the back island. In addition, they provide elevation and width as a temporary line of defense against wind and waves.

The primary dunes are the natural main line of defense against erosion and storm damage to man-made structures, albeit a leaky one because of the overwash passes between the dunes. When development interferes with

Figure 6.5 Well-vegetated grassy dune typical of Southern Shores.

the dune system, both the natural and the built environments suffer. We must recognize the mobility of dune systems, even those stabilized by vegetation. Off-road vehicles, foot traffic, drought, and fire destroy vegetation, and therefore dune stability. In North Carolina, primary dunes are protected, and local ordinances may dictate even stricter regulations. Wooden dune walkovers are encouraged, although their construction must meet standards set by the N.C. Coastal Area Management Act (CAMA) to prevent their interference with dune processes (fig. 6.5). By prohibiting vehicles on the dunes, and by building boardwalks and footbridges over them rather than building footpaths through them, we may be able to preserve the dunes.

In areas where dunes (oceanfront or interior) have been destroyed or are being threatened, remedial steps can be taken to restore or stabilize them. Planting dune grasses and sea oats in bare areas stabilizes existing dunes and encourages additional dune growth (appendix C, ref. 49). Sand fencing, elsewhere called snow fencing, is commonly used to trap sand and increase dune growth.

The high elevation of a dune does not in itself render a site safe. An area adjacent to the shore with a high erosion rate is likely to lose its dune protection during the average lifetime of a house. Even setback ordinances, which require that structures be placed a minimum distance behind the dune (see chapter 8), do not ensure long-term protection. Setbacks are based on historical erosion rates, but there is no guarantee that future erosion rates will be the same as past ones. If your house is located on a primary dune you should expect to lose it during the next major storm. Many existing houses were constructed by notching the landward side of the frontal dune: built-in destabilization in regard to the next storm.

Dune Fields

Dune fields are open, bare-to-grassy sand dune areas found between the primary dunes and the maritime forest (if present) or on the back side of the island. Stable dune fields offer sites that are at relatively low risk from wave erosion, overwash, and storm-surge flooding, if their elevation is sufficiently high. However, digging up the dunes for construction may cause blowing sand, destabilize vegetation, and increase sand movement. In the pre-bulldozer days, houses were either moved or abandoned when threatened by dunes.

Do not build where the dunes show bare, unvegetated surfaces; these are active dunes. Not far from Corolla on Currituck Bank, lots on top of 40- to 50-foot-high active dunes have been offered for sale. Avoid such areas. On the northern Outer Banks, some houses that were buried during the early part of this century have reappeared as the sand has shifted. In some of the

Dare County developments, and in Sunset Beach at the opposite end of the North Carolina coast, sand from active dunes drifts onto, and sometimes covers, roads. When this occurs, the sand should be returned to the area from which it came rather than hauling it away, as is often done.

Overwash Fans

Overwash fans (also called washover fans) develop when water thrown up by waves and storm surge flows between and around dunes. Surge waters carry sand and stained, bleached, and natural-colored shells that are deposited in flat, fan-shaped masses (fig. 6.2). Sand from these fans forms and maintains dunes and builds up the island's elevation. Where primary dunes are high and continuous, overwash is relatively unimportant and restricted to the back-beach and nearshore areas (e.g., along Bogue Banks, parts of Topsail Island, portions of Onslow Beach, and other islands). In areas where dunes are absent, low, or discontinuous, overwash fans may extend across the entire island, as on Masonboro Island, No Name Island, parts of Lea Island and Figure Eight Island, and most of Core Banks.

During severe hurricanes, only the highest elevations (generally above 15 to 20 feet) are safe from overwash. Hurricane Fran caused extensive overwash along much of Carolina Beach and all of Topsail Island. When low-elevation islands are struck by major hurricanes, the overwash fans created are so extensive as to coalesce into sheets called *overwash terraces*. Overwash may damage or bury structures and roads (fig. 6.6), in the latter case blocking escape routes.

Roads built to expand development may contribute to its destruction. Level roads cut straight to the beach may become overwash passes during storms, especially where they cut through dunes. Roads should end landward of the dunes and should curve or cross the island obliquely rather than perpendicular to the shore. The only roads that should go over the dunes are emergency vehicle accesses. The problem created by such roads was well demonstrated by Hurricane Fran on North Topsail Beach, where shore-perpendicular driveways, their effects exacerbated by shore-perpendicular channels cut into the marsh, led to the creation of three deep storm-surge scour channels (see fig. 2.6).

Try to avoid building on overwash fans, especially fresh and unvegetated ones. Unfortunately, such areas may be difficult to recognize if the fans have been destroyed by bulldozing or sand removal. If no alternative site is available, elevate the building and allow overwash to continue and build up sand. Use overwash deposits removed from roads and driveways to rebuild adjacent dunes, or return the sediment to the beach. Do not remove the sand from the area. Planting dune grass and other natural vegetation on an overwash deposit may help stabilize the deposit and trap additional sand.

Grasslands

Grasslands are located either behind dune fields or on the back sides of is-lands just inside the salt marsh. These areas may be relatively flat, built up as a terrace of coalescent overwash fans, and are generally subject to future flooding and overwash. Natural grasslands may be difficult to distinguish from artificial bulldozer-flattened developments, but the former are charac-terized by a diversity of plants (e.g., saltmeadow cordgrass, yucca, cactus, and thistle).

Inlets

Inlets are the channels that separate islands. As a hurricane approaches a barrier island, strong onshore winds drive storm-surge waters and waves against the island and through the inlets into the estuaries. As the storm passes, the wind either stops blowing or shifts and starts blowing seaward, allowing the storm-surge waters to return to the ocean (see figs. 2.6, 2.7). If the existing inlets do not permit the water to escape fast enough, a new inlet will be cut through the island from the marsh side. Two of North Carolina's most famous inlets, Hatteras and Oregon, are said to have formed in this manner during a September 1846 storm.

Figure 6.6 This view of N.C. Highway 12 on Hatteras Island shows mounds of overwash sand on either side of the road. The sand was removed after storms. Overwash sand is an important aspect of island migration, furnishing elevation to the island as it migrates landward. Frequent flooding of Highway 12 creates a major evacuation hazard. So, which is more important, island migration or island evacua-tion? Rebuilding a gravel road after each overwash could be a compromise.

Low, narrow island areas that lack extensive salt marsh and are near the mouths of rivers or estuaries are likely spots for inlet development. Spits, which are common on the ends of barrier islands, are particularly vulnerable (e.g., the southern end of Figure Eight Island). The wise resident does not build on such bits of expanding sand because the inlet will eventually and suddenly change the location of its channel.

Islands, particularly low areas in inlet zones, are often breached by small channels during storms, either by the storm-surge flood or, more often, by strong storm-surge ebb currents. Such channels are not inlets in a strict sense; they develop and persist to accommodate internal island drainage. Temporary "swashes" off small creek mouths are similar. Although these features are temporary and often fill with sediment naturally, the likelihood of reactivation makes them extreme-risk zones with respect to development. Hurricane Fran cut several such channels on the northern end of Topsail Island (see fig. 2.3).

The U.S. Army Corps of Engineers or N.C. Department of Transportation is often prompt in filling in such channels after a storm, and the future property owner may not realize that the site is in the throat of a former channel, or that the access (and escape) route to and from the property may be cut. Such is the case for those who live north of the Holiday Inn in Wrightsville Beach. The hotel sits on the former site of Moore's Inlet, which was closed in 1965 to connect Wrightsville Beach and Shell Island (fig. 6.7). The parking lot next to the new Holiday Inn is only 5 feet above sea level, making this site easily flooded during a storm. The old Holiday Inn was heavily damaged by Hurricane Fran and had to be razed.

Once formed, inlets tend to migrate laterally along their barrier islands, although there is wide variation in individual inlet behavior (appendix C, refs. 49, 53). See *The Citizen's Guide to North Carolina's Shifting Inlets,* by Simon Baker (appendix C, ref. 46), for directions and rates of individual inlet migration. The N.C. Division of Coastal Management uses a statistical analysis of inlets based on previous migration rates, inlet orientation, and the nature of the land immediately bordering the inlet to determine inlet hazard areas. These inlet hazards are outlined on the erosion rate maps. Structures and property in the path of a migrating inlet have a short life expectancy.

You may recall from chapter 3 that tidal delta formation is an important means of island widening. Sediment carried seaward through the inlet builds an underwater ebb-tidal delta. In time the delta may fill the inlet, closing it naturally. The presence of tidal deltas in back of old inlets may make these sites relatively safe areas on which to build. The width promotes dune and vegetation growth, and provides ample room to build far back from the beach. Also, the likelihood of a new inlet forming at the site of an old, naturally closed one is relatively low. Dr. William J. Cleary, of the Uni-

Figure 6.7 A pre-Fran view of the Holiday Inn at Wrightsville Beach fronted by a nourished beach. This motel was largely destroyed in Hurricane Fran but will be rebuilt as a seven-story structure. Because the motel occupied the former site of Moore's Inlet, it was sometimes referred to as the "Holiday Inlet."

versity of North Carolina at Wilmington, has demonstrated that at least 40 percent of the coast between Cape Fear and Cape Lookout consists of old natural inlet fills. Where flood tidal deltas were incorporated, the areas of potential new inlet formation are reduced.

Artificially filled inlets are unstable areas for development. After the old inlet between Wrightsville Beach and Shell Island (fig. 6.7) was filled with sand pumped up from the sound, buildings were constructed on the site. Unfortunately, this fill sand was taken from the tidal delta. Once the island was robbed of its natural mechanism for increasing its width, the number of safe areas on which to build was reduced. Another artificially filled and engineered former inlet is located on the eastern part of Sunset Beach. Here the inlet was filled in and moved to create a bigger development!

Maritime Forest, Thicket, and Shrub Areas

Maritime forest, thicket, and shrub areas are generally the least risky places for cottage building sites. Under normal conditions, overwash, flooding, and blowing sand are not problems in these environments. The plants stabilize the underlying sediment and offer a protective screen. The problem is that building in these low- to moderate-risk sites requires disturbing the vegetation, thus destroying the very aspect that helps reduce risk! Large-scale clearing of vegetation for large structures or extensive development not only increases the vulnerability of the new buildings but also increases risk to adjacent properties.

If you build in a vegetated area, keep the building small and within the tree line and preserve as much of the vegetation as possible, including the undergrowth. Trees buffer wind energy and provide excellent protection from flying debris during hurricanes. Remove large, dead trees from the construction site, but conserve the surrounding forest to protect your home. Stabilize bare sand areas as soon as possible with new plantings because bare surfaces are the first to erode by wind or water. Use native plants when you revegetate. The presence of an active dune field on the margin of a forest may threaten the stability of forest sites.

Marshes

Marshes (see chapter 4) are prolific breeding and nursery areas for many fish and shellfish. Their extensive shallows provide considerable protection against wave erosion of the back sides of islands. In the past, marshes were filled to create more land on which to build, but that practice is no longer legal. Areas around finger canals are often built up with the material dredged from the marsh to form the canal. Examples are the large back-island area of Bogue Banks at the Atlantic Beach bridge; the finger canal area near the Onslow-Pender County line on Topsail Island; and the finger canal areas on Figure Eight Island, Holden Beach, and Ocean Isle Beach.

Nature usually takes revenge on those who occupy filled marshland. Buried marsh provides poor support for building foundations and does not provide a high-quality groundwater reservoir. Thus, such building sites typically have an inadequate supply of fresh water and septic systems that do not function properly. In addition, effluent waste from such sites has closed adjacent marshes to shellfishing. Because they have a low elevation, filled marshlands are susceptible to flooding during even minor storms. The finger canals surrounding the causeway in Atlantic Beach had some flooding, although minor, from weak Hurricane Gordon. A direct hit by a moderate hurricane will level this area.

Marshes can no longer be dredged or filled. It is often possible to plant marsh grass or cordgrass (*Spartina alterniflora*) and create new marshes to stabilize areas that might otherwise become mudflats and lead to high-ground erosion. Planting marshes is highly preferable to building bulkheads because it both protects the shoreline and creates a new habitat for marine plants and animals.

Water Problems: Are You Ready for More Infrastructure?

One of the more significant hazards of barrier island living is contaminated water. Basically the problem involves three factors: water supply, waste disposal, and any form of island alteration that affects the first two factors. Dredge-and-fill operations (e.g., inlet cutting, the channeling of islands for canals and waterways, and the piling of dredge spoil) and other construction activities may alter the groundwater system.

Just as the quality and availability of water determine the plant and animal makeup of an island's ecosystem, the water supply also determines, in part, the island's capacity to accommodate people. Water quality is measured by potability, freshness, clarity, odor, and the presence or absence of pathogens (disease-causing bacteria).

Availability implies the presence of an adequate supply. Unless an island has a public water supply, water availability may be highly seasonal. The only fresh water directly available to a barrier island without a municipal water system is from the rainfall that reaches the island. This water seeps through the porous and permeable sands and builds up as a lens or wedge of fresh water beneath the island's surface. This lens overlies salt water, which seeps into the sediments from the adjacent ocean, inlet, or marsh. The higher the island's elevation above sea level and the greater the accumulation of fresh water, the greater the thickness of the freshwater lens. Where clean sands underlie the island, the thickness of the lens should be about 40 feet for every 1 foot of average island elevation. This ideal is rarely the case in North Carolina, however, where mud, peat, or bedrock may underlie islands. The top of the freshwater lens is known as the groundwater table, and on many islands this shallow reservoir is the only supply of domestic fresh water.

Too many wells drawing on the groundwater will lower the water table and potentially cause saltwater intrusion. Early occupants of a development should not be surprised if their shallow wells dry up as the development grows; ultimately they will require another source of fresh water. As condominiums and high-rises replace cottages, the demand for water will increase. Alternative sources of water such as deep aquifers or municipal water systems (deep wells, pipelines, filtration plants, desalinization plants) are so expensive that they are feasible only on densely developed islands. The tendency is toward municipal systems and their necessary expansion, and property owners should expect to help pick up the costs.

Ocracoke and Nags Head exceeded the capacity of local wells to provide water, and salt water crept into the groundwater. Now, both communities have desalinization plants to provide potable water. Some saltwater intrusion, especially in Nags Head, Kill Devil Hills, and Kitty Hawk, will occur as a result of frequent overwash through gaps in the artificial frontal dune line, which is now eroding. The presence of any sort of municipal water system immediately increases the potential for development.

Some developments draw their water supply from rock units beneath the younger surface sands and muds. These aquifers are rock formations that are exposed on the Coastal Plain (their recharge area) and dip seaward beneath the coast. The fresh water in such aquifers has been accumulating over thousands of years, but large developments withdraw it faster than it can be replaced (recharged). In effect, the water is being mined and replaced with salt water, contaminating existing wells and destroying the adjacent aquifer as a freshwater source.

Water facilities and lines are vulnerable to storm impact, so long recovery periods without water should be expected as well. Consult the proper authorities about water quantity and quality before you buy (see appendix B, "Water Resources").

Waste Disposal

Wastewater disposal goes hand in glove with the water supply. On many North Carolina barrier islands the home septic system is the primary means of wastewater disposal. Such systems consist of a holding tank in which solids settle and sewage is biologically broken down, and a drain field that allows water to percolate into the soil. The soil then filters and purifies the water. Unfortunately, sometimes the same natural system that is used to cleanse the water is also used to supply potable water to residences.

Many communities are unaware of the potential water problems they face. Crowded development, improperly maintained systems, and systems installed in soils unsuitable for filtration have resulted in poorly treated or untreated sewage entering the surrounding environment. Polluted water is a primary source of hepatitis and other diseases. When polluted water enters sounds and marshes, shellfish are contaminated and that resource is ultimately destroyed.

Septic tanks have been blamed in the past for the pollution and subsequent closing of more than 200,000 acres of North Carolina's shellfishing areas. In 1996, 303,000 acres of shellfish waters were closed, and many other thousands of acres are conditionally approved to be closed as soon as a large rainfall occurs and flushes pollutants from the drainage basins into the estuaries and sounds. The area closed to shellfishing is 20 percent of the total available in North Carolina, but unfortunately, most of the closed acreage is in prime shellfishing areas.

The sad irony is that we have the understanding and technology to make environmentally safe septic systems, but we sometimes fall short of the enforcement capability to ensure that they are always used. Of course, not all pollution of coastal waters comes from coastal development. The frightening fish kills that occurred in the Neuse River in the late 1990s, for example, were caused by inland pollution.

If the amenities of barrier island living are to be preserved, development must be wisely planned. Public officials should require strict enforcement of existing codes and policing of existing systems, and proper site evaluation before issuing permits. In addition, homeowners should learn the mechanics of septic systems to prevent malfunctioning or to spot it early (see appendix B, "Sanitation" and "Septic System Permits"). Municipal waste-treatment plants may be one answer for larger communities, although such plants often become overloaded or inefficient.

Municipal sewer and water systems can make life less complicated for island dwellers in terms of dependability of sewer and water service. But such systems almost inevitably set the stage for increased development, turning low density, single-family-home communities into high-density and even high-rise communities. Wrightsville Beach and Carolina Beach both have municipal water and sewer systems.

Septic tanks are the most common waste-disposal system used on the Outer Banks, although some developments have so-called package plants, local sewer systems for a small number of houses. These can be satisfactory if well maintained and not overtaxed. In the past, a number of these systems have failed and caused local environmental crises. One such problem occurred at The Place at the Beach condominium in Atlantic Beach when sewage was noted flowing across the parking lot.

Bogue Banks has no municipal sewage system and is looking, along with a lot of other North Carolina communities, at the possibility of an offshore sewer outfall. Such an outfall would provide almost unrestricted sewage disposal and could lead to the New Jerseyization of our islands!

Finger Canals

A common island alteration of the 1960s and 1970s that still causes water problems on islands is the *finger canal* (fig. 6.8), a term applied to channels dug into an island for the purpose of providing additional waterfront lots. Finger canals can be found on almost every developed island in North Carolina.

Six major problems are associated with finger canals:

1. The lowering of the groundwater table
2. Pollution of groundwater by seepage of salt or brackish canal water into the groundwater table
3. Pollution of canal water by septic seepage into the canal
4. Pollution of canal water by stagnation resulting from lack of tidal flushing or poor circulation with sound waters
5. Fish kills generated by higher canal water temperatures
6. Fish kills generated by nutrient overloading and deoxygenation of the water

Compounding these problems is the fact that finger canals sometimes begin to fill with sediment. This leads to requests for dredging, which is expensive and may not be permitted for the above reasons.

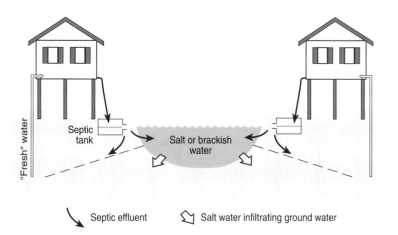

Septic effluent   Salt water infiltrating ground water

Figure 6.8 The finger canal saga. Saltwater intrusion ruins the freshwater supply. Intrusion of septic tank effluent pollutes the canal.

Bad odors, flotsam of dead fish and algal scum, and contamination of adjacent shellfishing grounds are symptomatic of polluted canal water. Thus, finger canals often become health hazards or simply places too unpleasant to live near. Residents along some older Florida finger canals have built walls to separate their homes from the canal.

If you do consider buying a lot on a canal, remember that canals are usually not harmful until houses are built along them. Short canals, a few tens of yards long, are generally much safer than long ones. Also, be aware that while most canals are initially deep enough for small-craft traffic, sand movement on the back sides of barrier islands results in the filling of the canals and subsequent navigation problems.

Finally, on narrow islands, finger canals dug almost to the ocean side offer a path of least resistance to storm waters and are therefore potential locations for new inlets. Although no such inlets formed during Fran, some roads next to finger canals on Topsail Island were scoured away by storm-surge flooding. Finger canals in Buxton brought storm surge into interior parts of the island that normally would not have been flooded (fig. 6.9). Property owners along finger canals on Dauphin Island, Alabama, found themselves owning tiny islands or open water after Hurricane Frederic in 1979. Because of the multitude of problems associated with finger canals, only modification or maintenance of existing canals is permitted in North Carolina.

Site Risk: Do You Know the Rules for Survival?

In order to determine the vulnerability or level of risk of a specific site on a barrier island it is necessary to evaluate all the prevalent dynamic processes on the island. Information on storm surge, overwash, erosion rates, inlet migration, longshore drift, and other processes can be obtained from maps, aerial photographs, scientific literature, or personal observations. Appendix C contains an annotated list of scientific sources, many available at little or no cost; you are encouraged to obtain those of interest to you. Although developers and planners usually have the resources and expertise to use such information in making decisions, they sometimes ignore it. In the past, the individual buyer was not likely to seek the information necessary to decide on the suitability of a given site. Today's buyers should be better informed.

Buyers, builders, and planners can assess the level of risk they are willing to take with respect to coastal hazards. The listing of specific dangers and cautions above provides a basis for taking appropriate precautions in site selection, construction, or evacuation plans. Our recommendation is to avoid extreme- and high-risk zones (see chapter 7). Keep in mind, however, that small maps of large areas must be generalized and that every site must be evaluated individually. Safe sites may exist in high-risk zones, whereas very dangerous sites may exist in moderate- and low-risk zones.

Below is a list of characteristics that are essential to site safety.

1. The site elevation is above the anticipated storm-surge level (tables 6.1, 6.2).
2. The site is behind a natural protective barrier such as a line of sand dunes, preferably 30 or more feet in height and 100 feet in basal width.

Figure 6.9 Frisco finger canal with wrecked boats and debris piled up by Hurricane Emily's storm surge. The funneling action of the canal made this the site of some of the highest sound-side storm-surge levels during Emily.

3. The site is well away from a migrating inlet (e.g., beyond even the state-designated inlet hazard zone).
4. The site is in an area of shoreline growth (accretion) or low shoreline erosion. Evidence of an eroding shoreline includes:
   a. sand bluff or dune scarp at back of beach
   b. stumps or peat exposed on beach
   c. slumped features such as trees, dunes, or man-made structures
   d. protective devices such as seawalls, groins, or replenished sand.

   You can also contact the North Carolina Department of Environment, Health and Natural Resources, Division of Coastal Management, or the local CAMA permit office (see appendix B for address and phone number) for calculated erosion rates.
5. The site is located on a portion of the island backed by healthy salt marsh.
6. The site is away from low-elevation, narrow portions of the island.
7. The site is in an area of no or infrequent historic overwash.
8. The site is in a vegetated area that suggests stability.
9. The site drains water readily.
10. The fresh groundwater supply is adequate and uncontaminated. There is proper spacing between water wells and septic systems.
11. The soil and elevation are suitable for efficient septic tank operation.
12. No compactable layers such as peat are present in soil. (The site is not on a buried salt marsh.)
13. Adjacent structures are adequately spaced and of sound construction.
14. The structure's design preserves natural protection (fig. 6.10).

Escape Routes: Do You Have an Emergency Plan?

The orderly evacuation that occurred on the North Carolina coast before the arrival of Hurricane Fran is a good example of effective and early evacuation. A majority of the coastal population relocated inland. As a result, few lives were lost. Fortunately, Bertha had reminded residents what a hurricane is like, so when the stronger Fran came around, those who had stayed in their homes for Bertha left. Of the few who stayed on the coast for Fran, most said they regretted doing so.

Although traffic was bumper to bumper on a few roads leading west, the early warning and direction by N.C. Emergency Management personnel led to a surprisingly smooth evacuation. Not all hurricane evacuations have been smooth, however, even in modern times. Hurricane Opal approached the Florida panhandle in October 1995. With the attention of the nation on the recent O. J. Simpson verdict, the hurricane's approach barely made an appearance on the news. After all, it was just a category 1 storm. The next morning, residents of the panhandle and surrounding areas awoke to the threat of a strong category 4 monster and immediate evacuation orders. The highways were jammed, and thousands of people faced the grim prospect of riding out Opal in their cars, stuck in traffic. Officials started telling residents not to try to leave the area, but to go to the nearest shelter. Fortunately, Opal weakened just before it made landfall. Had that not happened, there might have been carnage on the roadways.

The threat of hurricanes makes an escape route imperative for barrier island residents. You must have access to a route that will permit you to leave the island and reach a safe location inland within a reasonable length of time. The presence of a ready escape route near a building site is essential to site safety, especially in high-rise and high-density housing areas where the number of people to be evacuated, transported, and housed elsewhere is large.

Although one of the allures of a beach vacation is getting away from it all and being out of touch, coastal vacationers should make one exception. Always keep an eye and ear out for the weather. Remember: STAY INFORMED. DON'T WAIT. LEAVE EARLY.

Select an Escape Route in Advance

Examine your prospective escape route thoroughly. Check to see if any part of it is at a low elevation, and thus subject to blockage by overwash or flooding; if so, seek an alternate route. Several exit routes from North Caro-

Figure 6.10 Two houses atop a high dune in Salter Path illustrate differences in site safety. The one-story house on the right is tucked behind a dune and somewhat protected by the vegetation cover from the wind. The more distant dark house is exposed to the direct onslaught of storm winds.

lina islands are prone to flooding. Note whether there are bridges along the route. Remember that some residents will be evacuating pleasure boats and that fishing boats will be seeking safer waters; thus, drawbridges will be accommodating both boats and automobiles. Reevaluate the escape route you have chosen periodically—especially if the area in which you live has grown. With more people using the route, it may not be as satisfactory as you once thought.

Use the Escape Route Early

Be aware that several North Carolina islands have only one route for escape to the mainland and that in some cases exit is via another island (Hatteras Island and Nags Head are connected to the mainland via Roanoke Island). Ocracoke Island has no bridge or causeway, so evacuation is by ferry only. In the event of a hurricane warning, leave the island immediately; do not wait until the route is blocked or flooded. Anyone who has experienced the evacuation of a community knows of the chaos at such bottlenecks. Depend on it: excited drivers will cause wrecks, run out of gas, and have flat tires, and carloads of frightened occupants will be lined up for miles behind them. Be sure to have plans for where you will go. Keep alternative destinations in mind in case you find your original refuge filled or in danger. Finally, find a place of last refuge where you can go rather than being stuck in your car. Parking garages above the first floor or the lee side of high-rise condominiums and hotels are often good bets. Remember to plan, and then follow your plan. Nothing less than your life is at stake.

7 Ranking the Risks of Your Island

A growing number of people live and vacation along the coast, putting ever more lives, property, and dollars at risk. Given the tools with which to assess the historical and active processes, coastal hazards, vulnerability, and risk of a coastal area, you can evaluate your favorite island, community, neighborhood, existing house, or building site for your island dream home. Observations of barrier islands and their communities after several hurricanes and winter storms suggest that property damage can be lessened significantly by prudent site selection and proper location of structures. The coastal hazard assessments and maps in this chapter consider the risk of hurricane and winter storm damage based on a site's geologic and natural setting (appendix C, ref. 45).

This evaluation technique, known as *coastal risk mapping,* uses coastal physical processes and island landform characteristics to rate the overall risk of storm damage to property as "low," "moderate," "high," or "extreme." Island characteristics considered in making the risk maps (RMS) include elevation and forest cover; width; frontal and island interior sand dune height, width, and distribution; potential for inlet formation; modern inlet dynamics; erosion or accretion rates; historic storm response; engineering structures and projects; and other human modifications of the natural environment.

The conclusions represented on the risk maps are based on published data, aerial photographs, and maps, as well as personal communications and observations. The maps present risk zones (extreme, high, moderate, or low) relative to the potential property damage from passage of a moderate category 3 hurricane, such as Fran.

Risk maps are used to guide community planning and individual site selection, and to help determine viable property damage mitigation alternatives for individual coastal sites. Ultimately, mitigation measures will help reduce storm-loss expenditures, result in more affordable insurance for the property owner, and ease the burden on government disaster response and recovery programs. The risk categories used in the assessments and on the maps are defined below.

Extreme risk. The area or site is at low elevation, within the 100-year flood level, and exposed to open ocean or a wide lagoon so that waves greater than 3 feet are likely (FIRM V-zones; see chapter 8 for explanation and discussion). Vegetation consists of only sparse growth of beach or dune grasses, areas susceptible to scouring from storm-surge waters and heavy rains. These areas are most susceptible to wave attack and storm-surge ebb scour, and often are affected by erosional shoreline retreat. Extreme-risk areas are commonly, but not exclusively, oceanfront or near inlets.

High risk. The area or site is at low elevation and within the 100-year flood zone (FIRM A-zones), and is susceptible to flooding and wave attack. Vegetation is usually sparse, similar to that in extreme-risk zones. High-risk areas are likely to be flooded from storm-surge waters and heavy rains; overwash is less likely, although possible; and the areas are only slightly less susceptible to wind damage than extreme-risk zones.

Moderate risk. The area or site is above the 100-year flood zone (FIRM X-zone) but lacks maritime forest or dense shrub thicket, resulting in high vulnerability to wind attack. Moderate-risk areas are not generally subject to flooding and are unlikely to suffer direct wave attack, although such areas may lie within the 100-year flood zone (FIRM A-zones).

Low risk. The area or site is above the 100-year flood zone (FIRM X-zone) and well forested; generally not subject to flooding and wind hazards. Dense maritime forest growth or shrub thicket significantly reduces the impact of strong winds. Removing forest for development reduces the amount of protection and often leads to increased degradation of newly exposed portions of the forest from salt spray, resulting in a shift to moderate risk.

Virtually all coastal areas are at extreme risk from a category 4 or 5 hurricane. Differentiation into risk zones is useless for such storms. The relative risk zones presented here are based on the risk afforded to property by a low category 3 hurricane hitting directly at the site under question. A low category 3 hurricane will have winds of 111 to 120 miles per hour. The typical accompanying storm surge could range from 5 to 12 feet depending on coastal configuration and offshore bathymetry.

Note that this risk assessment involves *only* the risk of property damage and is not concerned with risks to inhabitants. In general, of course, areas with high potential for property damage are also areas of high risk for humans, but low-risk sites are not always safe for their inhabitants. Difficulty of evacuation is an example of a human risk that may be entirely independent of homesite safety (e.g., the only escape route from your moderate-risk site is through a high-risk zone). So, regardless of site location, always evacuate if ordered to do so and know your evacuation route ahead of time.

The coastal risk assessment method was developed and applied to the North Carolina coast from north to south to produce risk maps along nearly 110 miles of developed coastline. Most of the undeveloped islands are either military installations or within national seashores or state parks. These areas were not mapped because they will not be developed in the foreseeable future.

Results of the mapping indicate that 18 percent of the state's developable shore is at extreme risk and 31 percent is at high risk; thus 49 percent of the North Carolina coast is highly susceptible to damage from small, moderate, and large storms. The greatest portion, 36 percent, is rated moderate risk for property damage; only 15 percent of North Carolina's developed barrier system is in low-risk zones.

There Are Differences between Islands and Communities

Figure 7.1 is a comparison of property damage risks for large-scale segments of the North Carolina coast. The ranking is based on overall geologic setting and coastal processes of single barrier islands. It ignores political boundaries and does not consider risk to life and limb.

The risk ranking can be expanded to the community level by adding three additional human parameters and considering hazards on a community-by-community level.

1. *Management quality.* This judgment as to the quality of a community's environmental and risk management may change from election to election. Good management is important to maintaining frontal dunes, forests, construction standards, zoning laws, and the quality of life.
2. *People danger.* This measure refers to the risk to people during a storm. For example, evacuation difficulty is a critical issue. Some "safe" homesites may be difficult to evacuate safely.
3. *Crystal ball.* This factor concerns the future of the island. Will the frontal dunes be eroded away in a few years? Is the political situation ripe for beach nourishment and can the community afford it? Will the community plan and zone?

Community rankings were available in published form in *Living by the Rules of the Sea* (appendix C, ref. 45) before Hurricane Fran arrived in 1996. North Topsail Beach received the lowest ranking in North Carolina and was considered the highest-risk community in the state. Hurricane Fran proved this judgment to be correct, but the original ranking was an easy call to make. Any prospective homeowner with a knowledge of storm hazards

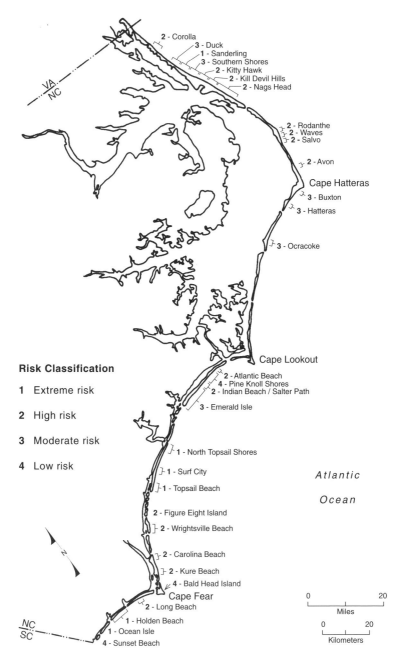

2 - Corolla
3 - Duck
1 - Sanderling
3 - Southern Shores
2 - Kitty Hawk
2 - Kill Devil Hills
2 - Nags Head

2 - Rodanthe
2 - Waves
2 - Salvo

2 - Avon

Cape Hatteras
3 - Buxton
3 - Hatteras

3 - Ocracoke

Cape Lookout

2 - Atlantic Beach
4 - Pine Knoll Shores
2 - Indian Beach / Salter Path

3 - Emerald Isle

1 - North Topsail Shores

1 - Surf City

1 - Topsail Beach

2 - Figure Eight Island

2 - Wrightsville Beach

2 - Carolina Beach

2 - Kure Beach

4 - Bald Head Island

Cape Fear

2 - Long Beach

1 - Holden Beach

1 - Ocean Isle

4 - Sunset Beach

Atlantic

Ocean

Risk Classification

1   Extreme risk

2   High risk

3   Moderate risk

4   Low risk

VA
NC

NC
SC

N

0   20
Miles

0   20
Kilometers

Figure 7.1   A generalized hazard ranking of all the islands on the North Carolina coast. Clearly, "islandwide" classification is painting with a broad brush because a range of risk-category sites exists on most islands. On the scale shown, 1 represents the highest risk and 4 represents low risk. The ranking is subjective, based entirely on natural oceanographic and geologic factors.

could have seen that North Topsail Beach was a community at extreme to high risk. The dunes were small and artificial, the island was extremely narrow and at a very low elevation, and it had been overwashed frequently in past small storms. All these were signs of pending trouble.

Regardless of a community's ranking or the regional ranking, the most important focus for homeowners is the individual property or specific site. Where you invest your money, time, and resources is important, and a low-risk community rating is not a guarantee that the building site in which you are interested is also at low risk. The clues that can be used to determine the risk to a particular house site on the North Carolina coast are outlined below.

The Outer Banks

The portion of the North Carolina coast north of Cape Lookout (see fig. 1.2) is referred to as the Outer Banks. The most striking features of the Outer Banks are the long, narrow islands separated from the mainland by large, shallow sounds. Much of the Outer Banks is part of the Cape Lookout and Cape Hatteras National Seashores. Only the northern islands are inhabited year-round. Portsmouth Island, Core Banks, and Shackleford Banks are undeveloped islands within the Cape Lookout National Seashore and are not rated here.

One of the great charms of the Outer Banks islands is their physical remoteness. Located many miles from the mainland, some areas are accessible only by ferry. Although this seclusion can be seductive, it can also be dangerous when a storm threatens. Ferries stop service when the sounds get too rough, which is generally long before a storm is near the coast. The islands are easily flooded, particularly from the sound side, slowing or preventing escape. Parts of N.C. Highway 12 flood from just a moderate wind during fair weather. Roads along the narrower sections of the Outer Banks are prone to being washed out or blocked by overwash.

There is only one escape route off Hatteras Island. You must take a two-lane bridge leading to the north, and then cross another two bridges to reach the mainland. There are other vulnerable locations along this escape route where early flooding may occur. On a given summer weekend, there are tens of thousands of visitors on the Outer Banks, and they cannot all get off the island at once. So don't wait until the last minute. Be prepared to leave in a hurry. If a storm threatens, pay close attention to weather forecasts and advisories from the local safety officials. If an evacuation is ordered, LEAVE AT ONCE! Preparedness and early evacuation are critical in all coastal areas, especially on the Outer Banks.

The portion of North Carolina's Outer Banks from the Virginia border to Oregon Inlet, a distance of more than 55 miles, is not technically an island;

it is a spit called Currituck Spit (it stretches over the length of Risk Maps 1–7). The main difference between a spit and an island is that a spit is connected to land (in this case, Cape Henry, Virginia), and an island is defined by inlets on either end. Numerous historic inlet locations (fig. 7.2), however, are testimony to the fact that there were many true islands along this stretch in the past, and likely will be again in the future. The natural processes on spits and true barrier islands are the same, and we use the terms *island* and *spit* essentially interchangeably here.

Figure 7.2   The location of historical inlets on the Outer Banks of North Carolina. Each of these inlets was open for a sufficient length of time to be named and put on a chart. Numbers 8, 13, 16, 25, 26, and 30 are present-day inlets. New inlets formed since the 1960s have been artificially filled. Most inlets are formed by water rushing from the estuary across the island in a seaward direction. The presence of a large body of water (such as Pamlico Sound) encourages this process.

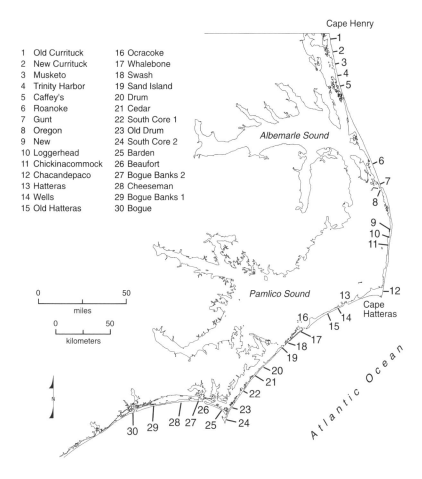

1 Old Currituck	16 Ocracoke
2 New Currituck	17 Whalebone
3 Musketo	18 Swash
4 Trinity Harbor	19 Sand Island
5 Caffey's	20 Drum
6 Roanoke	21 Cedar
7 Gunt	22 South Core 1
8 Oregon	23 Old Drum
9 New	24 South Core 2
10 Loggerhead	25 Barden
11 Chickinacommock	26 Beaufort
12 Chacandepaco	27 Bogue Banks 2
13 Hatteras	28 Cheeseman
14 Wells	29 Bogue Banks 1
15 Old Hatteras	30 Bogue

One of the most important events leading to the development of the Outer Banks was the construction in the 1930s of a continuous dune line from the Virginia border to the western end of Ocracoke Island, a make-work project of the Civilian Conservation Corps (CCC) and the Works Progress Administration. Intended to prevent shoreline retreat, the dune was built before it was understood that islands migrate and that erosion would not make the Outer Banks disappear. The large frontal dune changed the Outer Banks, especially south of Southern Shores, from an area dominated by overwash to a dune island. Development became possible in the protective lee of the artificial dune where it would once have been impossible because of frequent overwash.

Time marches on, shorelines retreat, and in the 1990s large portions of the CCC dune are disappearing. Frontal portions of Kitty Hawk, Kill Devil Hills, Nags Head, and Rodanthe are in desperate straits. Even small storms routinely flood the sections of these towns that lack the protection of the dune. Highway 12 south of Oregon Inlet is overwashed frequently. The prognosis is poor. More and more sections of towns and highways will become vulnerable as the dune continues to disappear.

Currituck County (RMs 1–3)

Currituck County, on the northern Outer Banks (fig. 7.2), has a long history of inlet formation along its coastline. The active inlets once made the area unsafe for development and prevented easy access. Today, however, these relict inlet sites provide wide areas and large volumes of sand on which to build (RMs 1–3). But nature has a way of reverting to former conditions.

Throughout the early history of North Carolina, Currituck Sound was a saltwater body continuously connected to the ocean by a series of inlets. The five historical inlets occurred alternately, but continuously, from the days of first discovery through the closure of the last inlet between 1828 and 1830 (fig. 7.2). Old Currituck Inlet, on the North Carolina–Virginia border, was used by trading vessels (especially New Englanders hoping to escape duty payment) until 1729–1731, when it closed. In the meantime, New Currituck Inlet had opened several miles to the south during a 1713 storm, but it, too, closed sometime between 1828 and 1830. The remnants of Musketo Inlet, which closed between 1672 and 1682, can be seen behind the town of Corolla. Farther south are the extensive marsh remnants that mark the position of Trinity Harbor Inlet, which closed sometime in the mid-1600s. The last inlet into Currituck Sound was Caffey's Inlet, which opened between 1790 and 1798 at the Dare-Currituck County line.

When Caffey's Inlet closed, sometime between 1811 and 1829, Currituck Sound began to freshen. Today this freshwater sound is an important hunt-

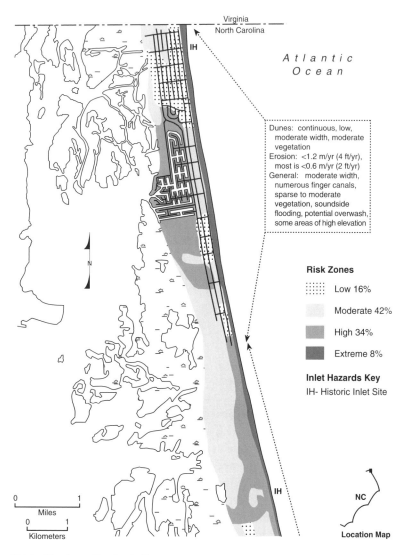

Virginia
North Carolina

IH

*Atlantic
Ocean*

Dunes: continuous, low,
   moderate width, moderate
   vegetation
Erosion: <1.2 m/yr (4 ft/yr),
   most is <0.6 m/yr (2 ft/yr)
General: moderate width,
   numerous finger canals,
   sparse to moderate
   vegetation, soundside
   flooding, potential overwash,
   some areas of high elevation

Risk Zones

:::::: Low 16%

   Moderate 42%

   High 34%

   Extreme 8%

Inlet Hazards Key
IH- Historic Inlet Site

IH

NC

Location Map

0   1
   Miles
0   1
   Kilometers

N

IH

RM 1   Northern Currituck County

ing and fishing area. If a new inlet were to form, the sound would revert to its former brackish state. There is a movement afoot by saltwater fishers to make an artificial inlet across Currituck spit to make the sound salty again.

The numerous historical inlets produced exceptionally wide portions of the barrier island. The inlets' flood-tide deltas, which once extended well into Currituck Sound, reverted to back-barrier marshes when the inlets closed (see chapter 3). Scattered maritime forests gradually developed in front of the old flood-tide deltas, and the widened areas of the island became sites for such communities as Corolla (RM 2) and Sanderling (RM 3).

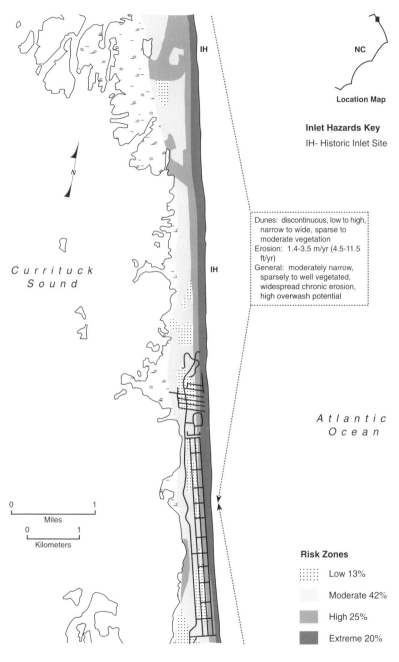

NC

Location Map

Inlet Hazards Key
IH- Historic Inlet Site

Dunes: discontinuous, low to high,
 narrow to wide, sparse to
 moderate vegetation
Erosion: 1.4-3.5 m/yr (4.5-11.5
 ft/yr)
General: moderately narrow,
 sparsely to well vegetated,
 widespread chronic erosion,
 high overwash potential

C u r r i t u c k
S o u n d

A t l a n t i c
O c e a n

0   1
  Miles
0   1
  Kilometers

Risk Zones

::::::: Low 13%

         Moderate 42%

         High 25%

         Extreme 20%

RM 2 Corolla

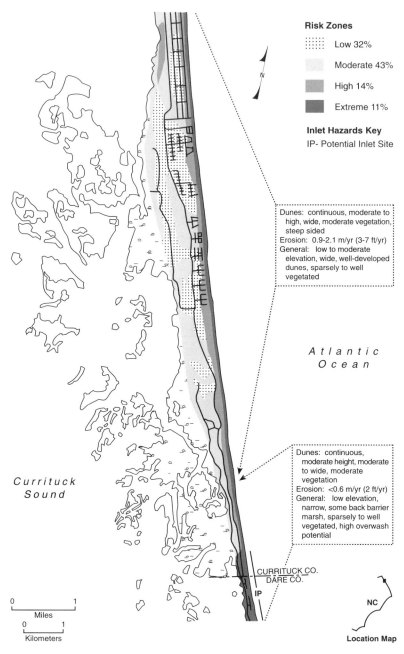

Risk Zones

- Low 32%
- Moderate 43%
- High 14%
- Extreme 11%

Inlet Hazards Key

IP- Potential Inlet Site

Dunes: continuous, moderate to high, wide, moderate vegetation, steep sided
Erosion: 0.9-2.1 m/yr (3-7 ft/yr)
General: low to moderate elevation, wide, well-developed dunes, sparsely to well vegetated

Atlantic Ocean

Dunes: continuous, moderate height, moderate to wide, moderate vegetation
Erosion: <0.6 m/yr (2 ft/yr)
General: low elevation, narrow, some back barrier marsh, sparsely to well vegetated, high overwash potential

Currituck Sound

CURRITUCK CO.
DARE CO.

IP

NC

Location Map

0 ————— 1
Miles
0 ————— 1
Kilometers

RM 3   Southern Currituck County

The oldest of the inlet deltas have been lost as a result of estuarine shoreline erosion and slow submergence over the centuries.

Almost all of Currituck County's shore is eroding, at rates ranging from 2.5 to 11.5 feet per year (RMS 1–3). Dunes are generally wide and high through most of southern Currituck County, but somewhat discontinuous farther north. Discontinuous central dune ridges extend along most of this coastal zone as well. Some of these dune ridges are actively moving and migrating, and great caution is necessary when selecting a building site on or near them. Forests are scattered throughout Currituck County, primarily along or near the sound. The rest of the barrier is a mix of dense and scattered shrub. Near the Virginia state line (RM 1), a series of finger canals built more than 20 years ago provide a reminder of opportunistic developers who rushed to construct the canals before they became illegal. Today these canals, cut halfway through the island, remain largely undeveloped and pose a serious flooding threat to the few buildings adjacent to them.

If floodwaters on a paved road make evacuation difficult, the same on unpaved sand roads may make escape impossible. Floodwaters pose a great threat to the residents of northern Currituck County. A new bridge from the northern part of the spit to the mainland has been proposed. Its proponents say the bridge is necessary for safe evacuation during storms. Opponents say the bridge will increase development pressures on the area because it will improve access to main roads from large population centers of the Tidewater area such as Norfolk, Virginia Beach, and Hampton Roads, Virginia; and more distant urban centers such as Richmond and Washington, D.C. The increased development will raise the population density on the spit far beyond safe limits.

Dare County (RMs 4–11)

Duck and Southern Shores (RM 4)
Not long ago Duck was a military firing and bombing range, but now the loudest noises are the cries of seagulls and the whine of carpenters' saws. A central dune ridge runs through Duck and continues into Southern Shores (RM 4), and the dunes through most of Duck are healthy (wide and tall). The northern part of Duck is narrow, and the dominant vegetation there is scattered shrub. Near the Currituck-Dare County line the island is so narrow and low that overwash and inlet formation are a threat. Areas along the sound are prone to frequent flooding and should be avoided. The southern part of Duck is wider and resembles its neighbor to the south.

Southern Shores is a wide, low-erosion (2 feet/year) area with three main dune ridges running parallel to the shore. One ridge extends down the center of the main part of the barrier; the other two flank Jean Guite Creek. Dunes in the area are continuous, wide, and high (see fig. 6.5). Most of the barrier's vegetation is forest and dense shrub, with scattered-shrub areas located mainly on the ridges. Thus there are numerous low- and moderate-risk areas. However, the areas between the ridges are low and susceptible to flooding.

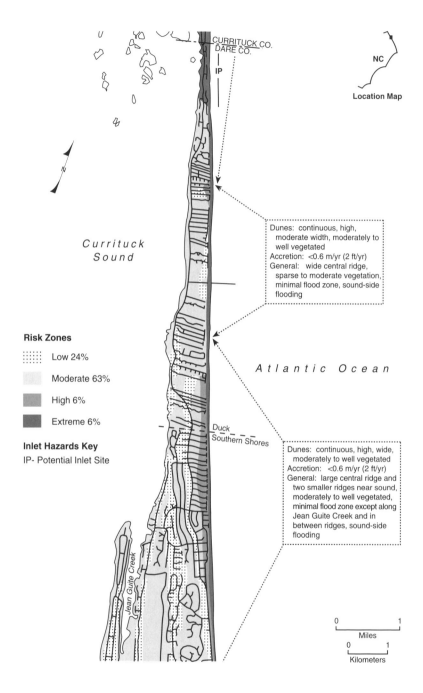

CURRITUCK CO.
DARE CO.

IP

NC

Location Map

Currituck
Sound

Dunes: continuous, high,
   moderate width, moderately to
   well vegetated
Accretion: <0.6 m/yr (2 ft/yr)
General: wide central ridge,
   sparse to moderate vegetation,
   minimal flood zone, sound-side
   flooding

Risk Zones

::::: Low 24%

Moderate 63%

High 6%

Extreme 6%

Inlet Hazards Key

IP- Potential Inlet Site

Atlantic Ocean

Duck
Southern Shores

Dunes: continuous, high, wide,
   moderately to well vegetated
Accretion: <0.6 m/yr (2 ft/yr)
General: large central ridge and
   two smaller ridges near sound,
   moderately to well vegetated,
   minimal flood zone except along
   Jean Guite Creek and in
   between ridges, sound-side
   flooding

Jean Guite Creek

0   1
     Miles
0   1
   Kilometers

RM 4 The Duck Area

Southern Shores must continue to grow wisely by preserving the natural vegetation and dunes, and avoiding high-density development. Project Blue Sky, an internationally recognized program to promote good construction practices, is located in Southern Shores (appendix C, ref. 69). Visit their exhibit to see firsthand what a well-built Outer Banks house looks like.

Because of its healthy frontal and interior dunes as well as its forest cover, this area has performed well in recent storms. Remember, however, that the northern Outer Banks haven't been hit by a major hurricane since Donna in 1960 (brushes with Gloria [1985], Charley [1986], and Emily [1993] notwithstanding), and haven't been crossed by a westward-tracking hurricane since 1933 (see chapter 3). This area was pounded by the Ash Wednesday Storm of 1962, and most of the dunes were overtopped. The seawardmost buildings in Nags Head were virtually destroyed. Southern Shores was in the early stages of development then.

Kitty Hawk and Kill Devil Hills (RM 5)

The area from the Kitty Hawk Fishing Pier at the Kitty Hawk–Southern Shores town line to just north of the Wright Brothers National Memorial is highly erosive, with erosion rates varying from 3 to 6.5 feet per year (RM 5). The slight embayment, or curve of the shore away from the sea, is due to the presence of more easily erodible material in the shoreface. The old CCC dune line from the 1930s is absent along much of this stretch, and some houses are sitting in the surf (fig. 7.3). The dunes that are present are low and narrow. Vegetation along the embayment is nonexistent to sparse, making much of this area an extreme-risk zone. The central dune is discontinuous north to the Kill Devil Hills–Kitty Hawk town line, but is continuous north of there. The island narrows considerably at Kitty Hawk Bay, but quickly widens to the north. Here sits Kitty Hawk Woods, a large area of dense maritime forest with small, very narrow ridges on an otherwise low area.

The town of Kill Devil Hills boasts an area of very well developed maritime forest and high dune ridges known as Colington Island. The history of this old flood-tidal delta dates back to a 1663 grant that established a plantation there. The plantation itself no longer exists, thanks to storms and severe water problems; however, a permanent community has survived from the mid-1700s to the present. The early residents understood the harsh environment they were living in and settled in the safest areas. Today, Colington Island remains much the same except for a number of finger canals cut deep into the back side of the island. These canals significantly reduce the site safety of Colington Island.

Like much of the Outer Banks, this area has not experienced a direct hit by a major hurricane in some time, but has been ripped apart by many northeasters. During the 1962 Ash Wednesday Storm, most of Kitty Hawk,

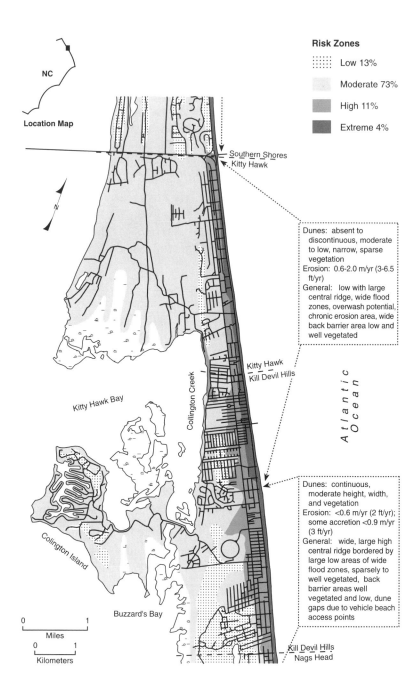

Risk Zones

:::::: Low 13%

    Moderate 73%

    High 11%

    Extreme 4%

NC

Location Map

N

Southern Shores
Kitty Hawk

Dunes: absent to
discontinuous, moderate
to low, narrow, sparse
vegetation
Erosion: 0.6-2.0 m/yr (3-6.5
ft/yr)
General: low with large
central ridge, wide flood
zones, overwash potential,
chronic erosion area, wide
back barrier area low and
well vegetated

Kitty Hawk
Kill Devil Hills

Kitty Hawk Bay

Collington Creek

Atlantic Ocean

Colington Island

Dunes: continuous,
moderate height, width,
and vegetation
Erosion: <0.6 m/yr (2 ft/yr);
some accretion <0.9 m/yr
(3 ft/yr)
General: wide, large high
central ridge bordered by
large low areas of wide
flood zones, sparsely to
well vegetated, back
barrier areas well
vegetated and low, dune
gaps due to vehicle beach
access points

Buzzard's Bay

0   1
Miles

0   1
Kilometers

Kill Devil Hills
Nags Head

RM 5 The Kitty Hawk area

Figure 7.3 An abandoned house in Kitty Hawk stands seaward of a makeshift "dune" (bulldozed pile of sand). This area is subject to chronic erosion, and this house indicates the fate that awaits the buildings across the street.

Kill Devil Hills, and Nags Head was flooded. Waves broke through the dunes, covering most of the island with 2 to 4 feet of water. A breach formed along the shore-perpendicular Soundside Road (formerly known as the Jigsaw Road), located just south of Jockey's Ridge State Park, cutting the area into two sections. This road remains in the same location, allowing the possibility of another breach.

The 1991 Halloween northeaster brought similar but less severe flooding (fig. 7.4). Although no breaches formed in this area, large waves pounded through the dunes, washing several houses away and leaving many others stranded on the beach. Interior flooding left several feet of standing water in some locations. A major, in part federally funded, beach nourishment project is in the planning stage at the time of this writing. The project will encompass portions of Kitty Hawk, Kill Devil Hills, and Nags Head. We believe, because of the relatively high wave energy here, that this beach will have a relatively short life span and will be quite costly to the communities.

Nags Head, South Nags Head, and Oregon Inlet (RMs 6 and 7)
North of Jockey's Ridge State Park and on the back side of Nags Head is an area of very well developed maritime forest called Nags Head Woods (RM 6). Nags Head Woods is owned by The Nature Conservancy and is thus protected from future development. The woods include high, steep-sided, ancient dunes with several freshwater ponds nestled among them. The first commercially successful resort in North Carolina got its start in this protected area in the 1830s.

At that time, the "bankers," who lived on the safe high land and maritime forests of Nags Head Woods on the back side of the island, began to sell open, unprotected land to outsiders from the mainland. A thriving tourist community called Old Nags Head sprang up on the sound side of the barrier. Shortly after the Civil War, development began to expand to the ocean side. The arrival of the first set of access bridges in the late 1920s and 1930s, and the second set in the early 1960s connecting the once-remote islands and barriers to the mainland, brought new waves of development. Almost immediately the newcomers began to have problems with the unstable and active dune fields and the very dynamic and actively eroding shoreline.

The barrier narrows southward from the Kill Devil Hills town line. From the Wright Brothers National Memorial to Jockey's Ridge the dunes also become narrower but are continuous. The dunes are generally in poor condition, and they diminish just south of Jockey's Ridge. A central dune ridge is discontinuous from Jockey's Ridge south to Baymeadow Drive. Where present, the dune offers excellent elevation for homesites, but protective vegetation is sparse. Erosion rates are generally less than 2 feet per year but are higher just south of Whalebone Junction and Jockey's Ridge. Much of the area west of Highway 158 is maritime forest; to the east is mostly scattered shrub. The extensive marshes behind Nags Head are highly erosive.

Figure 7.4   Until recently Kitty Hawk was protected by the dune constructed in the 1930s by the Civilian Conservation Corps. Since the dune was lost in the late 1980s, the first few blocks of the town have been flooded several times. This photo was taken after the 1991 Halloween Storm. It is not possible to replace the frontal dune because the beach has retreated past its former location. A new dune constructed on top of the frontal road could be a very effective and low-cost storm blocker, but blocking the road would not be popular with dwellers and business owners. Photo by Rob Young.

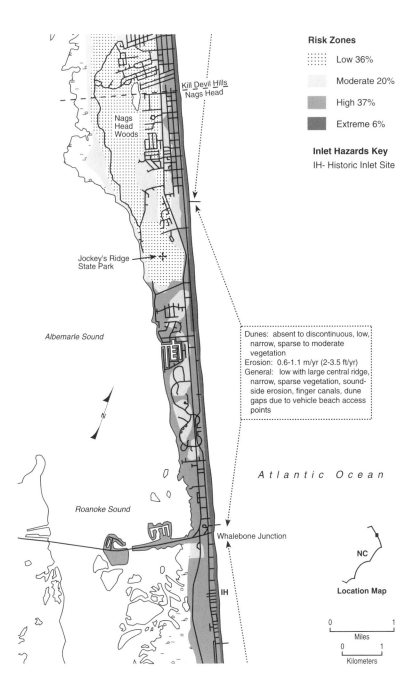

Risk Zones

:::::: Low 36%

Moderate 20%

High 37%

Extreme 6%

Inlet Hazards Key
IH- Historic Inlet Site

Kill Devil Hills
Nags Head

Nags
Head
Woods

Jockey's Ridge
State Park

Albemarle Sound

Dunes: absent to discontinuous, low,
  narrow, sparse to moderate
  vegetation
Erosion: 0.6-1.1 m/yr (2-3.5 ft/yr)
General: low with large central ridge,
  narrow, sparse vegetation, sound-
  side erosion, finger canals, dune
  gaps due to vehicle beach access
  points

Atlantic Ocean

Roanoke Sound

Whalebone Junction

IH

NC

Location Map

0 ———————————— 1
Miles
0 ———————————— 1
Kilometers

RM 6 Nags Head

Finger canals in the area flood easily, bringing high water into the interior parts of the island.

Nags Head is narrowest near Whalebone Junction, where Highways 64-264, 158, and 12 meet. Numerous inlets have been located here in the past, including Roanoke Inlet (just to the south of Whalebone Junction), the inlet most likely used by the Raleigh colonists in 1585. The low marsh islands on which the causeway to Roanoke Island is built are remnants of the tidal shoals of old Roanoke Inlet. This vital path off the island is less than 3 feet above Roanoke Sound. Even with the recently added rock revetment, this causeway will flood easily during a storm.

South Nags Head, just south of Whalebone Junction, is fairly wide, with extensive marshes along Pamlico Sound (RM 7). Like much of the Outer Banks, this area is low and highly erosive (see fig. 6.1). Erosion rates range from 4 to 11 feet per year, and generally increase to the south. The CCC dune has long since disappeared and flooding is almost an annual event. Along one shoreline block, the houses now on the front row were on the third row about 25 years ago! Some buildings now virtually on the beach are protected by large, ugly black sandbags, which the state is trying to remove.

The state inlet hazard area (see chapter 8) extends nearly 2 miles south of South Nags Head to Oregon Inlet. Development is concentrated on a narrow tract of land from the shoreline to the border of the Cape Hatteras National Seashore (about halfway to Highway 12). Vegetation is dominated by sparse shrub.

The Achilles heel of Nags Head and much of the Outer Banks is Whalebone Junction and the causeway leading off the island to the west. There is a large gap in the dune line at the pier, creating a path for storm waters to cut off the highway escape route from the island. The gap could be closed with a few truckloads of sand, reducing the flood overwash vulnerability. This area was completely flooded in the 1962 Ash Wednesday Storm, and even a small northeaster can flood the causeway (fig. 7.5). When this area floods in a major storm, the residents of South Nags Head, Hatteras Island, and Ocracoke will be cut off from the mainland and stranded.

Oregon Inlet, which separates Hatteras Island from the northern Outer Banks, is one of the most dynamic and energetic inlets on the East Coast. Through this single inlet the waters of Albemarle Sound and part of Pamlico Sound flow into the Atlantic Ocean. Since opening in 1846, Oregon Inlet has migrated 2 to 3 miles south to its present location, at an annual rate of between 75 and 125 feet per year. The construction of the Herbert C. Bonner Bridge over Oregon Inlet in 1962 marked a critical transition for Hatteras Island and Oregon Inlet. The bridge provided easy access for visitors, and Hatteras Island developed subsequently at a rapid pace.

Oregon Inlet necessarily became "fixed" in place by the bridge (see fig. 5.12) and could no longer continue to migrate southward as it had done for

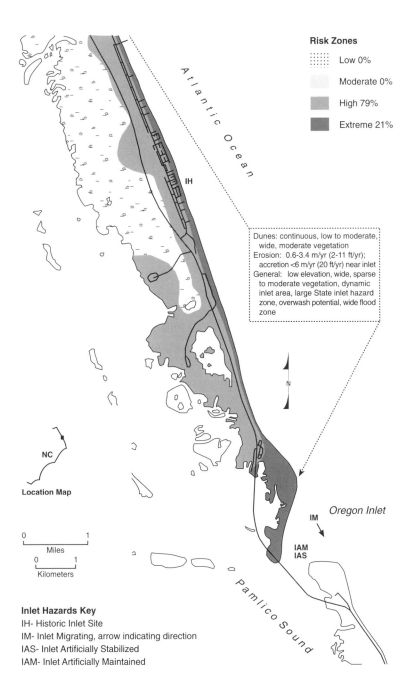

Risk Zones

  Low 0%

  Moderate 0%

  High 79%

  Extreme 21%

Dunes: continuous, low to moderate,
wide, moderate vegetation
Erosion: 0.6-3.4 m/yr (2-11 ft/yr);
    accretion <6 m/yr (20 ft/yr) near inlet
General: low elevation, wide, sparse
    to moderate vegetation, dynamic
    inlet area, large State inlet hazard
    zone, overwash potential, wide flood
    zone

Atlantic Ocean

IH

N

NC

Location Map

0   1
   Miles
0   1
   Kilometers

Oregon Inlet

IM

IAM
IAS

Pamlico Sound

Inlet Hazards Key
IH- Historic Inlet Site
IM- Inlet Migrating, arrow indicating direction
IAS- Inlet Artificially Stabilized
IAM- Inlet Artificially Maintained

RM 7   South Nags Head

Figure 7.5 Looking east along the causeway across Roanoke Sound during a small northeaster. The wind tide from Albemarle Sound has flooded the barrier, almost closing one of the only two escape routes off the Outer Banks.

more than 100 years. Over the years there have been several proposals to build jetties that would keep the inlet in a stable location relative to the bridge and improve access through the inlet for fishermen (see chapter 5). Such jetties would have a disastrous effect, particularly on areas south of the inlet. A jetty system would starve this low and narrow area of sediment, compounding the extreme to high risk that already exists here. Erosion rates would increase, dunes would deteriorate, and overwash and washing out of roads would become even more common than they already are.

Today, a rock revetment lining the southern side of Oregon Inlet prevents its migration to the south. The channel of the inlet is very narrow and deep, and clings to the southern side of the inlet. Large sand sheets are building out on the northern side. A new, longer bridge has been proposed, but such a structure would not solve the problem. Inevitably we will be forced to realize that the bridge is a fixed structure over a dynamic inlet that will not stay in one place, even when confined by jetties.

Rodanthe, Waves, and Salvo (RM 8)

The Pea Island Wildlife Refuge south of Oregon Inlet cannot be developed. The loss of the CCC dune here led to frequent overwash, making it necessary to relocate Highway 12 and build artificial dunes to protect the road. A few miles north of Rodanthe the island continues to narrow and erosion rates are high—5 to 22 feet per year (RM 8). This entire area has the potential to become an inlet.

Rodanthe, Waves, and Salvo (RM 8) are located at a spot where the island widens. The elevation is low in this area, and vegetation varies from none to dense shrubs and scattered maritime forest. That is about the only similarity between these three towns. In terms of coastal processes, the difference is like night and day.

Rodanthe is experiencing extremely high erosion rates along both the ocean (see fig. 3.11) and the sound sides. An aerial view shows that Rodanthe is actually on a small, deteriorating cape extending out to sea (see the shape of the coast in the center of RM 8). Rodanthe is an extremely high-risk community. From Holiday Boulevard north to Corbina Drive, average erosion rates along the ocean side are 15 feet per year (fig. 7.6)! The CCC dune line has long since been destroyed in this area. As a result, some of the oceanfront, shore-parallel roads have been abandoned—covered with sand or lost to the sea. Large washover fans cover the area, and houses sit in the ocean. Shore-perpendicular roads offer easy paths for storm-surge floodwaters entering the sound or exiting to the ocean. THIS AREA IS EXTREMELY DANGEROUS AND SHOULD BE AVOIDED! Sound-side erosion is indicated by the headstones of the old cemetery—which dates back to at least 1830—that now sit on the edge of Pamlico Sound. The headstones face west toward the sound, where the old road and much of the original town were located.

To the south, the town of Waves is in an area of transition. Here the dune field widens and erosion rates decrease. Some erosion is occurring along the northern part of Waves, but the southern beaches are accreting, or building seaward.

Salvo is buffered from the ocean by a multiridge dune field in excess of 200 feet wide and 13 to 20 feet high (fig. 7.7). Like Sunset Beach at the southern end of the state, Salvo is experiencing accretion at a rate of about 3 feet per year. Offshore of Salvo is Wimble Shoals, a shallow, sandy feature that absorbs much of the incoming wave energy and supplies sand to the beach (chapter 3). The shoals have allowed Salvo to accrete.

Between Salvo and Avon to the south, Hatteras island is low and narrow, with grass and scattered shrubs to the east of Highway 12 and dense shrubs and some maritime forest to the west. Erosion is generally less than 2 feet per year. The potential for overwash and flooding from Pamlico Sound is high. Although this area is part of the Cape Hatteras National Seashore and cannot be developed, take note of the potential for storm flooding here to sever the escape route off the island.

Historic storm response differs dramatically from Rodanthe to Salvo because of the variable nature of the offshore geology in this area (see figs. 3.10, 3.11). Rodanthe was overwashed during Hurricane Emily while Salvo experienced mostly wind damage to structures. Highway 12 north of Rodanthe is routinely overwashed during even small northeasters and was unpassable during the 1991 Halloween Storm. The same storm dumped a four-foot-thick layer of sand among the first few rows of houses in Rodanthe.

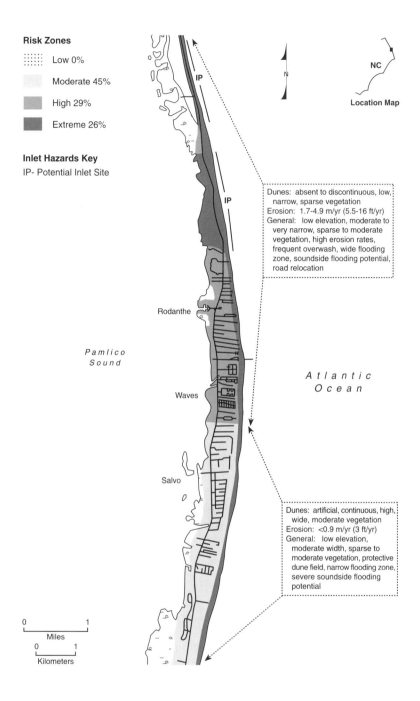

Risk Zones

Low 0%

Moderate 45%

High 29%

Extreme 26%

Inlet Hazards Key
IP- Potential Inlet Site

NC

Location Map

IP

IP

Dunes: absent to discontinuous, low, narrow, sparse vegetation
Erosion: 1.7-4.9 m/yr (5.5-16 ft/yr)
General: low elevation, moderate to very narrow, sparse to moderate vegetation, high erosion rates, frequent overwash, wide flooding zone, soundside flooding potential, road relocation

Rodanthe

Pamlico Sound

Atlantic Ocean

Waves

Salvo

Dunes: artificial, continuous, high, wide, moderate vegetation
Erosion: <0.9 m/yr (3 ft/yr)
General: low elevation, moderate width, sparse to moderate vegetation, protective dune field, narrow flooding zone, severe soundside flooding potential

0   1
Miles
0   1
Kilometers

RM 8 The Waves area

Figure 7.6 Rodanthe is one of North Carolina's most endangered coastal communities. Here, houses sit almost in the water on a calm day, indicative of extremely high erosion rates.

Avon, Buxton, Frisco, and Hatteras (RMS 9–11)
This reach of the Outer Banks ribbon is characterized by variable island width, including two wide areas separated by narrower segments. The wide sections typically have east-west dune ridge systems and maritime forest, while the narrow areas in-between are low and poorly vegetated.

South of Salvo and Wimble Shoals (see fig. 3.11) the island narrows and then widens again, and it is on this wide area that the town of Avon is located (RM 9). The island here is more than twice as wide as it is immediately to the south, and supports dense shrubs and some maritime forest. The older town of Avon, formerly known as Kinnakeet, was totally nestled among the maritime forest on the back side of the island. In fact, Kinnakeet was once known for the small schooners built of wood taken from the extensive maritime forests there and at Buxton and Frisco. Over the years development has driven Avon toward the ocean. Fortunately for the town of Avon, this seaward expansion is protected by a large, wide dune field. Erosion rates are minimal except along the very southern end of Avon, where the rate is 4.5 feet per year. Unfortunately, a small north-south canal was cut along the back side of the island, causing a hazard headache for mid-island residents.

Development has pushed Avon beyond its carrying capacity. The lack of adequate fresh water to support the summertime population necessitated the construction of a pipeline along Highway 12 from Frisco to supply Avon with fresh water, and now ever-increasing development density is assured. The area of Highway 12 between Buxton and Avon is prone to overwash and scouring. A washout of the pipeline during a storm could pose serious health problems.

The area south of Avon and immediately north of Buxton (RMS 9 and 10) is one of the most vulnerable to overwash and potential breaching along the

Figure 7.7 Along this shoreline reach in Salvo, the buildings are set well back from the dune ridge that was constructed by the ccc in the 1930s and 1940s. The damage from most storms will be much less in Salvo than in Rodanthe (see fig. 7.6).

entire Outer Banks. This stretch is only a few hundred feet wide and very low. The dunes, relics of the ccc dune project of the 1930s, are less than 10 feet high and very narrow, and are being eroded away at a rate of 4.5 to 10 feet per year from the southern border of Avon to Buxton. This area is prone to chronic dune breaching and overwash, and Highway 12 is frequently flooded, buried, or washed away. A very high potential for the formation of a new inlet exists in response to very large storm tides across Pamlico Sound. Indeed, there have been several inlets here in the past. Chacandepeco Inlet, which predated 1585, closed between 1657 and 1672. Buxton Inlet opened during the great 1962 Ash Wednesday Storm (see fig. 2.4) in the exact location of the former Chacandepeco Inlet. The new inlet, although it eventually filled in, was bridged by the state highway department. This area is prone to overwash and flooding from both the ocean and sound sides. As part of the Cape Hatteras National Seashore the land should remain undeveloped except for the highway lifeline and the water line to Avon.

Frisco and Buxton are located on the cuspate foreland of Cape Hatteras (RM 10). In the interior of the island are several dune ridges, some in excess of 32 feet high and covered with a dense maritime forest (see fig. 6.3), that offer one of the very few low-risk zones on Hatteras Island, as noted in the center of the cape (RM 10).

Despite the relatively safe nature of this area, there are serious concerns. In-between the large ridges sit low swampy areas that are easily flooded. While the south-facing shores of the cape are accreting at rates as high as 15 feet per year, the east-facing shores are eroding away at rates up to 11 feet per year (see fig. 1.7). Numerous erosion control and shoreline stabilization schemes have been tried in vain to halt the erosion and protect the Cape Hatteras Lighthouse (see chapter 1).

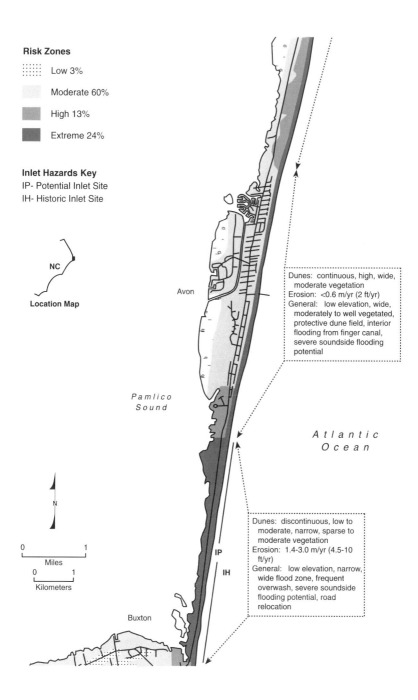

Risk Zones

:::::: Low 3%

 Moderate 60%

 High 13%

 Extreme 24%

Inlet Hazards Key
IP- Potential Inlet Site
IH- Historic Inlet Site

NC

Location Map

Avon

Pamlico Sound

Atlantic Ocean

Dunes: continuous, high, wide, moderate vegetation
Erosion: <0.6 m/yr (2 ft/yr)
General: low elevation, wide, moderately to well vegetated, protective dune field, interior flooding from finger canal, severe soundside flooding potential

Dunes: discontinuous, low to moderate, narrow, sparse to moderate vegetation
Erosion: 1.4-3.0 m/yr (4.5-10 ft/yr)
General: low elevation, narrow, wide flood zone, frequent overwash, severe soundside flooding potential, road relocation

N

0   1
  Miles
0   1
  Kilometers

IP

IH

Buxton

RM 9 Avon

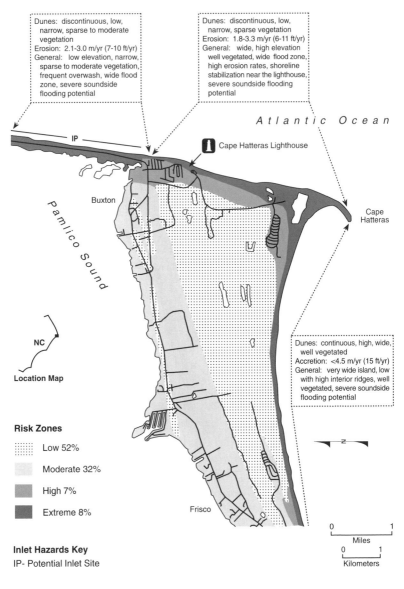

Dunes: discontinuous, low, narrow, sparse to moderate vegetation
Erosion: 2.1-3.0 m/yr (7-10 ft/yr)
General: low elevation, narrow, sparse to moderate vegetation, frequent overwash, wide flood zone, severe soundside flooding potential

Dunes: discontinuous, low, narrow, sparse vegetation
Erosion: 1.8-3.3 m/yr (6-11 ft/yr)
General: wide, high elevation well vegetated, wide flood zone, high erosion rates, shoreline stabilization near the lighthouse, severe soundside flooding potential

Atlantic Ocean

IP

Cape Hatteras Lighthouse

Buxton

Cape Hatteras

Pamlico Sound

NC

Location Map

Dunes: continuous, high, wide, well vegetated
Accretion: <4.5 m/yr (15 ft/yr)
General: very wide island, low with high interior ridges, well vegetated, severe soundside flooding potential

Risk Zones

Low 52%

Moderate 32%

High 7%

Extreme 8%

Frisco

0   1
Miles

0   1
Kilometers

Inlet Hazards Key
IP- Potential Inlet Site

RM 10 Buxton

Hurricane Emily (1993) seriously flooded the sound side of Buxton and Frisco; the floodwaters reached levels as high as 10 feet (see fig. 6.9). This level of flooding surprised local residents because the storm stayed 24 miles offshore and never crossed over land. Although gusts at Buxton National Weather Service Station reached 98 miles per hour (weak for a category 3 hurricane), the sustained winds never reached hurricane strength. The combination of high storm surge associated with weak winds is attributed to the storm track and the estuarine shoreline orientation (appendix C, ref. 12). As the storm approached the coast, the strongest winds at Buxton blew from the north-northwest, pushing Pamlico Sound water against the back side of Buxton and Frisco. The orientation of the island helped to keep the water in place. Finger canals then funneled floodwaters into the interior of the island (see fig. 6.9).

The local Cape Hatteras school, which had been considered a safe location, was flooded, and people were forced to wade though nearly chest-deep water. One distressing outcome of Hurricane Emily is that the people who stayed on the Outer Banks believe they survived a category 3 hurricane and have the impression that a category 3 storm is not to be taken seriously. Nothing could be further from the truth! In fact, the islands never felt the full force of the storm.

Between Frisco and Hatteras is a low, narrow stretch of coastline subject to flooding and overwash from the Atlantic Ocean and Sandy Bay (inlet potential zone on RM 11). This area might flood early in a storm, cutting off the escape route.

Although the village of Hatteras is located on a wide part of the island (RM 11), it is relatively low and there are extensive marshes in and around the village, some of which have canals dredged through them for boat access. Unfortunately, these channels also give floodwaters access to the interior of the island, increasing the risk to homeowners. Frontal dunes of 1930s CCC vintage are continuous and offer some protection from storm surge. The vegetation is a mixture of grasses, shrubs, and a discontinuous canopy of trees.

Hyde County (RM 12)

Ocracoke Island (RM 12)
Located almost 20 miles off the Hyde County mainland, Ocracoke is the most isolated coastal community in North Carolina, accessible only by ferry from either the mainland or the village of Hatteras. Most of this narrow 15.5-mile-long island is part of the Cape Hatteras National Seashore and is closed to private development. The island is bounded by Hatteras Inlet on the east and Ocracoke Inlet on the west.

Ocracoke Inlet, which separates Ocracoke Island from Portsmouth Island and the Cape Lookout National Seashore, has been open continuously since it was discovered in 1585. The inlet became a chief port of entry for North Carolina following the establishment of the town of Ocracoke as an important port in 1715. The inlet remained in use through the Revolutionary War and into the 1820s, but by then extensive dredging was necessary to maintain navigation channels. In the long run, the dredging proved futile; the channels filled faster than they could be dredged, and the effort was

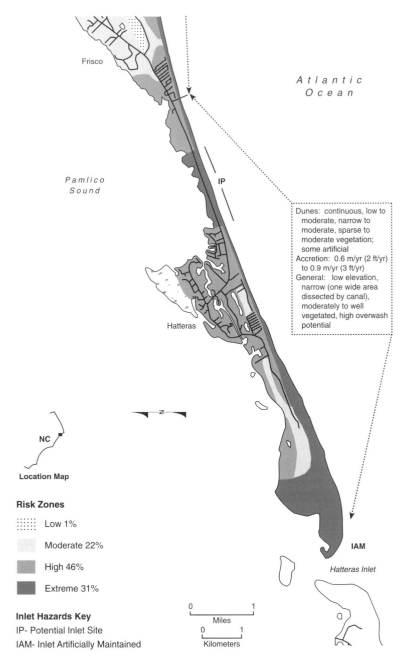

Frisco

Atlantic Ocean

Pamlico Sound

IP

Dunes: continuous, low to
moderate, narrow to
moderate, sparse to
moderate vegetation;
some artificial
Accretion: 0.6 m/yr (2 ft/yr)
to 0.9 m/yr (3 ft/yr)
General: low elevation,
narrow (one wide area
dissected by canal),
moderately to well
vegetated, high overwash
potential

Hatteras

NC

Location Map

Risk Zones

:::::: Low 1%

Moderate 22%

High 46%

Extreme 31%

Inlet Hazards Key
IP- Potential Inlet Site
IAM- Inlet Artificially Maintained

IAM

Hatteras Inlet

```
0          1
    Miles
0          1
 Kilometers
```

RM 11 Hatteras

abandoned in the 1830s. Shipping quickly shifted to use Hatteras Inlet after it opened during a hurricane in 1846, but by 1900 commercial shipping had been completely diverted to other ports.

Ocracoke Inlet's greatest notoriety comes from Edward Teach, better known as Blackbeard the Pirate, who sailed these waters until he was captured and beheaded just inside the inlet at Teach's Hole on November 22, 1718.

Ocracoke Island is generally narrow and low. Marsh extends along the back side of most of the island and around the village of Ocracoke. The artificial dune, constructed along most of the Outer Banks during the 1930s and actively maintained, extends the length of the island. For years, this dune ridge protected Highway 12 from much of the potential overwash from the ocean. The dune is now disappearing at the northern end of the island, and the road is frequently blocked by overwash.

The northeastern half of Ocracoke Island is almost entirely within the Cape Hatteras National Seashore. Sparse to dense shrub covers much of the back side of the island from Highway 12 to the marsh that stretches the length of the island. From the highway to the ocean, the vegetation cover is sparse shrubs and grass. Most of this side of the island is eroding at a rate of 4 to 9 feet per year. A wide inlet hazard zone and flooding area make the eastern side of the island a high- to extreme-risk area. The high overwash potential endangers this escape route for people fleeing an approaching storm. Dense shrub and maritime forest characterize much of the western half of Ocracoke Island (RM 12), on both sides of Highway 12 and in the village. The remaining areas are covered with grass and scattered shrubs.

Ocracoke village (RM 12), settled by local ship pilots and sailors in the early 1700s, is located on the only wide part of the island. Although the land here is not high enough to escape significant floodwaters, the surrounding maritime forest reduces the risk to moderate. Ocracoke's remote location, small size, and limited natural resources dictate that future development take into consideration the limited carrying capacity of the land.

Ocracoke has managed to survive for hundreds of years despite its remote location. As long as steps are taken to protect its forest, Ocracoke may weather future storms as well it has past ones.

Southern Islands

Carteret County: Bogue Banks (RMs 13–15)

Bogue Banks is a 25-mile-long barrier island comprising a variety of geological settings that present a variety of problems and concerns for its residents and visitors. It is the only developed island on the Carteret County shoreline. Undeveloped islands include Portsmouth Island, Core Banks, and Shackleford Banks. Bogue has examples of both good and bad development, and moderate- to extreme-risk settings.

Five communities call Bogue Banks home: (from east to west) Atlantic Beach (RM 13), Pine Knoll Shores (RMs 13 and 14), Salter Path (RM 14), Indian Beach (RM 14), and Emerald Isle (RMs 14 and 15). Each community has evolved differently in its own setting. The success of future development depends largely on how these communities resolve their problems politically.

RM 12 Ocracoke

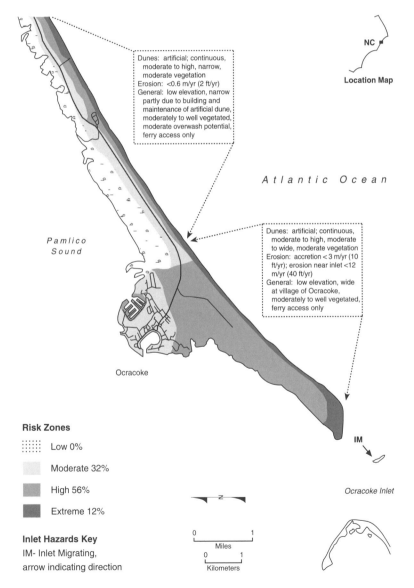

Dunes: artificial; continuous, moderate to high, narrow, moderate vegetation
Erosion: <0.6 m/yr (2 ft/yr)
General: low elevation, narrow partly due to building and maintenance of artificial dune, moderately to well vegetated, moderate overwash potential, ferry access only

NC

Location Map

Atlantic Ocean

Pamlico Sound

Dunes: artificial; continuous, moderate to high, moderate to wide, moderate vegetation
Erosion: accretion < 3 m/yr (10 ft/yr); erosion near inlet <12 m/yr (40 ft/yr)
General: low elevation, wide at village of Ocracoke, moderately to well vegetated, ferry access only

Ocracoke

Risk Zones

Low 0%

Moderate 32%

High 56%

Extreme 12%

IM

Ocracoke Inlet

Inlet Hazards Key
IM- Inlet Migrating,
arrow indicating direction

N

0 —————— 1
Miles
0 —————— 1
Kilometers

Bogue Banks may be the largest barrier island in the United States in terms of volume of sand deposited in the last 3,000 to 4,000 years. High dunes and dense forests abound. Some of the high, wide, and forested segments of the island provide the "safest" homesites anywhere on a barrier island. At least one community (Pine Knoll Shores) prohibits unnecessary tree cutting, helping to ensure its long-term safety. A few island reaches are low and narrow and should be avoided. Evacuation is difficult from most sections of Bogue Banks.

Beaufort Inlet to Pine Knoll Shores (RM 13)
Beaufort Inlet is both stabilized and maintained (by dredging) by the U.S. Army Corps of Engineers. Thus the inlet presents few direct problems for the town of Atlantic Beach (RM 13). Dredge material, although sometimes of poor quality, is used to renourish the beach at Atlantic Beach. Large oyster shells, mud balls, and a sharp erosional scarp are common on the replenished beach.

Rapid and uncontrolled development in Atlantic Beach has resulted in narrowed dunes, filled marshlands, finger canals, and removal of most of the protective vegetation. In some places the central dune ridge has been leveled. A striking example of destructive development is the amusement park at the end of the Atlantic Beach Causeway. To the east and west are areas of higher elevation, continuations of a dune ridge removed to make room for the amusement facility. All vegetation was removed from this area, and a paved notch in the dune ridge exposes downtown Atlantic Beach to storm surge and imperils the main escape road junction at the Morehead City bridge.

Behind the notch are several marsh-filled finger canals on either side of the causeway (fig. 7.8). These low-elevation, nonvegetated areas flood easily during storms and could flood or wash out the causeway long before a storm arrives. During Hurricane Gordon, a weak category 1 storm, many of the parking lots along the causeway were flooded.

East of downtown Atlantic Beach is a high-risk, low-elevation, sparsely vegetated area. A significant overwash hazard exists along this narrow section. To the east of this area the central dune ridge continues for the length of the island, but the poor vegetation cover places much of this area at moderate to high risk. The dense shrubs and forest at the eastern end of the island are located in the undevelopable Fort Macon State Park.

Eastern Pine Knoll Shores is mostly high and well vegetated. Much of this area has a thick forest canopy. Low areas along the sound are subject to some flooding and are at moderate risk. The discontinuous vegetation canopy of the Bogue Banks Country Club golf course turns what would be a low-risk zone into a moderate-risk zone.

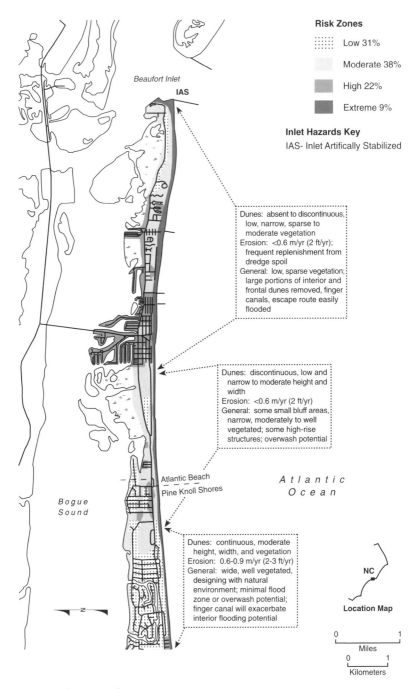

Risk Zones

- Low 31%
- Moderate 38%
- High 22%
- Extreme 9%

Inlet Hazards Key

IAS- Inlet Artifically Stabilized

Beaufort Inlet

IAS

Dunes: absent to discontinuous, low, narrow, sparse to moderate vegetation
Erosion: <0.6 m/yr (2 ft/yr); frequent replenishment from dredge spoil
General: low, sparse vegetation; large portions of interior and frontal dunes removed, finger canals, escape route easily flooded

Dunes: discontinuous, low and narrow to moderate height and width
Erosion: <0.6 m/yr (2 ft/yr)
General: some small bluff areas, narrow, moderately to well vegetated; some high-rise structures; overwash potential

Atlantic Beach
Pine Knoll Shores

Atlantic Ocean

Bogue Sound

Dunes: continuous, moderate height, width, and vegetation
Erosion: 0.6-0.9 m/yr (2-3 ft/yr)
General: wide, well vegetated, designing with natural environment; minimal flood zone or overwash potential; finger canal will exacerbate interior flooding potential

N

NC

Location Map

| 0 | | 1 |
Miles

| 0 | | 1 |
Kilometers

RM 13 Atlantic Beach

Figure 7.8 Aerial view of a dredge-and-fill area on the sound side of Atlantic Beach. Many of the buildings shown here are house trailers. This development, begun shortly after World War II, was made by dredging salt marsh, a process no longer allowed. Note how narrow the island is at this critical escape route off the island.

The relative safety of Pine Knoll Shores offers a stark contrast to Atlantic Beach. Both areas initially had similar settings, but unwise development decisions made Atlantic Beach the more risk-prone community. Much of Atlantic Beach was damaged by Hurricane Hazel in 1954. In response to the threat to the town's buildings, Atlantic Beach built a seawall in front of much of the downtown area. The wall now is hidden by sand. The less heavily developed Pine Knoll Shores area did not perceive any need for a seawall. But good choices aren't always rewarded, and today the balance is tilted a bit less toward Pine Knoll Shores, as Atlantic Beach gets free beach nourishment sand from the Army Corps of Engineers. Both communities suffered dune loss and shoreline retreat during Bertha and Fran.

Pine Knoll Shores to Eastern Emerald Isle (RM 14)
Along the stretch of Highway 58 from Pine Knoll Shores to eastern Indian Beach are numerous examples of good site design where natural vegetation and topography have been preserved, including the Loop Pole Woods development in eastern Pine Knoll Shores (RM 14). Although high and well forested, Loop Pole Woods has a large, horseshoe-shaped finger canal that disrupts the fresh water supply and will bring floodwaters into the interior of the island. In Salter Path (see fig. 6.10) and eastern Indian Beach, dunes increase in width and height, and vegetation is entirely dense maritime forest. Highway 58 runs along the top of a high, forested ridge that slopes off sharply to the ocean.

Salter Path and Indian Beach (RM 14) are fairly wide and high. Parts of the coast, mainly western Indian Beach, are blufflike, with little frontal dune at all, and are currently being eroded. Finger canals and poor vegetation cover create areas of high risk. The Summer Winds condominium and Squatters Camp Site have taken measures to abate erosion of the bluff via beach bulldozing and sand dumping, respectively. Bertha and Fran took big bites out of their properties.

The narrow width of eastern Emerald Isle (RM 14) and the removal of interior dunes resulted in the formation of two inlets there during Hurricane Hazel in 1954—one located between 19th and 23rd Streets and the other near 2nd Street. The old inlet sites are characterized by noticeable dips in the road and a lack of any interior dune ridge. The dip at the Indian Beach Fishing Pier, near the Indian Beach–Emerald Isle town line, is particularly noticeable. These areas are "weak links" in the chain of the island. The overwash potential here is high, and an inlet could form again in the future. Reestablishment of the interior dune could help prevent future inlet formation, but developers tend to flatten topography rather than add to it. The dunes are discontinuous and narrow, and define only a single line of poor natural protection. Near Indian Beach Fishing Pier, dunes are absent.

Eastern Emerald Isle to Bogue Inlet (RM 15)

With its natural setting of high central dune ridges, thick forest cover, and locally generous width, Emerald Isle has some of the lowest-risk sites on the North Carolina coast (RM 15). Great care should be taken to preserve these natural protective features during development. Thoughtless removal of dunes or vegetation, reduction of elevation, and tract developments that bare the island raise the risk to levels that both individual property owners and the collective community should find unacceptable.

West of the Indian Beach town line, N.C. Highway 58 runs on top of a high central ridge, in and out of areas of dense shrub and forest. To the north and south the island quickly slopes off to sea level (fig. 7.9). The dune field alternates between one and two ridges, and is often more than 16 feet high and 65 feet wide, although these dimensions decrease toward the east. The sparse vegetation cover of shrubs and thick grasses between the ocean and Ocean Drive offers little protection from strong winds (moderate risk), but the denser shrub cover between Ocean Drive and Highway 58 reduces the risk of wind damage, provided such cover is maintained when a property is developed. West of Pelican Point, the island abruptly widens to almost twice its width to the east.

The western two-thirds of Emerald Isle is wide and high in elevation, much of it above the 500-year flood level. Vegetation varies, but forest dominates. Developers should not be allowed to remove large tracts of vegetation (fig. 7.10). Much of the sound side is low risk because of the high elevation and dense forest. Several homes along Sound Drive are examples of how homes can be built without disrupting the natural environment.

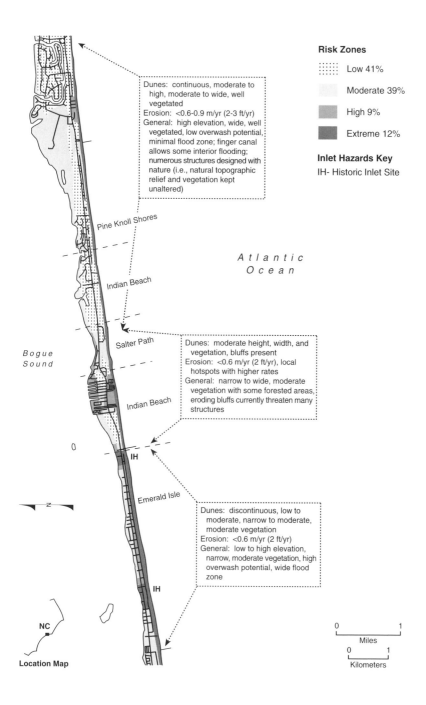

Risk Zones

- Low 41%
- Moderate 39%
- High 9%
- Extreme 12%

Inlet Hazards Key

IH- Historic Inlet Site

Dunes: continuous, moderate to high, moderate to wide, well vegetated
Erosion: <0.6-0.9 m/yr (2-3 ft/yr)
General: high elevation, wide, well vegetated, low overwash potential, minimal flood zone; finger canal allows some interior flooding; numerous structures designed with nature (i.e., natural topographic relief and vegetation kept unaltered)

Dunes: moderate height, width, and vegetation, bluffs present
Erosion: <0.6 m/yr (2 ft/yr), local hotspots with higher rates
General: narrow to wide, moderate vegetation with some forested areas, eroding bluffs currently threaten many structures

Dunes: discontinuous, low to moderate, narrow to moderate, moderate vegetation
Erosion: <0.6 m/yr (2 ft/yr)
General: low to high elevation, narrow, moderate vegetation, high overwash potential, wide flood zone

Atlantic Ocean

Pine Knoll Shores

Indian Beach

Bogue Sound

Salter Path

Indian Beach

IH

Emerald Isle

IH

NC

Location Map

0 Miles 1

0 Kilometers 1

RM 14 Bogue Banks

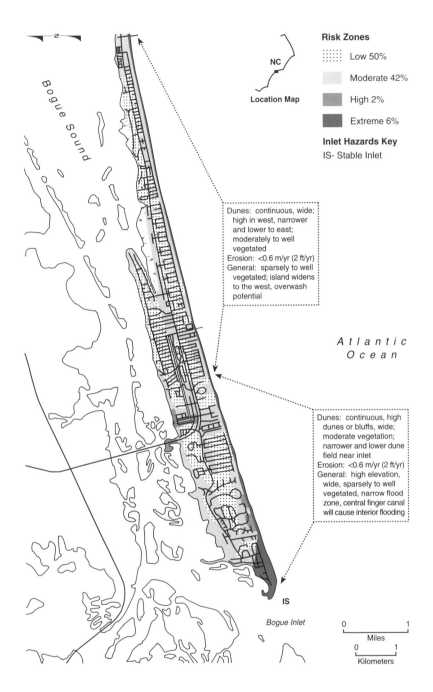

Risk Zones

:::::: Low 50%

Moderate 42%

High 2%

Extreme 6%

Inlet Hazards Key
IS- Stable Inlet

NC

Location Map

Dunes: continuous, wide;
high in west, narrower
and lower to east;
moderately to well
vegetated
Erosion: <0.6 m/yr (2 ft/yr)
General: sparsely to well
vegetated; island widens
to the west, overwash
potential

Atlantic Ocean

Dunes: continuous, high
dunes or bluffs, wide;
moderate vegetation;
narrower and lower dune
field near inlet
Erosion: <0.6 m/yr (2 ft/yr)
General: high elevation,
wide, sparsely to well
vegetated, narrow flood
zone, central finger canal
will cause interior flooding

IS

Bogue Inlet

0   1
Miles

0   1
Kilometers

RM 15 Emerald Isle

Figure 7.9 On Emerald Isle, dunes were removed to build the front row of houses, making them highly vulnerable to the next storm. The buildings on the second row are at a higher elevation, which offers greater protection. Houses in the mid-island area have both good elevation and protective vegetation cover.

Figure 7.10 Maritime forest was cleared and high dunes leveled to build this housing development on Emerald Isle. An area of moderate risk has been transformed to one of high risk.

Separating the sound side from Highway 58 is a low marsh and canal area. A canal was dug between the Bridge View Campground and the Forest Hill Mobile Home Court and connected to Archer Creek. No permit was granted to unplug the canal, so although it does not reach open water, the canal does provide a conduit for water to reach far into the island. This kind of reckless development presents a risk not just to the people immediately around the canal but also to those who live to the north of the canal and must cross it to escape floodwaters.

Much of the coastline in this area is bluff, and only small, low dunes are present. Erosion is not generally a problem. Landowners along most of this reach have little worry about property damage from direct wave attack, but erosion will undermine this high area during storms and threaten to topple structures.

Bogue Inlet is currently not migrating, but that does not mean it poses no danger. The inlet is a "breathing" inlet, meaning that it widens and narrows periodically. People should not be lulled into a false sense of security because the inlet is currently in a narrow state; further development of this part of the island should not be allowed. Fortunately, the N.C. Division of Coastal Management has designated this an inlet hazard area in the hope of preventing future development.

Much of eastern Emerald Isle suffered significant erosion during Hurricane Fran that removed dunes, exposed septic tanks, and undermined pilings. Subsequent bulldozing has done little to restore the protective dunes. Many residents returned to find their homes still standing, but teetering on the edge. Long-term beach replenishment most likely will be very costly, so a long-term plan of abandonment and relocation is the most effective means of reducing damage from future Frans.

Onslow and Pender Counties (RMS 16–18)

Hammocks Beach State Park

We encourage readers to visit this park to see an undeveloped barrier island. During the summer months a passenger ferry operated by the state transports visitors to the island from Swansboro. The small (3.5 miles of beach) island is backed by extensive salt marsh and covered with active dunes. Hammocks Beach is the most accessible island in North Carolina that is close to being in its natural state. Like Bogue Banks, its northeast-southwest orientation places the beach sand source perpendicular to southerly winds. Overall historic shoreline accretion suggests an ample sand supply. The result is active dune fields with maximum elevations ranging from 30 to 60 feet. Only a few small areas are well vegetated. This island is put to excellent use as a recreational beach and dune park. Ferries carry passengers only; the prohibition of vehicles protects the natural environment.

Bear (Shacklefoot) Island

Access to this island is highly restricted; the only way to get there is by boat. As part of a military reservation, the western end of the island has been used for target practice. Although smaller in area than Hammocks Beach,

Bear Island has about the same length of beachfront and more vegetation. The active dune field has elevations of around 15 feet, although most of the island contains stabilized dunes with elevations up to 30 feet. Historically the shoreline has shown low to moderate erosion. Bear Inlet and Brown's Inlet have histories of active migration.

Onslow Beach
Parts of this 11-mile-long island are similar to Topsail Island, and if the island were publicly owned rather than a military preserve, it would undoubtedly be developed. A bridge connects the island to the mainland. The northern end of the island, although narrow, has some moderately high elevations (greater than 30 feet) in a fairly continuous dune ridge. Military vehicles, however, threaten dune stability.

On the western portion of the island the dune ridge becomes lower and broken, subjecting the area to overwash. This zone also suffers moderate to high shoreline erosion. In addition, the New River Inlet has a history of migration and associated erosion-deposition problems. The eastern end of the island is also eroding from inlet migration.

Topsail Island (RMs 16–18)
Before the U.S. government acquired Topsail Island as a military reservation in 1941, the island was used as grazing land. During the period of military ownership the first drawbridge and a paved road that runs the length of the island were constructed, as were the still-visible concrete towers built to observe rocket tests. The island was returned to private ownership in 1947. Since then its population has grown, with the 1980s and 1990s experiencing an explosion of growth.

In the summer of 1996, it seemed that Topsail Island had been returned to the military and was being used once again for bombing exercises as the island became ground zero for two hurricanes within eight weeks (fig. 7.11). The scenes flashed on television screens looked like images from a war zone, not a vacation destination. Such complete devastation hadn't been seen along this stretch of coast in more than 40 years. But if ever there was an island primed for disaster, Topsail Island was it. To understand why, we need to look at the internal makeup of the island.

Topsail Beach has a troublesome geologic setting along its entire 22-mile length. The island is very narrow and flat, with no significant areas higher than the 500-year flood elevation; in fact, most of the island lies on the 100-year floodplain. As one would expect, historical storm damage on Topsail has been extensive. Hurricane Hazel, which made landfall near the South Carolina border in 1954, generated a storm surge of 9.5 feet (the average island elevation is 9 feet) and destroyed 210 of the 230 homes on Topsail. Ha-

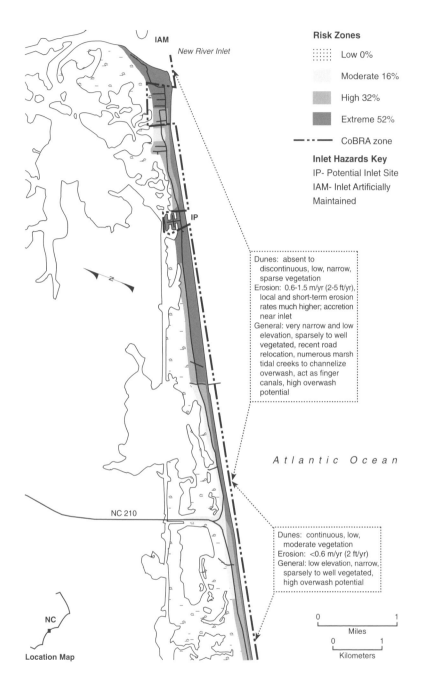

Risk Zones

Low 0%

Moderate 16%

High 32%

Extreme 52%

— ·· — CoBRA zone

Inlet Hazards Key
IP- Potential Inlet Site
IAM- Inlet Artificially
Maintained

IAM

New River Inlet

IP

Dunes: absent to
discontinuous, low, narrow,
sparse vegetation
Erosion: 0.6-1.5 m/yr (2-5 ft/yr),
local and short-term erosion
rates much higher; accretion
near inlet
General: very narrow and low
elevation, sparsely to well
vegetated, recent road
relocation, numerous marsh
tidal creeks to channelize
overwash, act as finger
canals, high overwash
potential

A t l a n t i c   O c e a n

NC 210

Dunes: continuous, low,
moderate vegetation
Erosion: <0.6 m/yr (2 ft/yr)
General: low elevation, narrow,
sparsely to well vegetated,
high overwash potential

0   1
Miles

0   1
Kilometers

NC

Location Map

RM 16   North Topsail Beach

zel caused an estimated $2.5 million (in 1954 dollars) worth of property damage on Topsail and destroyed the drawbridge in the process.

A 1987 evaluation by the N.C. Department of Emergency Management indicated the island would be largely underwater in a category 1 or 2 hurricane (such as Bertha), and nearly completely submerged in a category 3 hurricane (such as Fran; see appendix C, ref. 6). Both predictions proved to be correct. The dune ridges along Topsail were generally 10 to 15 feet high but often very narrow prior to Bertha and Fran. In many places the frontal dune was narrowed by back-side notching to accommodate construction, thus weakening the natural protection.

Because of the uniformly low elevation of Topsail Island, risk zones depend largely on vegetation. After Hurricanes Bertha and Fran, the Division of Coastal Management couldn't reestablish the setback line (see chapter 8) because there was no vegetation left! If you plan to buy or build on Topsail Island, pay particular attention to the vegetation around the site and also to your building's proximity to other buildings. Your neighbors may not want to preserve the native vegetation, making your site more risk-prone. Notice also the number and extent of sound-side bulkheads. These indicate a sound-side erosion problem, which exacerbates the island's problems.

The vegetation varies along Topsail's length. The ends of the island typically have sparse vegetation, mainly grasses and a few shrubs. The middle part of the island is a patchwork of forest and clearings where forest was removed for development.

Figure 7.11 A post-Fran view of a trailer park in North Topsail Beach. Overwash is clearly visible; the rows between trailers acted as overwash passes.

New River Inlet to Highway 210 Bridge (RM 16)

If Topsail Island was ground zero for Bertha and Fran, North Topsail Beach (RMs 16 and 17) and Surf City (RM 17) were where the bomb detonated. This stretch was particularly hard hit, and hundreds of homes were destroyed.

The Army Corps of Engineers maintains the New River Inlet channel, which helps to stabilize the northeastern tip of Topsail Island. The area is still very low, however, and much of it is in an inlet hazard zone. Most of the area is high to extreme risk, with local moderate-risk sites where forest remains.

Northeast of the Highway 210 bridge, dunes are discontinuous but well vegetated with grass. North of New River Inlet Road, forest is continuous, resulting in moderate risk north of the road to the Villa Capriani development. The Villa Capriani condominium and St. Regis Hotel are good examples of out-of-place buildings. Large buildings such as these do not belong on a narrow, eroding, and very low island.

After a long political battle, the developer of most of North Topsail Beach was forced by the state to move the road because it was threatened with immediate erosion. Most of the road along North Topsail Beach east to Bay Court has been relocated back from the beach a few tens of yards toward the island center, but to a lower spot. Unfortunately, homesites are now being sold where the road was once located. Avoid these short-lived "building" sites!

Figure 7.12 A post-Fran aerial view of North Topsail Beach showing five small bridges (marked by road-parallel dark lines) that once extended across marshes. Overwash sand, extending into the marsh behind the island, is clearly visible. The Villa Capriani condominium is visible at the top of photo.

In less than 2 miles the access road crosses approximately 10 small bridges that span marsh fingers, some of them with open water (fig. 7.12). Before Bertha and Fran, some of the fingers reached nearly to the back of the dune, effectively reducing the width of the island. These marsh fingers acted like conduits for storm surge during both storms, ripping up pavement and making roads nearly impassable (see fig. 2.3). During Hurricane Fran, two of the marsh fingers were actually scoured into inlets. The threats from the back side are coupled with erosion rates as high as 4.5 feet per year on the ocean side. The area is at extreme risk, and no further development should be allowed here.

A similar situation exists from Bay Court into the rest of the North Topsail Beach area. Erosion has forced the relocation of the road all the way to Marine Drive. The island is narrow and extremely low. Dunes are absent, and the area is poorly vegetated with only grass. Storm overwash completely covered this area and scoured deep breaches into the island. Nothing is safe here!

In general, the area north of the Highway 210 bridge should not be developed any further. Relocation of roads, high erosion rates, low elevation, recent inlet formation, poor vegetation, frequent overwash, and absence of dunes should sound the alarm for the residents of North Topsail Beach. The alarm sounded for the federal government in 1982, when much of this area became a designated unit under the Coastal Barrier Resources Act (see COBRA in chapter 8). The federal government will not issue flood insurance to buildings built after the COBRA start date. You build here at your own risk, *not* the government's (taxpayers')!

Highway 210 Bridge to Surf City Area (RM 17)
Before Hurricane Fran, the dunes south of the Highway 210 bridge were discontinuous. Where they were present, the dune field consisted of a single discontinuous ridge, 13 to 23 feet wide and generally no higher than 11.5 feet (RM 17). Now the dune is absent and vegetation varies from sparse shrub to forest, although forest is restricted to the lagoon side of the road.

There are several examples of poor development planning from the Highway 210 bridge southwest to the St. Moritz development. The areas on the southeast side of the highway were cleared of all vegetation and leveled. Large homes with elaborate roof lines were built right up into the backs of the dunes. Now the dunes are gone and these homes are at extreme risk. Across the road, the maritime forest remains. This will be a moderate-risk zone if the forest is preserved.

Approximately two-thirds of a mile south of the Roger's Bay Campground the island is extremely narrow and low. In this area, three deep storm-surge scours formed during Hurricane Fran. The channels scoured the road and undercut the foundations of at least two buildings (fig. 7.13).

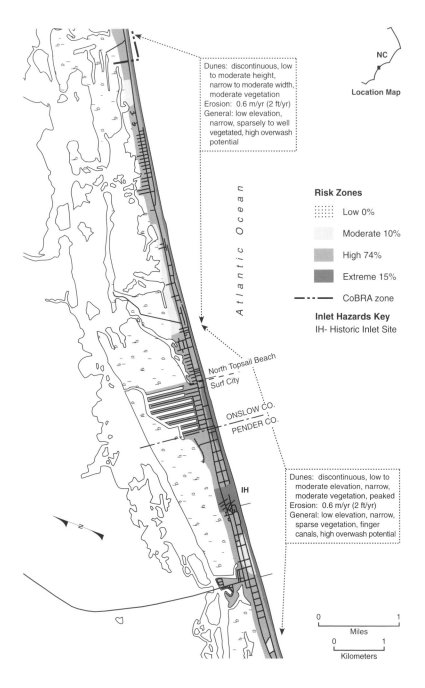

Dunes: discontinuous, low
    to moderate height,
    narrow to moderate width,
    moderate vegetation
Erosion: 0.6 m/yr (2 ft/yr)
General: low elevation,
    narrow, sparsely to well
    vegetated, high overwash
    potential

NC

Location Map

Atlantic Ocean

Risk Zones

:::::: Low 0%

Moderate 10%

High 74%

Extreme 15%

─ ─ ·· ─ CoBRA zone

Inlet Hazards Key
IH- Historic Inlet Site

North Topsail Beach
Surf City

ONSLOW CO.
PENDER CO.

IH

Dunes: discontinuous, low to
    moderate elevation, narrow,
    moderate vegetation, peaked
Erosion: 0.6 m/yr (2 ft/yr)
General: low elevation, narrow,
    sparse vegetation, finger
    canals, high overwash potential

N

0   1
        Miles
0   1
      Kilometers

RM 17 Surf City area

Figure 7.13 The house in the foreground fell into the new channel or inlet excavated by the storm-surge ebb on Topsail Island during Hurricane Fran. This channel is an extension and deepening of a natural channel in the salt marsh that extended into the island.

Interestingly, two of the scour channels line up with shore-perpendicular navigation channels cut into the marsh and the driveways that face them. This lineation indicates that the shore-perpendicular features channeled the water and enhanced scouring. Another deep scour occurred at the Onslow County Regional Beach access.

South to the Pender-Onslow County line, dunes were largely absent before Bertha. Some houses sat out on the beach, and their owners dumped sand and bulldozed it against them in a desperate attempt to protect them. Bertha overwashed this entire area with up to 2 feet of sand in some locations. The few dunes Bertha left behind, Fran consumed! Dozens of homes were lifted off their foundations and destroyed. Others simply disappeared. The devastation from here to downtown Surf City was awesome.

From the North Topsail Beach–Surf City town line to the south are seven finger canals. These cuts create a very dangerous situation in conjunction with the low elevation, poor or absent dunes, lack of significant vegetation, and narrow width. Development here is at high to extreme risk. If another Hazel (1954) should occur here, the area would be leveled. Fortunately for the current residents, Fran was not as strong as Hazel, although the damage it caused was severe enough.

The front row of houses along North Shore Drive from the North Topsail Beach town line south to the Surf condos was almost completely destroyed (see fig. 1.6). A group of 10 houses on one stretch vanished with nary a trace.

This area was extremely low and had virtually no protective dunes long before Fran.

Just north of Barnacle Bill's Pier is the scar of an inlet opened by Hurricane Hazel. Because of the low elevation, lack of significant vegetation, and narrow dunes, this zone is susceptible to inlet formation in the future. Avoid it. From Barnacle Bill's Pier to Surf City Pier (both heavily damaged during Fran) the dunes increase in both height and width.

Immediately north of the Surf City Pier, the dune field varies from 20 to 30 feet in width and may be as high as 15 to 20 feet. The dunes are continuous and well vegetated. The central portion of the island remains low and flat with sparse shrubs. A continuous canopy of vegetation is absent. The dunes, although heavily eroded, protected many structures in this area from Fran.

The area centered on Surf City is low, flat, and densely developed, marking the end of the continuous maritime forest cover that starts north of the Jolly Roger Pier in Topsail Beach to the south. Much of the central part of the island is covered with grass lawns and occasional clumps of shrubs. The dune field width decreases northeastward toward the Surf City Pier, narrowing to about 13 feet. The dunes are 6 to 10 feet high and well vegetated with grass. Houses are bunched up and notched into the back of the dunes. Many of the dunes remained intact during Fran, reducing the storm damage, especially compared with other parts of Surf City.

Surf City Area to New Topsail Inlet (RM 18)

Significant island interior vegetation composed of thick shrubs and maritime forest begins in the Surf City area. This cover is fairly continuous from the sound up to Ocean Boulevard and extends southwest to just north of the Jolly Roger Pier (RM 18). An exception is the area around Queen's Grant condominium, where the leveling of the forest and emplacement of finger canals have created a high-risk zone.

A section of N.C. Highway 50 was washed out near the Topsail Beach–Surf City town line by Fran. This road was the only escape route on this section of the island, and those foolish enough to stay on the island were stranded.

Between the Surf City town line and the Jolly Roger Pier in Topsail Beach, the dunes are well vegetated with thick grasses and occasional shrubs. The single dune ridge is nearly continuous, 11 feet high, and generally less than 30 feet wide. The entire dune is scarped, indicating erosion. Although erosion rates are not high here, the narrow dune width coupled with house sites often notched or cut into the dunes makes this a hazardous area for the near future. From the Jolly Roger Pier south to the Sea Vista Motel, the dunes can best be described as sparsely vegetated mounds of

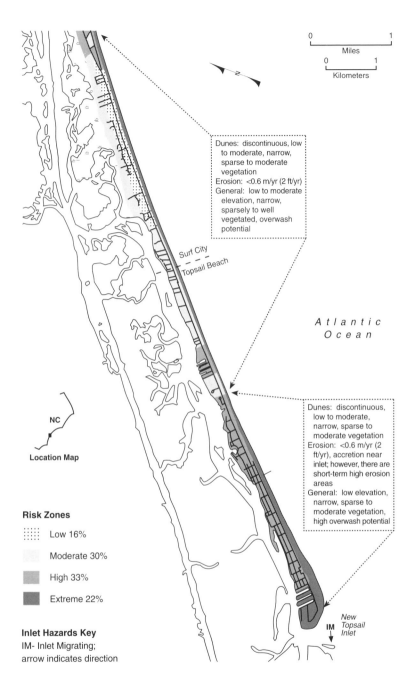

0 ————————— 1
Miles

0 ————————— 1
Kilometers

Dunes: discontinuous, low
to moderate, narrow,
sparse to moderate
vegetation
Erosion: <0.6 m/yr (2 ft/yr)
General: low to moderate
elevation, narrow,
sparsely to well
vegetated, overwash
potential

Surf City
Topsail Beach

*Atlantic
Ocean*

NC

Location Map

Dunes: discontinuous,
low to moderate,
narrow, sparse to
moderate vegetation
Erosion: <0.6 m/yr (2
ft/yr), accretion near
inlet; however, there are
short-term high erosion
areas
General: low elevation,
narrow, sparse to
moderate vegetation,
high overwash potential

Risk Zones

:::::: Low 16%

Moderate 30%

High 33%

Extreme 22%

Inlet Hazards Key
IM- Inlet Migrating;
arrow indicates direction

*New
Topsail
IM   Inlet*

RM 18   Southern Topsail Island

sand that afford little if any protection to the buildings behind them (fig. 7.14).

Before Hurricanes Bertha and Fran, a prominent artificial dune, 12 feet high and 50 feet wide, fronted much of the southern part of the island along Ocean Boulevard south of the Sea Vista Motel (fig. 7.15). Fran leveled this dune, and the entire area was overwashed by the storm surge. Up to 3 feet of washover sand was deposited in some parts of Surf City.

Three finger canals cut from the sound across the island to Ocean Boulevard create a potential inlet area. The owners of the Sea Vista Motel have

Figure 7.14 The beachfront road on Topsail Island, (A) before Hurricane Fran, and (B) after Fran. The low dune was washed out and overwash was deposited across the road into the island's interior. The new sand raises the elevation of the island.

Figure 7.15 View looking toward the Sea Vista Motel on the southern part of Topsail Beach (A) before Hurricane Fran struck, and (B) after Hurricane Fran. The dune in the foreground was completely removed by Fran's storm surge. Overwash buried the beachfront road as well as a shore-perpendicular access road.

learned the lessons of migrating inlets the hard way. So many storms have washed through the motel that the owners have wisely abandoned the first floor of rooms! The protective bulge of sand associated with New Topsail Inlet that once fronted the property moved to the southwest as the inlet migrated away, and the shorefront changed from accretionary to highly erosive.

New Topsail Inlet has been migrating to the southwest at a rate of 125 feet per year since 1738 (fig. 7.16). In modern times, as the inlet has migrated and built out the island, the new land has been heavily developed. This is a dan-

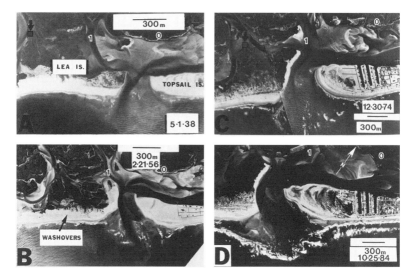

Figure 7.16 Shape changes in New Topsail Inlet from 1938 to 1984. The points labeled "o" and "1" are fixed reference points. Note that the bulge at the end of Topsail Island (*right*) moves as the island lengthens and the inlet migrates. As the bulge migrates south (*left*), the shoreline at the former position of the bulge retreats rapidly. Photo courtesy of William Cleary.

gerous practice for three reasons. First, inlets are fickle beasts; they can suddenly stop migrating or change direction. Second, the "new" part of the island is very low because there has not been enough time to build up the elevation of the interior through overwash and dune-building processes (see chapter 3). Third, the seaward bulge or wide beach area often associated with an inlet builds a false sense of security. But as the inlet migrates, this wide beach migrates with it, and so does the natural protection (as happened at the Sea Vista Motel). Thus, much of the southern part of the island is at extreme to high risk.

Lea Island

Lea Island was promoted by developers in the 1970s as "exclusive" and "secluded," both of which were true, as the island is accessible only by boat. The island is not included here on a risk map because it is 100 percent extreme risk, unsuitable for development.

Most of Lea Island has an elevation less than 10 feet; much of it is less than 5 feet above mean sea level. A continuous foredune is absent over most of the island. Where present, the dune is usually less than 10 feet above mean sea level. Overwash is common, and the island has been flooded by past hurricanes. The entire island, with its approximately 2 miles of beachfront, is within the migration zone of its bounding inlets. New Topsail

Inlet, at the northeastern end of Lea Island, is migrating into the island as the Topsail spit grows. Although Old Topsail Inlet on the southwestern end may be migrating to the southwest, the sand spit that forms this end of the island is simply too low and unprotected for safe development.

The original development plan called for 48 lots ranging in size from more than 1 acre to less than 4 acres. Developers had the right to subdivide any lot into two lots. It is difficult to imagine 48 low-risk cottage sites on Lea; 96 developed sites is inconceivable! Some of the land that was "exclusive" in the 1970s is now under the sea.

No Name Island

No Name Island is a 2.5-mile-long barrier backed by wide marsh. Similar in size and shape to Figure Eight Island, it lacks high elevations and has numerous overwash passes in the low dunes. A vegetated, 15-to-20-foot-high dune ridge on the back side of the northeastern end of the island could provide a few moderate-risk building sites, but most of the island is simply too low and unprotected for development. High rates of shoreline erosion and inlet migration are added hazards. Although this island is not shown on a risk map, most of it is extreme to high risk.

New Hanover County (RMs 19–21)

Figure Eight Island (RM 19)

Figure Eight Island, an exclusive private island just north of Wrightsville Beach (RM 19), is a vacation destination for people such as Vice President Al Gore and a number of media stars. Before beginning construction, the developers elevated the ocean side of a portion of the island using sand excavated from finger canals dug on the back side of the island. The shoreline steadily eroded, however, and two beach nourishment projects were carried out with local funding prior to 1997. Both nourishments were substantially lost in short periods, indicating that future continuous protection by nourishment will be a heavy financial burden on the island's property owners.

Hurricane Fran eroded much of the protective frontal dune, leaving many buildings without protection from future storms. Mason Inlet to the south has a history of changing its location rapidly as a result of storms. Property owners should be aware of this and ensure that no additional development occurs near the inlet. The channel in Rich Inlet at the northern end of Figure Eight Island migrates back and forth, and its position at any given time determines the erosive state of the shoreline at the tip of the island. That is why the position of the shoreline has oscillated so dramatically here. Figure Eight is a short island with good roads, but the drawbridge leading off the island could be a dangerous evacuation route obstacle. Early storm evacuation is highly recommended.

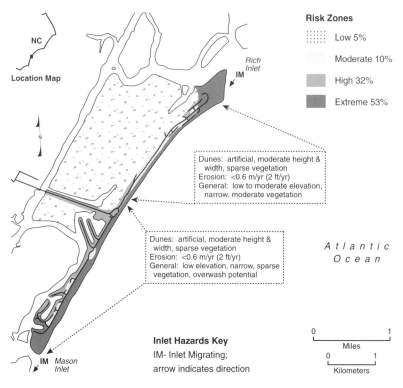

Risk Zones

Low 5%

Moderate 10%

High 32%

Extreme 53%

Dunes: artificial, moderate height &
width, sparse vegetation
Erosion: <0.6 m/yr (2 ft/yr)
General: low to moderate elevation,
narrow, moderate vegetation

Dunes: artificial, moderate height &
width, sparse vegetation
Erosion: <0.6 m/yr (2 ft/yr)
General: low elevation, narrow, sparse
vegetation, overwash potential

*Atlantic
Ocean*

Inlet Hazards Key
IM- Inlet Migrating;
arrow indicates direction

0   1
Miles

0   1
Kilometers

RM 19   Figure Eight Island

One of the unfortunate aspects of the development of Figure Eight Island was the dredging of the adjacent marsh during the construction of the
access causeway. The dredge-spoil barrier altered the original circulation in
the marsh.

Wrightsville Beach (RM 20)
Wrightsville Beach is a composite of two barrier islands. In 1965,
Wrightsville Inlet (Moore's Inlet) was artificially closed, filling the gap between Wrightsville Beach and Shell Island to the north and creating one
continuous island (RM 20). Before Hurricane Fran, a Holiday Inn occupied
the site where the old inlet was located (see fig. 6.7). Geologists familiar
with the area referred to it as the "Holiday Inlet." This extreme-risk area is
characterized by low elevation (approximately 5 feet) and an absence of
vegetation and dunes. It should be avoided.

The Holiday Inn was heavily damaged during Hurricane Fran and was
razed. The owners of the hotel sued the town of Wrightsville Beach for correctly denying them a permit to build a nine-story replacement for the
original four-story structure. An out-of-court settlement allows a seven-
story hotel to be built—on a former inlet site! This is a good example of

why property losses increase in successive hurricanes. The builders plan to put the new structure at a higher elevation, which may prevent a repeat of the Fran damage in future small hurricanes. Nevertheless, this will remain a very hazardous site.

Virtually all frontal dunes on Wrightsville Beach are made of nourished sand and sit atop the storm berm constructed by the U.S. Army Corps of Engineers as part of the beach nourishment program. On the south end of the island, a wide, healthy, well-vegetated dune field offers some protection to the structures behind the dunes. The dunes along the central portion of the island, including the old inlet area, are generally in poor condition: low, narrow, and with sparse vegetation cover.

RM 20 Wrightsville Beach

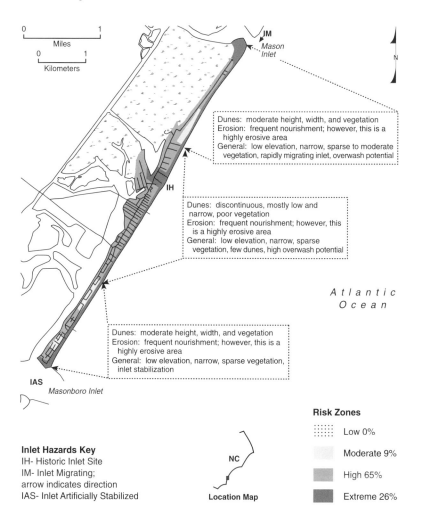

Dunes: moderate height, width, and vegetation
Erosion: frequent nourishment; however, this is a highly erosive area
General: low elevation, narrow, sparse to moderate vegetation, rapidly migrating inlet, overwash potential

Dunes: discontinuous, mostly low and narrow, poor vegetation
Erosion: frequent nourishment; however, this is a highly erosive area
General: low elevation, narrow, sparse vegetation, few dunes, high overwash potential

Dunes: moderate height, width, and vegetation
Erosion: frequent nourishment; however, this is a highly erosive area
General: low elevation, narrow, sparse vegetation, inlet stabilization

Atlantic Ocean

JM — Mason Inlet

IH

IAS
Masonboro Inlet

Inlet Hazards Key
IH- Historic Inlet Site
IM- Inlet Migrating; arrow indicates direction
IAS- Inlet Artificially Stabilized

NC
Location Map

Risk Zones
Low 0%
Moderate 9%
High 65%
Extreme 26%

Compared with the extensive damage on Topsail Island, the damage from Hurricane Fran was relatively light in Wrightsville Beach. Undoubtedly the nourished beach played a major role in damage prevention. But it is important to note that Fran's hurricane-force winds lasted for only one hour on Wrightsville Beach versus seven hours on Topsail Island (appendix C, ref. 11). Most of the damage in Wrightsville Beach was caused by wind; floodwaters did some damage as well, but there was little wave damage. The flooding occurred primarily from the lagoon side. Note again that one of the most severely damaged buildings in Wrightsville Beach was located on a former inlet site.

Wrightsville Beach's two inlets are in extreme contrast. Masonboro Inlet, to the south, has been stabilized by jetties. Although residents of the southern end of the island should be somewhat concerned with possible inlet formation across the high-risk areas at this end, they need not worry about Masonboro Inlet migrating. In contrast, Mason Inlet, which separates Wrightsville Beach on the north from Figure Eight Island (a private community), is rapidly migrating southward. Shell Island Resort, a high-rise at the northern tip of the island, is threatened by the migrating inlet (see fig. 5.11).

Residents of Shell Island Resort sued the state of North Carolina because they were denied a permit to build hard stabilization structures along the inlet. After several tries and some political shenanigans, the resort owners were allowed to build a "temporary" sandbag seawall via an exemption granted by the Coastal Resources Council (see chapter 8). At the time of this writing, less than six months after the wall was built, the channel of Mason Inlet has migrated up to the sandbags and has started to undermine them. It is now only a matter of time before they fail and the inlet channel threatens the resort. There is an important lesson to be learned from the Shell Island situation: Building in dynamic high-risk zones leads to continuing and increased costs to ward off the threat of hazards, with little likelihood of long-term success. Shell Island Resort is a twin to the Holiday Inn in its expected storm response.

Numerous hurricanes have raked this island. Hurricane Hazel (1954) destroyed 89 buildings—mainly the row fronting the beach—and damaged several hundred others. Hurricane Diane (1955) covered the island's streets with water and sand from the beach. Since the early 1920s, techniques ranging from the emplacement of groins in 1923 to the beach nourishment projects of the 1960s and 1970s have been employed to combat shoreline erosion. Wrightsville Beach may be one of the nation's most nourished beaches; a total of 20 nourishment projects have been carried out since 1939 (see fig. 5.9). The first federally funded (in part) project was completed in 1965, followed through 1995 by 15 more nourishments. This beach also seems to be one of the most successful beaches in terms of retention of the nourished sand. Nevertheless, as discussed in chapter 5, many questions remain about beach nourishment, including the biological impacts of such heavy engineering and whether or not such projects should be paid for with federal funds.

Masonboro Island

This low, narrow, frequently overwashed, state-owned barrier is another example of a nearly natural system. Subject to rapid change, and thus highly unsuitable for development, the island is best left untouched to serve a recreational (8 miles of beach) and preservation role, with access limited to boats and no recreational roads or support facilities.

Carolina Beach (RM 21)

Carolina Beach comprises a low-lying, narrow spit of sand backed by a narrow marsh that is attached to the mainland near Atlanta Avenue (RM 21). Like Wrightsville Beach, this community depends on beach replenishment (see fig. 5.9). Since 1955, at least 20 sand pumpings have been necessary to hold the shoreline in place. Carolina Beach was once a community of small single-family houses and cottages, but after the very large 1982 nourishment, the erosion problem was no longer apparent and the town quickly boomed into a multifamily home and high-rise community. The beach in front of the stone revetment at the north end of Carolina Beach has experienced rapid loss of nourishment sand (fig. 7.17).

The earliest storm accounts on record, from the 1880s, mention the Carolina Beach area. In October 1889, the U.S. Navy lookout station was destroyed by heavy storm surf. A year later, numerous resort cottages were washed away or damaged. The island was struck again by a severe storm in 1893. Carolina Beach continued to grow, however, as did the dollar value of the damage resulting from each successive storm. During the storm of August 1, 1944, the most destructive storm of the first half of the twentieth century, Carolina Beach incurred some of the heaviest damage on the entire North Carolina coast. Fortunately, the area was evacuated before being hit by the storm's 40-foot waves. Two piers were destroyed; trees were blown down; and the water rose high enough to flood second-story levels.

In 1952, the artificial Carolina Beach Inlet was opened to provide a shorter access route to the ocean from the waters in back of Carolina Beach and Masonboro Island. Although shoreline engineers pointed out that opening the inlet would interrupt the natural southerly flow of sand along the beach, boating and fishing interests triumphed. The inlet was constructed (illegally, as it turns out, by a company that dissolved the day after the inlet opened), and the longshore sand flow was indeed interrupted. Sand was trapped updrift or moved into the inlet, and erosion accelerated on the downdrift shoreline. The major hurricanes of the 1950s would have

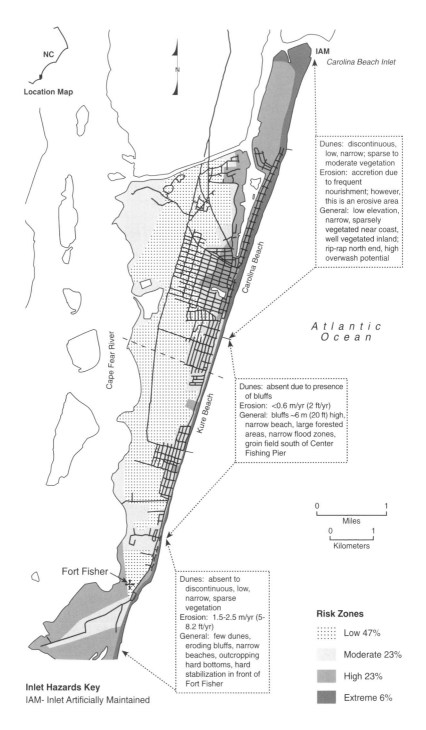

NC

Location Map

IAM
Carolina Beach Inlet

Dunes: discontinuous, low, narrow; sparse to moderate vegetation
Erosion: accretion due to frequent nourishment; however, this is an erosive area
General: low elevation, narrow, sparsely vegetated near coast, well vegetated inland; rip-rap north end, high overwash potential

Carolina Beach

*A t l a n t i c
O c e a n*

Cape Fear River

Kure Beach

Dunes: absent due to presence of bluffs
Erosion: <0.6 m/yr (2 ft/yr)
General: bluffs ~6 m (20 ft) high, narrow beach, large forested areas, narrow flood zones, groin field south of Center Fishing Pier

0 _____ 1
Miles
0 _____ 1
Kilometers

Fort Fisher

Dunes: absent to discontinuous, low, narrow, sparse vegetation
Erosion: 1.5-2.5 m/yr (5-8.2 ft/yr)
General: few dunes, eroding bluffs, narrow beaches, outcropping hard bottoms, hard stabilization in front of Fort Fisher

Risk Zones

::::::: Low 47%

Moderate 23%

High 23%

Extreme 6%

Inlet Hazards Key
IAM- Inlet Artificially Maintained

RM 21   Kure/Carolina Beach

Figure 7.17 A post-Fran view of the rock revetment constructed by the Corps of Engineers at the northern end of Carolina Beach. Hurricane Fran removed the nourished beach in front of this wall and also scattered some of the rocks from the revetment.

caused shoreline erosion under any circumstances; however, the undernourished downdrift beach was unable to maintain a natural protective buffer or to rebuild itself after the storms. For this reason, artificial nourishment commenced in 1955.

Hurricane Hazel destroyed more than 370 buildings and damaged 700 others on Carolina Beach. Streets and structures were buried by shifting sand, but high winds and flooding caused most of the damage. Less than a year later, in August 1955, the successive Hurricanes Connie and Diane caused additional damage. In 1959, Hurricane Grace flooded parts of the area. Well over 30 years passed before Hurricane Bertha hit Carolina Beach with pounding waves and extensive overwash, leaving behind 1 to 2 feet of sand in some locations. Fran, which followed soon after Bertha, brought much deeper storm-surge waters and left another 1 to 2 feet of sand. Many houses floated off their foundations or were smashed by waves. All of the Carolina Beach spit area had 3 to 4 feet of water above ground level. Carolina Lake flooded downtown Carolina Beach with several feet of lake and overwash water. The nourished beach here was much less successful in preventing damage from Fran than the nourished beach on Wrightsville Beach.

The risk distribution of Carolina Beach is correlated to its two different geologic settings: the spit area and the mainland area. The spit is low and overwashed frequently (mostly as a result of human intervention, discussed above), and is never allowed to build up, making it a high- to extreme-risk area. The mainland area is high enough to be untouched by all but the largest storms, thus making it a low- to moderate-risk zone.

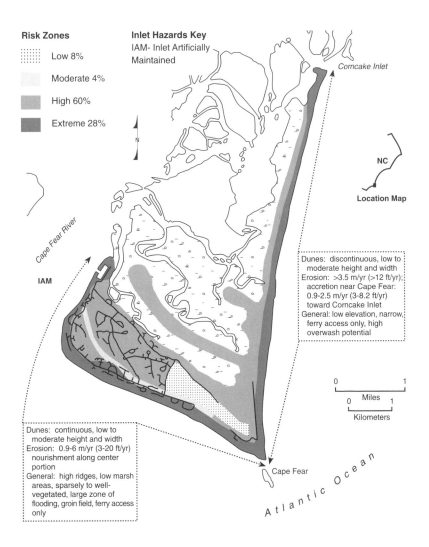

Risk Zones

::::::: Low 8%

Moderate 4%

High 60%

Extreme 28%

N

Inlet Hazards Key
IAM- Inlet Artificially
Maintained

Corncake Inlet

NC

Location Map

IAM

Cape Fear River

Dunes: discontinuous, low to
moderate height and width
Erosion: >3.5 m/yr (>12 ft/yr);
accretion near Cape Fear:
0.9-2.5 m/yr (3-8.2 ft/yr)
toward Corncake Inlet
General: low elevation, narrow,
ferry access only, high
overwash potential

0   1
‾‾‾‾‾‾‾‾‾‾‾‾‾‾‾‾‾‾‾‾‾‾
0   Miles   1
‾‾‾‾‾‾‾‾‾‾‾‾‾‾‾‾‾‾‾‾‾‾
         Kilometers

Dunes: continuous, low to
moderate height and width
Erosion: 0.9-6 m/yr (3-20 ft/yr)
nourishment along center
portion
General: high ridges, low marsh
areas, sparsely to well-
vegetated, large zone of
flooding, groin field, ferry access
only

Cape Fear

Atlantic Ocean

RM 22 Bald Head Island

Kure Beach (RM 21)

The stretch from the Carolina Beach border south to Fort Fisher is entirely mainland coast, but the location of the Cape Fear River gives this area the appearance of a barrier island (RM 21). The dense forest here has been removed in some spots for development, and the elevation is at least 20 feet in most places. As a result, much of the coast is bluff, and the dunes are generally small. The bluff is retreating, but at a relatively slow rate. Residents along the bluff, particularly those in downtown Kure Beach, should nevertheless keep an eye on the erosion. Fran proved that even elevated bluffs can undergo serious erosion. Some of the buildings destroyed by Fran in Kure

Beach may never have been hit by a wave until they fell into the ocean. As a whole, though, Kure Beach is low to moderate risk.

Because of its geologic setting, Kure Beach has historically fared well in storms, especially when compared with other beaches in the area. Hurricane Hazel, for example, severely damaged or destroyed hundreds of buildings at Carolina and Wrightsville Beaches, but damaged only 80 buildings at Kure Beach. Kure Beach survived most of the other 1950s storms with only minor damage. The Kure Beach fishing pier has been destroyed at least 12 times, including by Fran, which also caused erosion and road and building damage in the downtown area.

At the time of this writing, a first-time nourishment project is being carried out on Kure Beach. The replenished beach should decrease the storm hazard to some extent, but we believe the risk categories in Risk Map 21, which were determined before the nourishment, should remain unchanged because the nourished beach is likely to erode relatively rapidly.

Fort Fisher marks an area of sudden beach orientation change, primarily because it is located not on the mainland, but rather on relict stream sediments (see chapter 3) that erode more easily than do the mainland sediments. The average erosion rate in the vicinity of Fort Fisher is 8 feet per year, but the construction of a rip-rap revetment will slow the retreat. This seawall, built by the Corps of Engineers, is one of only a few major exceptions to the North Carolina antihardening regulations established by the Coastal Area Management Act (see chapter 8). The wall was built to protect Civil War earthworks, but several decades from now erosion rates will greatly increase on the adjacent beaches in both directions because of the wall. Civil War forts, lighthouses, and many other structures have been allowed to fall into the sea elsewhere. As precious as Fort Fisher may be, its preservation may prove to be a pyrrhic victory.

Brunswick County (RMs 22–27)

Bald Head Island/Cape Fear (RM 22)

Accessible only by boat, this private community sits on the remains of a series of forested dune and beach ridges separated by low areas, including active marsh (RM 22). Bald Head's status as a private community put it at the center of a long battle with the N.C. Division of Coastal Management regarding the use of shoreline engineering structures. Although initially the owners' application to build groins was rejected, pressure from Governor James Hunt pushed an exception through the Coastal Resources Council (see fig. 5.5 and chapter 8). Like the Fort Fisher seawall, the Bald Head groin field may be a pyrrhic victory. And if this exception is used as a legal "hole" in the regulations that other communities can follow, the old ways of destructive shore hardening could return. Allowing the Bald Head exception was an irresponsible act from the standpoint of preserving the state's beaches for future generations. Ironically, the erosion problem that led to the construction of the groins was evident, even to the untrained eye, when some of the houses that are now protected by the groins were constructed. Figure 5.5 illustrates the extreme risk that persists even with the groin field. The front-row houses are in a "bald" situation, facing the sea without the natural protection of elevation, dunes, or forest cover.

The northern part of the eastern shore of Bald Head Island is rapidly eroding at rates ranging from 4 to 8 feet per year. The region near Cape Fear, however, is accreting at rates exceeding 10 feet per year. This area is frequently overwashed, and the only lower-risk zones are the forested ridges inland. The southern shore of Bald Head is highly erosive, losing 4 to 11 feet per year. Overwash is common, but the several wooded east-west-trending dune ridges offer some less dangerous sites.

Fran's pass over Bald Head Island caused serious erosion along the southern and eastern shores. Some structures were left sitting out on the beach with little or no protection from groins or anything else.

Oak Island (RMS 23 and 24)

Two distinct geologic settings are divided among the three Oak Island communities of Caswell Beach (RM 23), Yaupon Beach (RM 23), and Long Beach (RMS 23 and 24). The back side of the island is heavily forested, high-elevation, relict mainland, extending in the west from the Intracoastal Waterway to Big Davis Canal, and reaching the ocean in the vicinity of Yaupon Beach to the east. Marshes border this former piece of mainland (most of which is more than 20 feet above sea level). This area is protected from open wind and water, well forested, and sufficiently elevated above most storm-surge flooding to be at low to moderate risk.

Fronting this high former mainland area is a low, narrow, modern barrier island that stands in sharp contrast to the back side of the island. Because the mainland intersects the barrier, conditions along the front of the island vary. Although it was close to the tracks of both Bertha and Fran, Oak Island escaped with only minor scrapes and bruises. Numerous houses were damaged by wind, water, or erosion.

Caswell Beach (RM 23) is a mostly low, narrow strip of sand that forms the approximate eastern third of Oak Island. Next to Cape Fear Inlet is old Fort Caswell, now the grounds of the North Carolina Baptist Assembly retreat. Slight accretion near the inlet, and the wise location of most construction away from the beach and inlet, have allowed this area to remain stable and well protected. However, sound-side erosion is active, as indicated by the junk rip-rap placed near the small pier at the end of the island.

West of Fort Caswell to just east of the Carolina Power and Light facility, development is set well back and the dune field is vegetated with grass and shrubs. Although extensive marshlands back this area, the dry-land portion is very narrow (typically less than 600 feet) and overwash scour is a significant risk. From the Carolina Power and Light facility east to the Yaupon Beach line, setback and dunes narrow considerably and there is

RM 23   Oak Isle

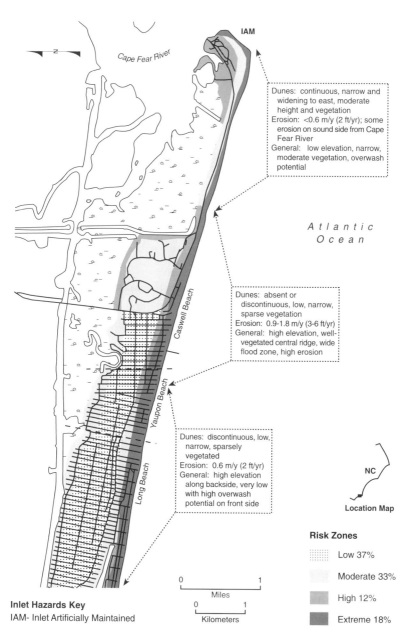

Dunes: continuous, narrow and widening to east, moderate height and vegetation
Erosion: <0.6 m/y (2 ft/yr); some erosion on sound side from Cape Fear River
General: low elevation, narrow, moderate vegetation, overwash potential

Dunes: absent or discontinuous, low, narrow, sparse vegetation
Erosion: 0.9-1.8 m/y (3-6 ft/yr)
General: high elevation, well-vegetated central ridge, wide flood zone, high erosion

Dunes: discontinuous, low, narrow, sparsely vegetated
Erosion: 0.6 m/y (2 ft/yr)
General: high elevation along backside, very low with high overwash potential on front side

NC

Location Map

Risk Zones

Low 37%

Moderate 33%

High 12%

Extreme 18%

Inlet Hazards Key
IAM- Inlet Artificially Maintained

0   1
Miles
0   1
Kilometers

significant erosion. Although generally well vegetated with thick shrubs and some forest, poor to nonexistent dunes and erosion rates as high as 6 feet per year make waterfront development here unsafe.

Erosion has been so rapid along this section and into Yaupon Beach that the forest extends right to the ocean, and old tree stumps and some black peat layers are exposed on the beach (see fig. 3.6). At the back of the beach, a wave-cut scarp exposes roots of shrubs growing on old, stabilized dunes. The red sand exposed on some of these small bluffs indicates old soils. All of these features are natural signs that a forested barrier island (around 1,000 years ago) and then a younger salt marsh once occupied the present beach's position. Erosion and shoreline migration have changed what was once a low-risk zone to an extreme-risk zone. Avoid it.

Yaupon Beach (RM 23) is a community with a diverse setting. The central part of the island is relict mainland with high elevation and extensive forest. Development is dense in some areas, but much of the forest remains, making this area an example of good low- to moderate-risk development.

From the high central area the land slopes to the beach without an intervening marsh. The V-zone extends one to two blocks landward of Ocean Drive because of the low elevation. Dunes are either absent or are very low piles of sand. The erosion rate is high (3–6 feet per year), and tree stumps outcrop on the beach near the border with Caswell Beach. Although portions of the beachfront are vegetated with grasses, the low elevation, rapid erosion, and frequent overwash render the area unsafe for development. In sharp contrast to the other part of Yaupon Beach, developers in this area stripped the original vegetation, removing all natural protection.

Long Beach (RMS 23 and 24) looks and acts like two different islands separated by Big Davis Canal. A high-elevation, forested mainland area occupies the expanse from the Intracoastal Waterway south to Big Davis Canal. As on the rest of Oak Island, development on this mainland area is generally 20 feet above sea level in a low-risk zone. The approximate elevation change of 10 feet across Big Davis Canal is dramatic when compared with the gentle slope between these two areas in Yaupon Beach. As in Caswell Beach and Yaupon Beach, the front of the island is extremely low, with poor to moderate vegetation cover. Low, narrow, scarped, and discontinuous dunes back a narrow, often eroding beach. One exception is a high, well-vegetated dune ridge between 51st Place West and 42nd Place West. The dune ridge here is nearly 40 feet high and is the only low-risk section of the island. From 1949 to 1956, however, an inlet was open just to the west of this area, which today represents a potential new inlet site. Lockwood Folly Inlet has been migrating westward; however, this trend could stop or a new inlet could cut across the spit farther to the east. The low elevation and lack of protective or significant dunes and continuous vegetation cover make any development in this area of Long Beach inadvisable.

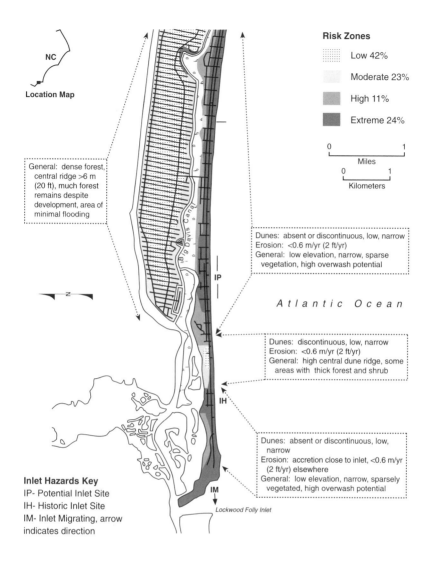

Location Map

NC

Risk Zones

Low 42%

Moderate 23%

High 11%

Extreme 24%

0   1
Miles

0   1
Kilometers

General: dense forest, central ridge >6 m (20 ft), much forest remains despite development, area of minimal flooding

Dunes: absent or discontinuous, low, narrow
Erosion: <0.6 m/yr (2 ft/yr)
General: low elevation, narrow, sparse vegetation, high overwash potential

IP

Atlantic Ocean

Dunes: discontinuous, low, narrow
Erosion: <0.6 m/yr (2 ft/yr)
General: high central dune ridge, some areas with thick forest and shrub

IH

Dunes: absent or discontinuous, low, narrow
Erosion: accretion close to inlet, <0.6 m/yr (2 ft/yr) elsewhere
General: low elevation, narrow, sparsely vegetated, high overwash potential

IM

Lockwood Folly Inlet

Inlet Hazards Key
IP- Potential Inlet Site
IH- Historic Inlet Site
IM- Inlet Migrating, arrow indicates direction

RM 24   Oak Isle (Long Beach)

Long Beach was hit hard by Hurricane Hazel; more than 95 percent of its buildings were destroyed or knocked off their foundations. Although this island, especially the seaward portion, remains highly vulnerable to hurricanes, better standards of construction will reduce damage, at least in weaker hurricanes. The long stretch of the seawardmost row of buildings in Long Beach is in imminent danger of falling into the sea during the next moderate storm. The three beach nourishment projects that have been conducted since 1986 indicate a serious erosion problem in Long Beach.

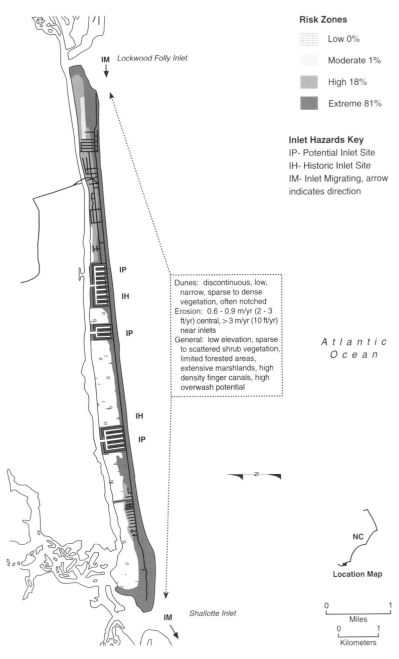

IM Lockwood Folly Inlet

IP

IH

IP

Dunes: discontinuous, low,
  narrow, sparse to dense
  vegetation, often notched
Erosion: 0.6 - 0.9 m/yr (2 - 3
  ft/yr) central, > 3 m/yr (10 ft/yr)
  near inlets
General: low elevation, sparse
  to scattered shrub vegetation,
  limited forested areas,
  extensive marshlands, high
  density finger canals, high
  overwash potential

Atlantic
Ocean

IH

IP

N

NC

Location Map

0   1
Miles

0   1
Kilometers

IM Shallotte Inlet

RM 25 Holden Beach

Holden Beach (RM 25)
The developers of Holden Beach, which was leveled by Hurricane Hazel
(1954) and battered by Hurricane Hugo (1989), seem to have learned little

during the last 40 years. The island is low and narrow (RM 25). Its vegetation consists mainly of dune and lawn grasses, with a small patch of significant vegetation on the back side of the far eastern end of the island. Dunes are almost nonexistent on the eastern third of the island, and there are numerous buildings in or near the surf zone. The erosion rate is high in this area. Dunes increase in height and width to the west along the central part of the island. Houses in this section have been cut into the backs of dunes, increasing the dunes' vulnerability to breaching. Frontal scarping of these dunes and a very narrow beach indicate active erosion. The eight nourishment projects between 1971 and 1987 have done little to solve the problem. A significant dune fronts the far western end of the island. Unfortunately, most of this area lies in either an inlet hazard zone or a V-zone.

Finger canals are abundant on the island; there are 17 in all. These channels dissect the island, creating potential inlet sites, increasing flooding potential, and contributing to the demise of the ecology on the back side of the island. The largest group of finger canals, around the Salisbury Street area, is located on the historic location of Mary's Inlet, which reopened as recently as 1954 during Hurricane Hazel. Another historic inlet, Bacon Inlet, formed just east of Swordfish Drive. That area is now another finger canal complex. Because of low elevations relative to storm-surge floodwaters and wave heights, plus the numerous finger canals cutting Holden Beach and the absence of protective dunes and vegetation cover, all of the area is rated extreme risk. Much of the island suffered significant erosion during Fran, leaving many oceanfront homes in the swash zone. The island's vulnerability is increasing!

Ocean Isle Beach (RM 26)

Most of the development on Ocean Isle Beach is based on finger canals (RM 26); there are 21 open canals and 15 plugged canals. The highest density of canals is just east of the causeway, in the central part of the island. Much of this area is densely developed with single-family homes. The two easternmost canals have yet to be developed and should not be, as this is an extremely hazardous area. A moderate storm overwashing into this area will result in erosional scouring by flood- and ebb-surge currents.

Apart from the canal areas, Ocean Isle Beach is a very low, narrow island with poor dune development and no significant protective vegetation. The last remaining natural dune was bulldozed in 1994 (fig. 7.18)! The dune ridge is discontinuous and narrow, generally only 16 to 32 feet wide and 3 to 6 feet high. The western one-third of the island lies in an inlet hazard zone. Erosion associated with Shallotte Inlet on the eastern end of the island is destroying roads and houses and forcing some owners to move their buildings. Portions of the eastern end of the island lack dunes and are overwashed periodically.

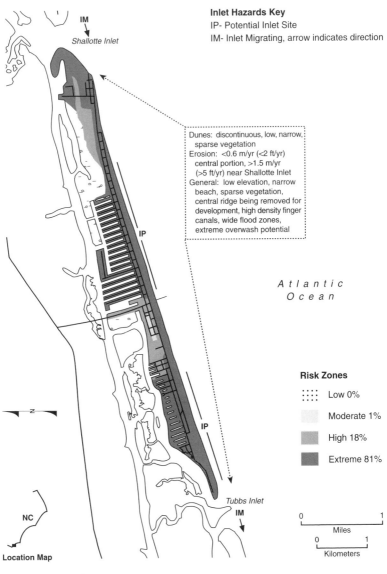

Inlet Hazards Key
IP- Potential Inlet Site
IM- Inlet Migrating, arrow indicates direction

IM
Shallotte Inlet

Dunes: discontinuous, low, narrow,
     sparse vegetation
Erosion: <0.6 m/yr (<2 ft/yr)
     central portion, >1.5 m/yr
     (>5 ft/yr) near Shallotte Inlet
General: low elevation, narrow
     beach, sparse vegetation,
     central ridge being removed for
     development, high density finger
     canals, wide flood zones,
     extreme overwash potential

IP

A t l a n t i c
O c e a n

Risk Zones

::::: Low 0%

Moderate 1%

High 18%

Extreme 81%

IP

Tubbs Inlet
IM

NC

Location Map

0 ———— 1
Miles
0 ———— 1
Kilometers

RM 26 Ocean Isle

As you might expect given its setting, Ocean Isle Beach has not fared well
in past storms. The Flood Insurance Study produced by FEMA for Ocean Isle
Beach states: "Because of the relatively low elevations and the lack of a continuous dune ridge, the beach development of the town is particularly susceptible to damages caused by tropical storms." Hurricane Hazel completely
overwashed Ocean Isle Beach in 1954, destroying 33 of 35 homes and washing the remaining 2 homes nearly a mile away (appendix C, ref. 9). Hazel,

the most destructive hurricane ever to hit Brunswick County, destroyed everything in its path from the South Carolina border to Cape Fear. More recently, Hurricane Hugo (1989) destroyed several homes on Ocean Isle, despite crossing the coast some 200 miles to the south near Charleston, South Carolina. Even small storms or storms far out to sea can cause serious erosion on Ocean Isle, and the most casual observer should be able to see that there will be very extensive property loss in the next direct strike by a hurricane.

Fran stranded many homes out on the beach. A beach nourishment project has been proposed to remedy this situation, but seven previous nourishment projects on Ocean Isle between 1974 and 1984 did not hold the beach in place. The proposed new project is simply putting a Band-Aid on a compound fracture. The new beach will provide limited short-term protection and will encourage continued development on one of North Carolina's most dangerous islands.

Sunset Beach (RM 27)
Sunset Beach, the southernmost developed island in North Carolina, has a varied geologic setting for such a small island (RM 27). The central portion of the island has what most coastal communities wish for: an accreting

Figure 7.18 On Ocean Isle, the central dune ridge of the island was largely removed by bulldozing in 1994! The ridge was the only portion of the island above the 100-year flood line. A low-risk development site has been transformed into an extreme-risk site.

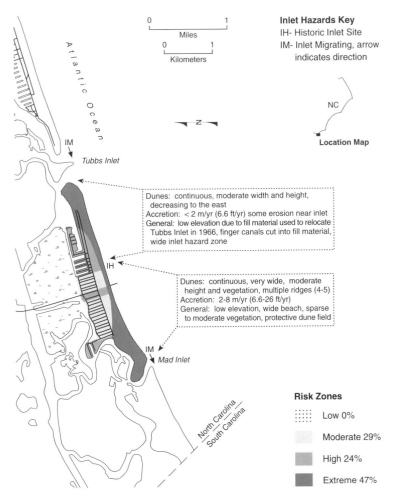

Inlet Hazards Key
IH- Historic Inlet Site
IM- Inlet Migrating, arrow
indicates direction

Location Map

Dunes: continuous, moderate width and height,
decreasing to the east
Accretion: < 2 m/yr (6.6 ft/yr) some erosion near inlet
General: low elevation due to fill material used to relocate
Tubbs Inlet in 1966, finger canals cut into fill material,
wide inlet hazard zone

Dunes: continuous, very wide, moderate
height and vegetation, multiple ridges (4-5)
Accretion: 2-8 m/yr (6.6-26 ft/yr)
General: low elevation, wide beach, sparse
to moderate vegetation, protective dune field

Risk Zones
Low 0%
Moderate 29%
High 24%
Extreme 47%

RM 27 Sunset Beach

shoreline, with 50-year average accretion rates as high as 10 feet per year. A wide, continuous dune field (ca. 600 feet) extends the length of the zone of accretion, with three to four dune ridges, 13 to 16 feet in height. The dune field extends from 40th Street east to the 15th to 7th Street area, where it becomes discontinuous and narrows significantly to about 300 feet and approximately 6.5 feet high. The dune field continues to narrow toward the east end of the island, becoming as narrow as 100 feet. The dune field on Sunset Beach offers protection to what is otherwise a very low, flat island.

Sunset was battered by several hurricanes during the 1950s. In particular, Hurricane Hazel (1954) passed just to the south of Sunset Beach, near the border with South Carolina. Nearly everything from the border to Cape Fear was annihilated. The accretionary dune field on Sunset Beach has enabled the island to bear the brunt of recent storms well, however. Hurricane Hugo caused significant damage to nearby Myrtle Beach, but damage was minimal on Sunset Beach. In fact, none of the more than 120 buildings reported destroyed or condemned in New Brunswick County was on Sunset Beach (appendix C, ref. 9). Hugo destroyed two of the dune ridges, but they have since built back, with some help from artificial sand trapping (fences).

Sunset Beach is not without problems. To begin with, the island is very low and generally very flat behind the main dune field. Development, mostly single-family homes, is dense. Inlets play an important role in the history of Sunset Beach. Tubbs Inlet, which separates Sunset Beach from Ocean Isle Beach, was located at the approximate location of Cobia Street as recently as 1966. At that time, the area was filled and the inlet was moved back to the location it occupied in the late 1930s (fig. 7.19). This hazardous, artificially filled area has subsequently become heavily developed. Although Tubbs Inlet has yet to return to its original westward migration rate of 150 feet per year, there is a strong possibility that the inlet might relocate west of its current position during a storm.

Mad Inlet to the west separates Sunset Beach from undeveloped Bird Island. Mad Inlet has a history of migrating, leaving a narrow spit on the

Figure 7.19 An aerial photograph of Sunset Beach taken in 1977 clearly shows the portion of the island that was reformed by dredging and relocation of Tubbs Inlet a decade before the photograph was taken. Fortunately for the property owners on this now totally developed artificial spit, Sunset Beach is the only island in North Carolina that is accreting seaward.

western end of Sunset Beach. The inlet could migrate quickly to the east, or a storm could open an inlet east of its current position. This area has wisely been left undeveloped and should remain in a natural state. Residents of the western end of Sunset Beach need to keep a watchful eye on Mad Inlet and the tidal creeks behind the island.

Bird Island

The southernmost island in North Carolina is too small to support development, and its low elevation and dynamic inlets place all of the island in the extreme-risk zone.

Past Reflections, Future Expectations

Living at the shore calls for greater prudence than is needed in inland environments. First, shore environments are less uniform than inland ones. Topography, sediment, and vegetation change abruptly from beach, to dune, to overwash terrace, to forest, to marsh. None of these systems is stable in the long term, however; they change or shift in response to changes in sea level and shoreline migration. Look to the future when selecting a site. The future comes sooner on barrier islands.

Second, coastal hazards such as hurricane winds, storm-surge flooding, wave attack, overwash, and persistent erosion are unlike anything you might have experienced in the relative quiet and stability of the Coastal Plain or Piedmont. Choose your site with such forces in mind, and reinforce your construction to improve its ability to survive these forces. Expect maintenance to be more frequent and more expensive.

Third, North Carolina's islands are numerous and varied in geologic setting. As a result, each island has a unique flavor, unique inhabitants, and unique politics. Laws designed to control development cover all the islands, however, unifying their communities in an attempt to save North Carolina's beaches for our enjoyment today and in the future.

8 The Law and the Shore

The previous chapters have shown that barrier islands are dynamic systems. The philosophy of shoreline development should be that if development must occur at all, it must be in harmony with the natural processes and environments that constitute these systems. This wisdom dictates that development should be prohibited in some areas. Various segments of society view the coastal zone differently and, as a result, hold very different philosophies of land use. At the two poles are adherents of untouched preservation and those who favor totally unplanned urbanization.

Like other decisions affecting the public good, decisions on land use are controlled in part by government. Special-interest groups create political pressure that often leads to compromise legislation. Thus, regulations have been and will continue to be established with the intentions of ensuring reasonable, multiple land use of the coastal zone and protecting inhabitants as well as the natural environment. Current and prospective owners of barrier island property should be aware of their responsibilities under the current laws with respect to development and land use, and also of the likelihood of future regulation.

Following is a partial list of the current land-use regulations applicable to the North Carolina coast. The explanations provided are general; appendix B lists the agencies that can supply more specific information. Always remember to check local county and community codes, regulations, and laws before starting any project, as local laws may have changed or may be stricter than the state's laws.

National Flood Insurance Program

One of the most significant legal pressures applied to encourage land-use planning and management in the coastal zone is the National Flood Insurance Program (NFIP), which is implemented by the Federal Emergency

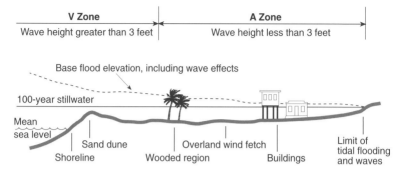

V Zone	A Zone
Wave height greater than 3 feet	Wave height less than 3 feet

Base flood elevation, including wave effects

100-year stillwater

Mean sea level

Shoreline — Sand dune — Wooded region — Overland wind fetch — Buildings — Limit of tidal flooding and waves

8.1 The V-zone and A-zone in a coastal flood zone, as defined by the Federal Emergency Management Agency. Modified from *Managing Coastal Erosion* (appendix C, ref. 60).

Management Agency (FEMA). Private insurance companies long ago stopped offering flood insurance to coastal residents because it was simply too risky. The premiums they would have had to charge to cover that risk would have been unaffordable. As a result, when coastal storms struck or floods came down rivers, the federal government had to step in and provide disaster relief.

In an effort to reduce flood disaster relief costs, Congress passed the National Flood Insurance Act of 1968 (P.L. 90-448), which established the NFIP. Amended by the Flood Disaster Protection Act of 1973 (P.L. 92-234), the NFIP requires that a homeowner meet certain conditions to be eligible to purchase flood insurance. Persons living in flood zones who do not purchase such insurance will not, in the event of a flood, receive any form of federal financial assistance. Most banks will not provide a mortgage loan for a structure that does not have flood insurance.

Communities must adopt certain land-use and control measures in order to make flood insurance available at reasonable rates for their residents. Federal funds for shoreline engineering, waste disposal, or water treatment systems are available only when the individual and community involved comply with the requirements of the law. To encourage involvement, the Community Rating System was implemented so that communities that exceeded the minimum standards set by the NFIP could receive reduced rates. The initiative for qualifying for the program rests with the community, which must contact FEMA. Once the community adopts initial land-use measures and applies for eligibility, FEMA designates the community as eligible for subsidized insurance.

Individual insurance rates are determined primarily by two factors: (1) the community's insurance rating, and (2) the flood zone within which the building to be insured is located. Flood zones are represented on Flood Insurance Rate Maps (FIRMS) and are designated as V-, A-, or X-zones (V-, A-, B-, or C-zones on older maps). These zones represent flood probabilities (fig. 8.1).

V- and A-zones are areas inundated in what is commonly referred to as a 100-year flood. V-zones are subject to 100-year floods with waves greater than 3 feet on top of the flood level; A-zones have waves smaller than 3 feet. As explained in chapter 6, the term *100-year flood* is misleading. *A 100-year flood does not happen only once every 100 years!* Rather, the term means there is a 1 percent chance that this level of flooding will occur in any given year. Thus, residents of Topsail Island should not think they are safe for another 100 years after Fran.

The X-zones shown on the FIRMS are divided into two categories: gray zones and white zones. The gray X-zone is the area between the 100- and 500-year floods (the B-zone on older maps); the white X-zone (C-zone on older maps) is above the 500-year flood level. X-zones are much safer places to build than V- or A-zones (fig. 8.2).

Most flood zones on FIRMS are divided into subzones that include a number in parentheses, such as "A7 (EL14)." EL14 in this example refers to the minimum base elevation of the structure that FEMA requires, in this case 14 feet above sea level. (For more information on how to interpret FIRMS, see appendix C, ref. 66.) Other FEMA building regulations include requirements

8.2 Portion of a Flood Insurance Rate Map (FIRM) from Atlantic Beach. The FIRMS show flood zones and are used in management and zoning decisions. Such maps are available for public examination in all coastal town and city halls.

for ground-floor breakaway walls, which reduce overall damage by allowing storm surge to pass unobstructed under the building.

The NFIP undoubtedly has its flaws. Some people feel that requirements for insurance eligibility should be more stringent and suggest denying flood insurance and federal disaster assistance to current property owners in coastal high-hazard areas whose structures do not meet the standards for new construction. Other problems include establishing actuarial rates, funding the necessary coastal studies to define high-hazard areas, and understanding the effects of long-term federal subsidies. Perhaps the greatest obstacles to the success of the program are the uninformed individuals who stand to gain the most from it. A study that examined public response to flood insurance found that many people know little about the threat of floods or the cost of insurance, and view insurance as an investment with the expectation of a return rather than as a means of sharing the costs of a natural disaster.

Purists may debate the merits of taxpayer-subsidized federal programs, but the National Flood Insurance Program's objectives are worthwhile in that the program applies pressure to ensure wiser management of hazardous flood zones. As taxpayers, we hope that in the long run this program will cost less than the growing expense of disaster relief needs generated by flooding.

Coastal Barriers Resources Act

In 1982, Congress passed the Coastal Barriers Resources Act (COBRA) (P.L. 97-348), which established the Coastal Barrier Resources System (CBRS). The CBRS is a group of environmentally sensitive areas designated by the federal government as ineligible for direct or indirect federal financial aid. The purpose of COBRA was to discourage development in sensitive and unstable environments. Structures built after COBRA was enacted cannot receive federal assistance in any form for either building or rebuilding. Such development is ineligible for federal flood insurance.

Most COBRA zones in North Carolina are undeveloped marshlands. However, much of the northern end of North Topsail Beach is in a COBRA zone, and newly constructed homes and businesses there are not eligible for federal flood insurance (see chapter 7). Although many North Topsail Beach residents whose homes were destroyed by Hurricane Fran did not have flood insurance because of COBRA, FEMA was required to provide assistance to the town to rebuild its infrastructure (e.g., roads and bridges).

Upton-Jones Amendment and National Flood Mitigation Fund

The Upton-Jones Amendment, an amendment to the National Flood Insurance Program passed in 1987, allowed homeowners of threatened buildings to use up to 40 percent of the federally insured value of their homes for building relocation. The law recognized relocation as a more economical, more permanent, and more realistic way of dealing with long-term erosion problems. Under this law the federal government (i.e., the taxpayers) agreed to pay a relatively small amount to help a homeowner relocate a threatened house rather than paying a larger amount to help rebuild it—only to see the rebuilt house destroyed in a subsequent storm, and paying to rebuild again . . . and again. By March 1995, North Carolina had made claims for more than 70 relocations and 168 demolitions, and accounted for more than 60 percent of all coastal claims under the program.

The National Flood Insurance Reform Act of 1994 terminated the Relocation Assistance Program as of September 23, 1995, and replaced the Upton-Jones program with the National Flood Mitigation Fund. Financed from penalty revenues collected for noncompliance with NFIP requirements, the new program provides state and local governments with grants for planning activities and mitigation assistance that will reduce the risk of flood damage to structures covered under the NFIP. Demolition and relocation activities are eligible for grant assistance under this program, but they now compete with other mitigation approaches, including elevation and flood-proofing programs, acquisition of flood-zone properties for public use, beach nourishment, and technical assistance. Limits are placed on how much a state or community can receive in a five-year period (state, $10 million; local community, $3.3 million; $20 million total for any one state).

Rivers and Harbors Act of 1889

The U.S. Army Corps of Engineers is the federal agency responsible for regulating dredging and filling, as administered through the Rivers and Harbors Act of 1889 (33 U.S.C. 403) and the federal Water Pollution Control Act of 1972 (P.L. 92-500), as amended. If your project is within the Corps's jurisdiction, you must obtain one of the following authorizations: (1) a nationwide permit, a general permit issued by the Chief of Engineers in 1982; (2) a regional permit, a general permit issued by the Wilmington district of the Corps authorizing certain minor activities in specific geographic areas within North Carolina; or (3) an individual permit, if your project exceeds the scope of the nationwide and regional permits.

Before building or buying a home on the coast, you should determine the answers to seven basic questions:

1. Is the community I'm locating in covered by the nfip program?
2. If not, why?
3. Is my building site above the 100-year flood level?
4. Is my building or community in a cobra zone?
5. What are the structural requirements for my building?
6. What are the limits of coverage?
7. What is the town's Community Rating? What is the town doing to improve its rating?

The North Carolina Coastal Area Management Act

The federal Coastal Zone Management Act of 1972 (CZMA) set in motion an effort by all coastal states to manage their shorelines and thereby conserve a vital national resource. Key requirements of the CZMA are coastal land-use planning based on land classification, and identification and protection of critical areas.

In 1974, the North Carolina Coastal Area Management Act (CAMA) was passed in compliance with the federal CZMA, qualifying North Carolina for federal aid in implementing effective coastal management. CAMA was intended to ensure good land use and resource development, and to conserve resources to protect the quality of life for citizens of the coastal zone. The act was prompted by the growing recognition of the barrier island system as a natural resource, and the increasing realization that the actions of one person on one piece of island property may affect all other property within the system. CAMA created the Coastal Resources Commission (CRC) to oversee the development of a coastal-zone management program. The state's Division of Coastal Management (DCM) is responsible for implementing CAMA. Coastal counties prepare additional plans based on their own needs.

CAMA sets aside Areas of Environmental Concern (AEC) to which CAMA is applicable. The four categories of AECs are (1) the estuarine system, (2) ocean hazard areas, (3) areas of public water supplies, and (4) unique natural and cultural features. Broad summaries appear below, but do not substitute this information for a complete and thorough reading of CAMA.

The Estuarine System

CAMA recognizes both the commercial value to local fisheries and the "considerable nonmonetary value associated with aesthetics, recreation, and education" of North Carolina's estuaries. Estuarine AECs are the areas within 75 feet of the high or normal water level for most areas, and within 575 feet of the high or normal water level in Outstanding Resource Waters (as determined by the Environmental Management Commission). Development within these zones is subject to various CAMA regulations, including a maximum impervious surface area (e.g., roads, parking lots) less than or equal to 30 percent of the total lot area, and rules aimed at reducing siltation in estuarine waters.

Ocean Hazard Areas

These areas are the most commonly discussed under CAMA regulations because of the setback and hard stabilization rules. CAMA defines *setback* as the minimum distance from the ocean that houses and buildings can be constructed. Hard stabilization structures such as seawalls and groins are banned in these areas. The four ocean hazard areas are:

1. *Ocean erodible area:* the distance from the first line of stable vegetation landward a distance that is equal to 60 times the annual erosion rate, or 120 feet, whichever is greater, plus the estimated erosion for a 100-year flood.
2. *High hazard flood area:* any V-zone on a firm.
3. *Inlet hazard area:* an area close to an inlet. These zones are particularly susceptible to erosion and flooding.
4. *Unvegetated beach area:* a backbeach with no stable vegetation to offer protection and anchor dune ridges.

The setback regulations within ocean hazard areas are as follows: for small structures (less than 5,000 square feet total floor area) the setback line is a distance equal to 30 times the annual erosion rate (minimum of 120 feet) landward of the first line of stable vegetation, unless this line is seaward of the primary dune. In that case, structures must be located behind the primary dune to preserve these protective features. For large structures (greater than 5,000 square feet total floor area) the setback line is a distance equal to 60 times the annual erosion rate (minimum of 120 feet), or 30 times the annual erosion rate plus 105 feet if the erosion rate is more than 3.5 feet per year.

Frontal and primary dunes in ocean hazard areas are protected from development that would weaken them. Many towns have additional local ordinances regarding development on or near dunes.

Perhaps the single most important CAMA regulation is the one that bans "erosion control structures" such as seawalls, bulkheads, groins, revetments, jetties, and offshore breakwaters. Forced to choose between its beaches or buildings (see chapter 5), North Carolina chose its beaches, and CAMA's crowning jewel has given North Carolinians a legacy of hundreds of miles of beautiful beaches.

The only erosion control devices allowed by law are "temporary" sand-bags. These bags may be no larger than 3 to 5 feet wide and 7 to 15 feet long, and must be tan in color. The sandbag pile may not exceed 20 feet in width or 6 feet in height. The sandbags may remain in place for up to two years for small structures (less than 5,000 square feet total floor area) and up to five years for large structures (greater than 5,000 square feet total floor area). Temporary sandbags may be placed only once in the lifetime of a structure, regardless of changes in ownership. Unfortunately, these sandbags are never removed after their permitted time. The bags are left to waste away at the mercy of the waves, which strew their ragged black and tan fabric all over the beach.

Beach bulldozing is another temporary erosion control method regulated by CAMA. The simple bulldozing of beach sand into small mounds is highly ineffective as a method of erosion control. Although sand is piled up, increasing the elevation, the width of the beach is reduced, bringing the ocean waters that much closer to the threatened property. Permits are required before bulldozing, but in the case of an emergency such as Hurricane Fran, the permitting process may be temporarily suspended. Bulldozing is allowed landward of the low-water line to a depth of 1 foot. Although permits are required, bulldozing is poorly policed. Unfortunately, bulldozing often goes beyond the low-water line and deeper than 1 foot.

Public Water Supplies

Fresh water is a valuable and scarce resource on barrier islands. In an effort to protect the sources of fresh water from the potential harmful effects of development, CAMA restricts construction near certain areas. The state has designated three protected areas: the freshwater pond on the Nags Head–Kill Devil Hills border, Toomers Creek Watershed in Wilmington, and the Cape Hatteras Well Field. Regulations try to keep construction and septic tanks a safe distance from these areas to prevent contamination (see T15A: 07H.0400 of the North Carolina Administrative code for site-specific details and regulations).

Natural and Cultural Resource Areas

Unique or endangered features of the coastal environment are also protected under CAMA. Any person or group can nominate an area "containing environmental, natural or cultural resources of more than local significance" to the CRC for protection from development. If approved, the area becomes an AEC subject to CAMA regulations. Such areas are divided into five groups: (1) areas with remnant species, (2) complex natural areas, (3) unique geological formations, (4) coastal archaeological resources, and (5) coastal historic architectural resources.

The goal of CAMA is not to stop or prohibit development, but rather to control it. Nevertheless, CAMA has met with opposition from coastal residents. The CAMA regulations require planning, which some regard as inconvenient, and a change in attitude or behavior that interferes with the get-rich-quick motives of others. North Carolina residents who oppose CAMA need look no further than our neighboring cities of Myrtle Beach and Virginia Beach to see what uncontrolled development looks like. We are truly fortunate.

Waste Disposal

Protecting barrier island water resources is essential to safeguarding the many uses of the islands. Fisheries, all forms of water recreation, and the general ecosystem depend on high-quality surface waters. The potable water supply is drawn mainly from groundwater, which must be of high quality. Coastal development is threatening our water resources, and the existing pollution is costly to both local communities and the state. Improper land use relative to waste disposal and inadequate planning for treatment of the increasing waste necessitate additional regulation at all levels of government.

Title 15A, subchapter 18A, section .1900 of the North Carolina Administrative Code addresses wastewater systems. Systems with flows less than 3,000 gallons per day must be placed a minimum of 50 feet from the high-water mark, or 100 feet from waters that are suitable for commercial fishing. Systems with flow rates greater than 3,000 gallons per day must be at least 200 feet away from the high-water mark. Additional regulations apply to public water supplies, AECs, and relocation of structures under CAMA. Remember, these are just the state guidelines. Local communities will probably have slightly different regulations, consistent with CAMA but possibly stricter. Always consult the local building inspector's office.

Building Codes

Most progressive communities require new construction to adhere to the provisions of a recognized building code. If you plan to build in an area that does not follow such a code, you would be wise to insist that your builder do so anyway to meet your own requirements. Local building officials in storm areas often adopt national codes, such as the Uniform Building Code, that contain building requirements for protection against high wind and water. These codes, compiled by knowledgeable engineers, officials, and architects, regulate the design and construction of buildings and the quality of building materials. In North Carolina, builders must adhere to the North Carolina State Building Code.

It is emphasized that the purpose of these codes is to provide *minimum* standards to safeguard lives, health, and property. These codes protect you from yourself as well as your neighbor. We recommend that coastal residents exceed the minimum standards set by their local communities whenever possible. Addition of permanent shutters or dry flood-proofing can drastically reduce storm damage to a house (see chapter 9 and appendix C).

Mobile Home Regulations

Mobile homes differ in both construction and anchorage from "permanent" structures. The design, shape, lightweight construction materials, and other characteristics required for mobility or for staying within axle-weight limits create a unique set of potential problems for residents of these dwellings. Because of their thinner walls, for example, mobile homes are more vulnerable to wind and windborne projectiles than are permanent homes. Thus, North Carolina has a separate building code for mobile homes. Mobile-home dwellers in North Carolina may wish to obtain a copy of the *North Carolina Manufactured/Mobile Homes Regulations* (appendix C, ref. 94). Recognizing the effects of coastal-zone processes, the code requires that mobile homes manufactured after October 1, 1973, and offered for sale on the North Carolina coast meet the state's hurricane-zone requirements. Most counties and municipalities also have ordinances pertaining to mobile homes.

Mobile-home anchorage is commonly regulated by local ordinances. Tie-downs should be and often are required to make the structure more stable against wind stress (see chapter 9). Violations of anchorage or foundation regulations may go undetected unless there is a sufficient number of conscientious inspectors to monitor trailer courts. One poorly anchored mobile home can wreak havoc on adjacent homes whose owners abided by sound construction practices. Some mobile-home park operators or managers are alert to such problems and see that they are corrected; others simply collect the rent.

Wherever you choose to build or live on the North Carolina coast, remember to use CAMA and FEMA regulations as a minimum requirement. Exceed all regulations whenever possible. Follow prudent construction practices to help minimize risks.

9 Building, Retrofitting, and Buying a House Near the Beach

Initially you may think this chapter is at cross purposes with the book's underlying philosophy. But this apparent contradiction is more rational than it might at first seem. For those who will heed the warning, we have described the risks of owning shorefront property. But we realize that coastal development will continue because there will always be some individuals willing to gamble with their fortunes to be near the shore. For those who disregard our warning and elect to play the game of real estate roulette, we offer some advice on improving the odds—on reducing (but not eliminating) the risks. We do not, however, recommend that you play the game!

Can We Learn from Past Experience?

Although the memory of Fran may fade, coastal property owners in North Carolina would be foolish to ignore the problems the hurricane brought to light. Similarly, hurricanes in other areas (e.g., Andrew, Gilbert, Hugo, and Iniki) have taught lessons that must be heeded as well. Why, for example, did Habitat for Humanity houses, built by amateurs, stand up to Andrew while houses built by professionals blew apart? Posthurricane damage inspections have been very revealing and have led to useful recommendations (see appendix C, "Coastal Construction").

Coastal Realty versus Coastal Reality

Coastal property is not the same as inland property. Do not approach it as if you were buying a lot in a developed woodland of the Carolina Piedmont or a subdivided farm field in the Coastal Plain. The previous chapters illustrate that the shores of North Carolina, especially the barrier islands, are composed of variable environments subject to nature's most powerful and persistent forces. The reality of the coast is its dynamic character. Property lines are an artificial grid superimposed on this dynamism. If you choose to place yourself or others in this zone, prudence is in order.

A quick glance at the architecture of most of the structures on our coast provides convincing evidence that the sea view and aesthetics were the primary considerations in their construction, not the reality of coastal processes. Except for meeting minimal building code requirements, no further thought seems to have been given to the safety of many of these buildings. The failure to follow a few basic architectural guidelines may have disastrous results when structures are required to stand up to major storms.

In the case of coastal property, two general factors should be considered: site safety and the integrity of the structure relative to the forces to which it will be subjected. We discussed site safety in chapter 7; here we concentrate on building safety.

The Structure: Concept of Balanced Risk

A certain chance of failure exists for any structure built within the constraints of economy and environment. The objective of the building design is to create a structure that is both economically feasible and functionally reliable. Every homeowner wants a house with a reasonable life expectancy. In order to obtain such a house, a balance must be achieved among financial, structural, environmental, and other special conditions. Most of these conditions are intensified on the coast: property values are higher, the environment is more sensitive, the likelihood of storms is increased, and there is greater pressure to develop as more and more people want to move into the coastal zone.

Anyone who builds or buys a home in an exposed coastal area should fully comprehend the risks involved and the chance of harm to his or her home and family. The risks should then be weighed against the benefits to be derived from the residence. Similarly, the developer who is putting up a motel should weigh the possibility of destruction and deaths during a hurricane against the money and other advantages to be gained from such a building. Only with an understanding of the risks should construction proceed. For both the homeowner and the developer, proper construction and location reduce the risks.

The concept of balanced risk should take into account six fundamental considerations:

1. A coastal structure exposed to high winds, waves, or flooding should be stronger than a structure built inland.
2. A building with a planned long life, such as a year-round residence, should be stronger than a building with a planned short life, such as a mobile home.

3. A building with high occupancy, such as an apartment building, should be safer than a building with a low occupancy, such as a single-family dwelling.
4. A building that houses elderly or sick people should be safer than a building housing able-bodied people.
5. Construction costs that incorporate a higher than usual margin of safety will be higher than costs for an average home.
6. The risk of loss may make the project unfeasible.

Using the principles of structural engineering, structures can be designed and built to resist all but the largest storms and still be reasonably economical. These principles utilize an estimate of the forces to which the structures will be subjected and an understanding of the strength of building materials. The effectiveness of structural engineering design has been known for a long time, and was reflected in the aftermath of Cyclone Tracy, which struck Darwin, Australia, in 1974: 70 percent of the housing that was not based on structural engineering principles was destroyed, 20 percent was seriously damaged, and only 10 percent weathered the storm. In contrast, more than 70 percent of the large, structurally engineered commercial, government, and industrial buildings came through with little or no damage, and less than 5 percent of such structures were destroyed. The importance of building codes requiring standardized structural engineering for houses in hurricane-prone areas is apparent.

Can We Rely on Building Codes?

The North Carolina State Building Code is an adaptation of the Standard Building Code that incorporates significant changes made by the North Carolina Building Code Council. Since the 1960s, North Carolina has had a special building code for one- and two-family dwellings, called the Residential Building Code, which is based on the Council of American Building Officials Code with amendments from the North Carolina Building Code Council.

Since the 1960s, most houses on the North Carolina coast have been built on pilings. Before 1986, codes required pilings to be embedded 8 feet below grade. In 1986 the code was revised so that buildings closer than 60 times the long-term erosion rate to the seaward edge of the first line of stable vegetation must have pilings embedded 5 feet below mean sea level or 16 feet below grade, whichever is *less*. In order to improve stability against wind, the revised code requires cross-bracing between pilings. Potential problems with cross-bracing are considered later in this chapter. Since 1997, a strengthened Residential Code applies to new houses built up to 100 miles inland from the coast.

After Hurricane Fran, FEMA commissioned a study to assess the effect of embedment depth of foundation pilings on structural failures (see appendix C, ref. 76). Ninety percent of the oceanfront structures built since the 1986 code changes had no significant damage to their pilings. Of the leaning pilings tested, none met the code depth requirements (fig. 9.1); however, more than half of the nonleaning pilings also did not meet the code depth requirements. It may be concluded that construction and enforcement practices need improvement to ensure that pilings at least adhere to current code requirements.

Coastal Forces: Design Requirements

Although northeasters can be devastating, hurricanes produce the most destructive forces coastal residents have to reckon with (fig. 9.2). Even though coastal storms are discussed in detail in chapter 2, it will be useful to restate some of the most important points and to add more information here for emphasis.

Figure 9.1 Many oceanfront houses built before the current (1986) North Carolina State Building Code requirements were enacted were damaged or destroyed by Hurricane Fran. From *Building Performance Assessment: Hurricane Fran in North Carolina* (appendix C, ref. 76).

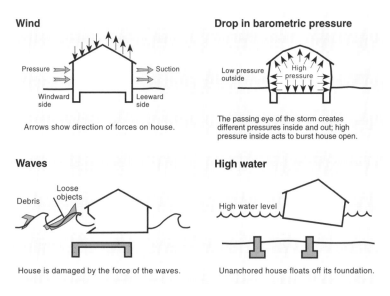

Wind

Pressure ⟹⟹   ⟹ Suction

Windward side   Leeward side

Arrows show direction of forces on house.

Drop in barometric pressure

Low pressure outside   High pressure

The passing eye of the storm creates different pressures inside and out; high pressure inside acts to burst house open.

Waves

Loose objects

Debris

House is damaged by the force of the waves.

High water

High water level

Unanchored house floats off its foundation.

Figure 9.2 Forces to be reckoned with at the shoreline.

Hurricane Winds

Hurricane winds can be categorized in terms of the pressure they exert. The pressure varies with the square of the velocity of the wind. Thus, doubling the velocity of the wind corresponds to increasing the pressure by a factor of four. A 50 mph (miles per hour) wind exerts a pressure of about 10 psf (pounds per square foot) on a flat surface. A 100 mph wind would exert a pressure of 40 psf, and a 200 mph wind would exert a pressure of 160 psf.

You can estimate the wind force that can be expected to be applied to a flat wall of a house by multiplying the expected force times the exposed area of the side of the house receiving that force. If the wall facing the hurricane is 40 feet long and 16 feet high, the area of the wall is 640 square feet. A 100 mph wind exerts a force of about 40 psf. Thus the total force on the wall will be 640 ft^2 40 lb/ft^2 = 25,600 lb, or about 13 tons of force. A 200 mph wind would exert a force of more than 50 tons on the wall. The amount of force the wind exerts on a building can be modified by several factors, which must be considered in building design. For instance, the pressure on a curved surface, such as a cylinder, is less than the pressure on a flat surface. Also, wind velocities increase with the height above the ground, so a tall structure is subject to greater pressure than a low structure. The pressures presented above were computed for a structure with a height of 33 feet. The damage that can be anticipated from various wind velocities is shown in table 2.2.

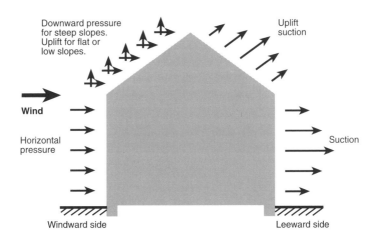

Figure 9.3 Wind-exerted pressures on a house.

A house or building designed for inland areas is built primarily to resist vertical, and mostly downward, loads. Generally, builders assume that the foundation and framing must support the load of the walls, floor, and roof, and relatively insignificant horizontal wind forces. A well-built house in a hurricane-prone area, however, must be constructed to withstand a variety of strong wind and wave forces that may come from any direction. Although many people think wind damage is caused by uniform horizontal pressure, most of the damage is caused by uplift (vertical), suctional (pressure-differential), and torsional (twisting) forces. High horizontal pressure on the windward side is accompanied by suction on the leeward side. The roof is subject to downward pressure and, more important, to uplift (fig. 9.3). Often roofs are sucked up by the uplift drag of the wind.

Usually, houses fail because the devices that tie their parts together fail. All structural members (beams, rafters, and columns) should be fastened together on the assumption that about 25 percent of the vertical load on each member may be a force coming from any direction (sideways or upward). Structural integrity is also important if it is likely that the building may be moved to avoid destruction by shoreline retreat. In a fanciful way, structural integrity means that you should be able to pick up a house (after removing its furniture, of course), turn it upside down, and shake it without it falling apart.

Storm Surge

Storm surge is an abnormal rise in sea level caused by a storm. During hurricanes, the coastal zone is inundated by storm surge and the accompanying storm waves, and these forces cause most of the property damage and loss of life.

Often the pressure of the wind backs water into streams or estuaries already swollen from the exceptional rainfall brought by the hurricane. The offshore storm piles water into the bays between islands and the mainland. In some cases islands are flooded from the bay side. This flooding is particularly dangerous when the wind pressure keeps the tide from running out of inlets, so that the next normal high tide pushes the accumulated waters back, and higher still.

People who have cleaned flood debris and mud out of a house retain vivid memories. Floodwaters can float an unanchored house off its foundation and bring it to rest against another house, severely damaging both buildings. Even if the house itself is left structurally intact, flooding may destroy its contents.

Proper coastal development takes into account the expected level and frequency of storm surge for the area. In general, building standards require that the first habitable level of a dwelling be above the 100-year flood level, the level at which a building has a 1 percent probability of being flooded in any given year.

Hurricane Waves

Hurricane waves can cause severe damage not only by forcing floodwaters onshore, but also by throwing boats, barges, piers, houses, and other floating debris inland against standing structures, a process known as "ramrodding." In addition, waves can cause coastal structures to collapse by scouring away the underlying sand. Buildings can be designed to survive crashing storm surf. Many lighthouses, for example, have survived hurricane waves. But in the balanced risk equation, it usually isn't economically feasible to build ordinary houses to withstand powerful wave forces. On the other hand, houses can be made considerably more stormworthy if the suggestions in this chapter are followed.

The force of a wave may be understood by considering that a cubic yard of water weighs more than three-fourths of a ton. A breaking wave moving shoreward at a speed of 30 or 40 mph can be one of the most destructive elements of a hurricane. A 10-foot wave can exert more than 1,000 pounds of pressure per square foot, and wave pressures higher than 12,000 psf have been recorded.

Figure 9.4 illustrates some of the actions a homeowner can take to deal with the forces just described.

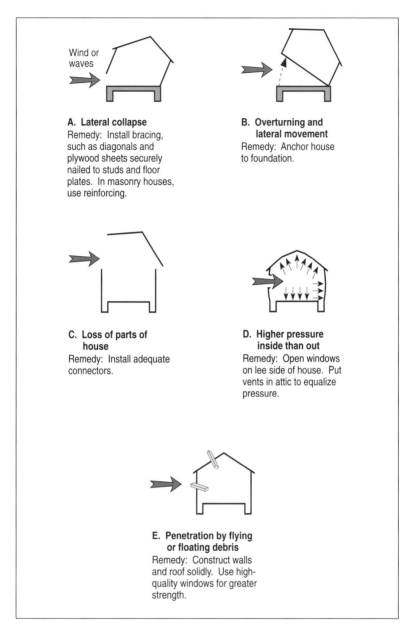

A. Lateral collapse
Remedy: Install bracing, such as diagonals and plywood sheets securely nailed to studs and floor plates. In masonry houses, use reinforcing.

B. Overturning and lateral movement
Remedy: Anchor house to foundation.

C. Loss of parts of house
Remedy: Install adequate connectors.

D. Higher pressure inside than out
Remedy: Open windows on lee side of house. Put vents in attic to equalize pressure.

E. Penetration by flying or floating debris
Remedy: Construct walls and roof solidly. Use high-quality windows for greater strength.

Figure 9.4 Modes of failure and how to deal with them.

According to the building code, the design wind speed for North Carolina is 110 mph, the fastest mile (the wind speed averaged over the time required for a mile-long volume of air to pass a fixed point) for a 50-year return frequency. Although the National Hurricane Center and the National Weather Service estimate that Fran's winds exceeded the design speed with a maximum one-minute sustained wind speed of 115 mph, most homes along the coast were probably subjected to winds lower than the design wind speed. The most severe home damage occurred in areas subjected to storm surge and waves in addition to high winds.

Hurricane Fran caused significant erosion and scour from Cape Fear to Cape Lookout. The erosion was exacerbated by the dune erosion that had occurred two months earlier when Hurricane Bertha made landfall in the same region. Beach profiles were lowered 2 to 3 feet in many places, and erosion of up to 4 to 6 vertical feet underneath oceanfront homes occurred. Localized scour around vertical foundation components tended to be 1 to 1.5 times the diameter or width of the components (fig. 9.5), typically adding a vertical foot to the erosion.

Many lessons can be learned from Fran. Damage to water, sewage, electrical, telephone, and cable TV utilities can often be avoided by proper installation. Appendages to houses such as porches or decks, whose support columns tend not to be deeply embedded, were particularly vulnerable. In spite of usually being improperly installed, breakaway walls did indeed break away (appendix C, ref. 76); however, several problems came to light about breakaway walls. First, breakaway wall panels installed seaward of cross-bracing can damage the cross-bracing when they break away. Second, utilities such as air conditioners installed on or next to the breakaway panels can inhibit a clean breakaway, resulting in damage to the utilities. Third, sheathing, when installed such that the breakaway panels are connected to the foundation columns, can retard a clean breakaway of the panels.

Many houses have a slab-on-grade as a floor for the breakaway area below the elevated structure. Most of these structures performed as intended, but some problems were noted (appendix C, ref. 76). Slabs attached to the vertical foundation members can have the undesirable effect of transferring hurricane-related loading to the foundation. Also, a solidly constructed slab (with wire mesh or without sufficient contraction joints) can provide too much resistance to break into fragments small enough to avoid damaging the foundation system when waterborne.

Particularly vulnerable were mobile homes, manufactured homes, and permanently installed RVs. The usual installation system of concrete-block foundations and metal tie-down straps with anchors to the ground performed poorly. Scour undermined the blocks, while the corrosion-weakened straps often failed. Also, the anchors frequently pulled out.

The National Flood Insurance Program

The National Flood Insurance Program FIRMS for the North Carolina barrier island communities led to a false sense of security because they did not consider the effects of waves above the still-water flood elevation. Accordingly, many oceanfront properties designated by the FIRMS as being outside the influence of 100-year flooding were in fact severely damaged by Fran. This problem resulted in revisions to some FIRMS (appendix C, ref. 76).

Construction Type

Building materials and construction methods have a profound effect on storm damage. Hurricane Gilbert, which struck the Caribbean and Mexico in 1988, was the most powerful storm to strike the Western Hemisphere in the twentieth century. Gilbert's central barometric pressure of 885 millibars is the lowest ever recorded in the Caribbean. After mauling Jamaica, Gilbert made landfall as a category 5 hurricane over the Yucatán Peninsula of Mexico near Cozumel and moved west-northwest across the peninsula.

Single-family structures on the Yucatán coast are built primarily of reinforced concrete because construction lumber is extremely expensive. There is an essentially limitless supply of limestone for making concrete, and most Mexican engineers and architects are trained in Mexico City, where reinforced concrete construction is used extensively to mitigate earthquake damage. Also, Yucatán homes are not usually elevated; many are built right into the frontal line of dunes.

In contrast, construction on the North Carolina coast uses a number of building materials. Single-family homes are typically built of wood, cinder block, or a combination of wood, brick, and cinder block. Newer structures

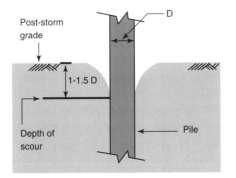

Figure 9.5 Piling scour was commonly observed after Hurricane Fran. From *Building Performance Assessment: Hurricane Fran in North Carolina* (appendix C, ref. 76).

are elevated on wooden pilings or cinder-block footings. Generally speaking, the older the structure, the less elevated it is likely to be.

In part because different construction materials are used in the two areas, the damage caused by Hurricane Fran on the North Carolina coast was substantially different from that caused by Hurricane Gilbert on the Yucatán Peninsula. When buildings along the Yucatán oceanfront collapsed, the reinforcing rods in the concrete held the large pieces in place. Their rubble formed a temporary seawall-like protection for landward buildings, reducing inland damage. When North Carolina cinder-block houses failed, they broke into small pieces that were tossed about and caused damage to other structures through missiling and ramrodding. In addition, inadequately elevated wooden houses were knocked off their foundations and carried some distance from their original locations, in the process colliding with other houses, trees, utility poles, and automobiles.

Reinforced concrete construction is not typically considered aesthetically or economically appealing in the United States, although it is common in some states such as Florida and Hawaii, and in Puerto Rico.

House Selection

Some types of houses are better than others for the shore, and an awareness of the differences will help you make a better selection, whether you are building a new house or buying an existing one.

Worst of all are unreinforced masonry houses, whether they are brick, concrete block, hollow clay-tile, or brick veneer, because they cannot withstand the lateral forces of wind and waves and the settling of a foundation. Extraordinary reinforcing, such as concrete-block stucco reinforced with tie beams and columns, will alleviate some of the inherent weaknesses of unit masonry, if done properly. Reinforced masonry performed well in Hurricane Andrew. Reinforced concrete and steel frames are excellent but are rarely used in the construction of small residential structures.

In Puerto Rico, where hurricanes are more a way of life than in North Carolina, residences are typically built of cast-in-place concrete or concrete masonry units with reinforced concrete columns and perimeter beams, and roof slabs approximately 4 to 5 inches thick. The design is governed by seismic codes like those used in Mexico. This class of structure performed extremely well in Hurricane Hugo.

It is hard to beat a wood frame or concrete house that is constructed properly, with bracing and connections for the roof, wall, and floor components, as well as anchors for the foundation. A well-built wood house will hold together as a unit even after it is moved off its foundation, when other types of structures disintegrate.

A new, inexpensive type of construction that fared well in both Hurricanes Hugo and Andrew is made from weldedwire sandwich panels, which consist of two parallel sheets of wire mesh connected diagonally by truss wires that pierce an insulating core of polystyrene, and are then sprayed on both sides with cement.

Strengthening the Exterior Envelope

The term *building envelope* refers to the entire system by which the building resists wind penetration. A breach in the envelope occurs when an exterior enclosure fails, as when the garage door or a window is open. When this happens during a strong wind, pressure may build up inside the structure, and roof uplift or wall suction may occur, leading to failure of the entire system (fig. 9.6). The most susceptible parts of the house are the windows, garage doors, and double-wide doors.

Doors

All doors in a home should be certified by the seller as to their strength under a given design wind load, especially garage doors and double-wide doors. The strength must be adequate to prevent damage from projectiles or flying objects such as tree limbs. To upgrade existing doors, a dead bolt added to the locking system can be used for reinforcement. The dead bolt will act as an additional rigid connection to the house frame. If the house has a double entry door, one door should be fixed at the top and bottom with pins or bolts (fig. 9.7). In most cases, the original pins are not strong enough to resist heavy wind forces. Homeowners should consider installing

Figure 9.6 Building envelope breach due to failure of external doors or windows. From *Building Performance: Hurricane Andrew in Florida* (appendix C, ref. 75).

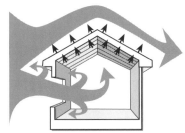
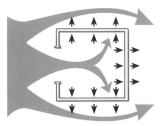

Wind pressure on roofs.
Internal pressure adds to roof uplift.

Wind pressure on walls.
Internal pressure adds to wall suction.

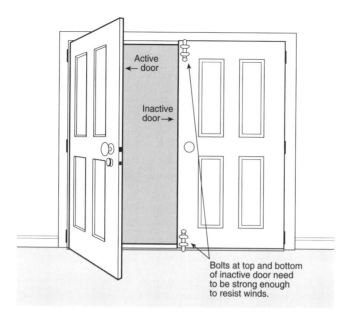

Active door →

Inactive door →

Bolts at top and bottom of inactive door need to be strong enough to resist winds.

Figure 9.7 Double-wide entry doors. Adapted from *Against the Wind* (appendix C, ref. 77).

heavy-duty bolts (your local hardware store will be able to advise you as to the strength of the bolts or pins).

Garage doors also pose a risk to the building envelope. They often fail because of inadequate thickness, and they tend to bend when subjected to strong winds. Double-wide or two-car garage doors are especially susceptible to high winds. When purchasing a new garage door, check the manufacturer's certification of its strength to verify the adequacy of the system. Retrofit existing garage doors by installing horizontal girts on each panel (fig. 9.8). A temporary strategy to reinforce a garage door during a wind storm is to back your car up against the inside of the door, providing extra support against bending. To prevent the garage door from falling off its tracks during high winds, strengthen the track supports and glider tracks. The rotation of the door along its edges can be reduced by chaining the door pin to the glider track connections.

Windows

All windows—including skylights, sliding glass doors, and French doors—must be protected from projectiles that could penetrate the building envelope. During a storm, missiles may be branches, roof pieces, lawn furniture, or anything else the wind can pick up. Protect windows by using storm shutters or precut plywood that is screwed to the outside of the windows (fig. 9.9). Strong windows are important in protecting the structure against high winds. Pay close attention to manufacturers' specifications of wind resistance for shutters and windows. On commercial or office buildings, where shutters are impractical, windows can be reglazed. (Reglazing is a method of strengthening the windows that replaces normal glass with tempered laminated glass.)

All windows and doors should be anchored to the wall frame to prevent them from being pulled out of the building. After missile impacts, this is the second most common mode of failure of the building envelope.

Structural Integrity

Building Shape

A hip roof, which slopes in four directions, resists high winds better than a gable roof, which slopes in two directions (fig. 9.10). The reason is twofold: the hip roof offers a smaller surface for the wind to blow against, and its structure is such that it is better braced in all directions.

The horizontal cross section of the house (the shape of the house as viewed from above) can affect the wind force exerted on the structure. The pressure exerted by the wind on a round or elliptical shape is about 60 percent of that exerted on a square or rectangular shape; the pressure exerted on a hexagonal or octagonal cross section is about 80 percent of that exerted on a square or rectangular cross section (fig. 9.10).

Figure 9.8 Double-wide garage doors. Adapted from *Against the Wind* (appendix C, ref. 77).

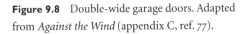

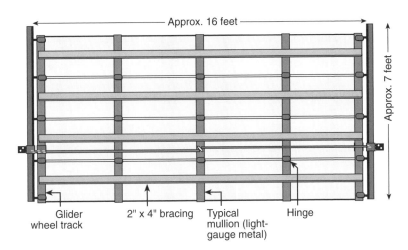

Approx. 16 feet

Approx. 7 feet

Glider wheel track   2" x 4" bracing   Typical mullion (light-gauge metal)   Hinge

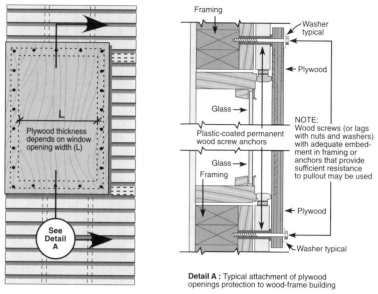

Light wood-frame wall

L

Plywood thickness depends on window opening width (L)

See Detail A

Framing

Washer typical

Plywood

Glass →

Plastic-coated permanent wood screw anchors

Glass →

Framing

NOTE:
Wood screws (or lags with nuts and washers) with adequate embedment in framing or anchors that provide sufficient resistance to pullout may be used

Plywood

Washer typical

Detail A : Typical attachment of plywood openings protection to wood-frame building

Figure 9.9 Typical installation of plywood over openings of wood-frame building. From *Building Performance: Hurricane Andrew in Florida* (appendix C, ref. 75), which also has information on how to install plywood to masonry.

The design of a house or building in a coastal area should minimize structural discontinuities and irregularities. There should be a minimum of nooks and crannies and offsets on the exterior, as damage to a structure tends to concentrate at these points. Award-winning architecture will be a storm loser if the design has not incorporated the technology for maximizing structural integrity with respect to storm forces. When irregularities are absent, the house reacts to storm winds as a complete unit (fig. 9.10).

Roofs

When a roof fails, either by losing its shingles or by flying off the house, it can spell disaster for the rest of the house and its contents. In high-wind areas, roofs can fail for a number of reasons, including inadequate tie-downs of the roof framing and poor connections of the roof to the wall components. Poorly attached roof sheathing or poorly placed asphalt-on-roof shingles can also cause roof failure.

To protect the contents of your home, judiciously select and adequately attach its roof covering. Shingles can be rated by the manufacturer and recommended as satisfactory for high-wind areas. Metal is the least acceptable of all roof coverings. Asphalt shingles perform poorly because poor fasten-

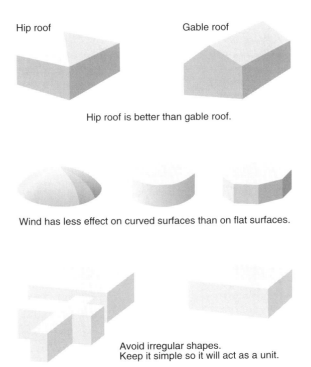

Hip roof   Gable roof

Hip roof is better than gable roof.

Wind has less effect on curved surfaces than on flat surfaces.

Avoid irregular shapes.
Keep it simple so it will act as a unit.

Figure 9.10   How building and roof shape influence wind resistance.

ing techniques are often used. If your roof is covered with metal or asphalt, it might be wise to change to wood shingles, which have a history of performing well in high-wind areas. Look around the neighborhood: what has worked in the past? Consult the building code.

Galvanized nails (two per shingle) should be used to connect wood shingles and shakes to wood sheathing, and they should be long enough to penetrate through the sheathing. Threaded nails should be used for plywood sheathing. For roof slopes that rise 1 foot for every 3 feet or more of horizontal distance, exposure of the shingle should be about one-fourth of its length (4 inches for a 16-inch shingle). If shakes (thicker and longer than shingles) are used, less than one-third of their length should be exposed.

Wind engineers, structural engineers, builders, and insurers are now working together to develop a new roof technology. The cry is, "Reinvent roofing for coastal areas." Specifically, the research involves a search for better re-covering materials. Perhaps the most important goal is to replace asphalt shingles with a continuous waterproof membrane that wind cannot lift up and tear off.

If you choose to use asphalt shingles in hurricane-prone areas, they should be exposed somewhat less than usual. Use a mastic or seal-tab type, or an interlocking heavy-grade shingle, along with a roof underlay of as-phalt-saturated felt and galvanized roofing nails or approved staples (six for each three-tab strip).

As indicated in figure 9.10, the shape of the roof is an important consideration. Aerodynamic building shapes are advantageous. For example, when feasible, use a low-angled hip roof rather than a steep-angled gable-end or clearstory roof.

The roof trusses must be strong enough to withstand design wind loads. Structural rigidity can be obtained by using bracing and connectors (see fig. 9.11 in general and figs. 9.12 and 9.13 for hip roof framing). Secondary bracing within the truss system can help the roof resist lateral wind forces. An inherent method of bracing is accomplished by substituting hip roofs for gable roofs. Retrofitting gable roofs may be necessary to strengthen them. In addition to strengthening the trusses, the overhang must be considered; there should be minimal overhang to prevent roof failure. Overhangs should extend only the distance required for proper drainage.

Figure 9.11 Roof-to-wall connectors. (*Top*) Metal strip connectors: rafter to stud (*left*); joist to stud (*right*). (*Bottom left*) Double-member metal plate connector, in this case with the joist to the right of the rafter. (*Bottom right*) A single-member metal plate connector.

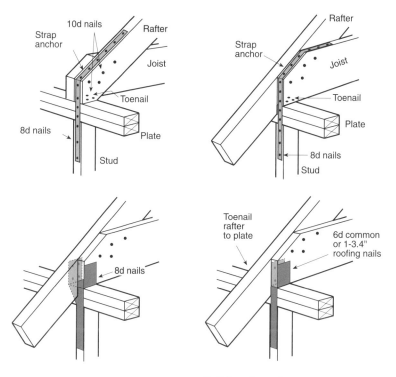

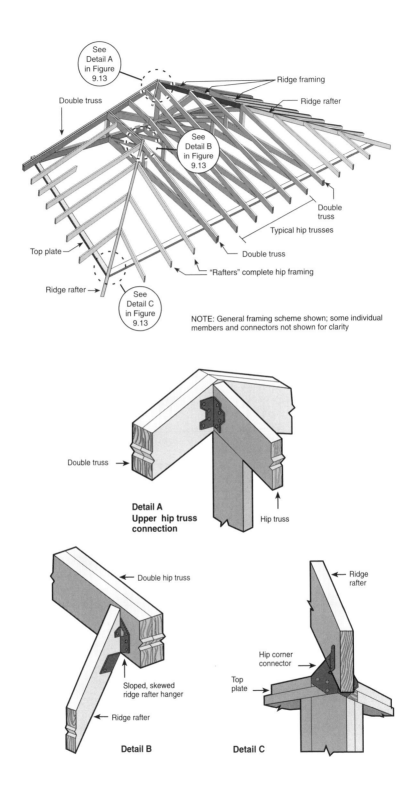

See Detail A in Figure 9.13

Double truss

Ridge framing

Ridge rafter

See Detail B in Figure 9.13

Double truss

Typical hip trusses

Double truss

"Rafters" complete hip framing

Top plate

Ridge rafter

See Detail C in Figure 9.13

NOTE: General framing scheme shown; some individual members and connectors not shown for clarity

Double truss

**Detail A
Upper hip truss connection**

Hip truss

Double hip truss

Sloped, skewed ridge rafter hanger

Ridge rafter

Detail B

Ridge rafter

Hip corner connector

Top plate

Detail C

Finally, roof venting is necessary to relieve internal pressures. The venting must exclude the entry of any uncontrolled air flow, which could result in a buildup of internal air pressure.

Connectivity, High-Wind Straps, and Tie-downs

A continuous load transfer path is needed if a house is to remain structurally intact under extreme loads. Everything must be connected to the foundation. This is done by using fasteners and connectors at all the joints, as in figure 9.14. In high-wind areas, these connectors are commonly called hurricane straps if they hold the roof to the walls (fig. 9.15), or tie-downs or anchor bolts if they hold the house to the foundation. See figures 9.16 and 9.17 for details. High winds cause uplift and lateral forces on the girders, trusses, and beams of the structure. Proper connectors can transfer the load away from these vulnerable areas, reducing the potential for structural damage and perhaps even saving the home. During wind storms, wood structures reinforced with metal connectors perform better than unreinforced structures.

A *shear wall* is an important addition to help a house resist lateral loads. Plywood is an excellent shear wall when it is nailed to the building frame accurately and completely. The larger the nails and the closer together they are, the better the plywood will perform as a shear wall. The use of nail guns during construction, which do not allow the carpenter to sense whether or not nails are going into the framing, sometimes results in whole rows of nails that missed the framing. When inspecting, make sure the plywood is attached at all levels of the building or house.

A multistory home must have floor-to-floor connectors to transfer the load path correctly. The first floor should be connected to the second floor with either nailed ties or bolted hold-downs to transfer the uplift forces from the upper stud to the lower stud. In addition, all houses must have connectors in the rafters and trusses.

The load transfer path must include a tie-down to the foundation of the building; generally this involves attaching a metal rod from the house frame into the concrete foundation. Have a professional check the foundation of an existing house for termite infestation and dry-rot damage and to make sure it is compatible with the planned tie-down system. Remember, if any component of the house is not connected, the whole house could fail.

Figure 9.12 Recommended hip roof framing. From *Building Performance: Hurricane Andrew in Florida* (appendix C, ref. 75).

Figure 9.13 Hip roof framing connectors. Adapted from *Building Performance: Hurricane Iniki in Hawaii* (fema–fia-23, 1993).

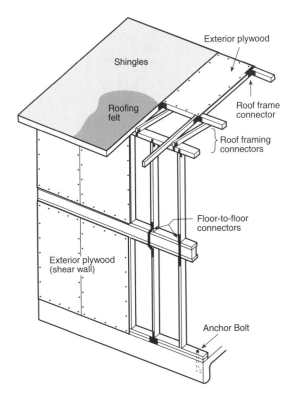

Figure 9.14 Recommended wood-frame construction. Continuous load path. Adapted from figures in *Building Performance: Hurricane Andrew in Florida* (appendix C, ref. 75).

Figure 9.15 Typical hurricane strap to roof framing detail. Rafter or prefabricated roof truss. From *Building Performance: Hurricane Andrew in Florida* (appendix C, ref. 75).

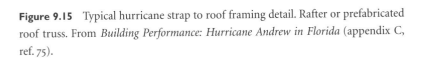

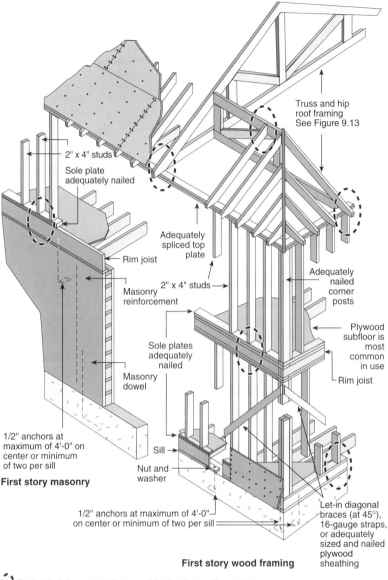

2" x 4" studs

Sole plate
adequately nailed

Truss and hip
roof framing
See Figure 9.13

Adequately
spliced top
plate

Rim joist

2" x 4" studs

Masonry
reinforcement

Adequately
nailed
corner
posts

Sole plates
adequately
nailed

Plywood
subfloor is
most
common
in use

Masonry
dowel

Rim joist

1/2" anchors at
maximum of 4'-0" on
center or minimum
of two per sill

Sill

First story masonry

Nut and
washer

1/2" anchors at maximum of 4'-0"
on center or minimum of two per sill

Let-in diagonal
braces (at 45°),
16-gauge straps,
or adequately
sized and nailed
plywood
sheathing

First story wood framing

Typical building connections requiring hurricane clips or straps

Figure 9.16 Primary wood framing systems: walls, roof diaphragm, and floor diaphragm. From *Building Performance: Hurricane Andrew in Florida* (appendix C,
ref. 75).

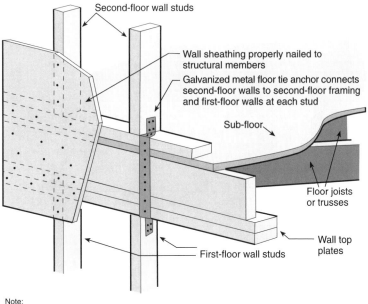

Second-floor wall studs

Wall sheathing properly nailed to
structural members

Galvanized metal floor tie anchor connects
second-floor walls to second-floor framing
and first-floor walls at each stud

Sub-floor

Floor joists
or trusses

Wall top
plates

First-floor wall studs

Note:
1. Horizontal sheathing joints should be minimized along second-floor line.
2. Straps should be sized appropriately for each building, i.e., maximum allowable uplift load resistance may
vary from 300 lbs. to 950 lbs., for 20-gauge to 16-gauge thickness, respectively

Figure 9.17 Upper-floor tie to lower floor for two-story buildings. From *Building Performance: Hurricane Andrew in Florida* (appendix C, ref. 75).

Keeping Dry: Pole or "Stilt" Houses

In coastal regions subject to flooding by waves or storm surge, the best and most common method of minimizing damage to houses is to raise the lowest floor above the expected highest water level. The first habitable floor of a home must be above a prescribed level to comply with regulations. Most modern structures built in flood zones are constructed on piling that is well anchored in the subsoil. Elevating the structure by placing it on top of a mound is not a suitable strategy in the coastal zone because mounded soil is easily eroded. Construction on piles or columns is a required design criterion for pole house construction under the National Flood Insurance Program. Regardless of insurance requirements, pole-type construction with deeply embedded poles is best in areas where waves and storm surge will erode foundation material. The materials used in pole construction include piles, posts, and piers. We will call all three "poles." Piles and posts are often referred to as "piling."

Piles are long, slender columns of wood, steel, or concrete driven into the earth to a depth sufficient to support the vertical load of the house and to withstand the horizontal forces of flowing water, wind, and waterborne debris. Pile construction is especially suitable in areas where scouring (soil washing out from under the foundation of a house) is a problem.

Posts are usually made of wood (if steel, they are called "columns"). Unlike piles, posts are not driven into the ground, but instead are placed in a predug hole which may or may not have a concrete pad at the bottom (fig. 9.18). Posts may be held in place by backfilling and tamping earth or by pouring concrete into the hole after the post is in place. Posts are more readily aligned than driven piles, and are therefore better to use if the poles must extend to the roof. In general, treated wood is the cheapest and most common material used for both posts and piles.

Piers are vertical supports, thicker than piles or posts and usually made of reinforced concrete or reinforced masonry (concrete blocks or bricks). They are set on footings and extend to the underside of the floor frame. This type of foundation is very vulnerable to water erosion; the pier footings topple and the piers buckle, leading to building damage or collapse.

Pole construction can be of two types. First, the poles can be cut off at the first floor to support the platform that serves as the dwelling floor. In this case, piles, posts, or piers can be used. Second, the poles can be extended to the roof and rigidly tied into both the floor and the roof, thus becoming major framing members for the structure and providing better anchorage for the house as a whole (fig. 9.19). Sometimes both full-height and floor-height poles are used, with the shorter poles restricted to supporting the floor inside the house (fig. 9.19).

Figure 9.18 Shallow and deep supports for poles and posts. Supplied by the Southern Pine Association. Check local regulations because supported pilings may not be permitted or recommended. In fact, *Building Performance: Hurricane Andrew in Florida* (appendix C, ref. 75) recommends that in areas subject to erosion and scour, concrete collars should not be placed around foundation pilings.

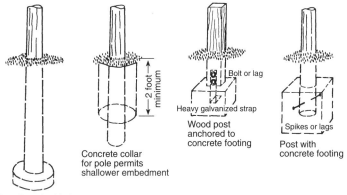

2 foot minimum

Bolt or lag

Heavy galvanized strap

Wood post anchored to concrete footing

Spikes or lags

Post with concrete footing

Concrete collar for pole permits shallower embedment

Deeply embedded pole on concrete pad

Piling Embedment

Erosion and scour can be devastating to coastal piling foundations. The loss of soil around a slender vertical member can have several deleterious effects. First, it increases the unsupported length of the member, which can result in more deflection or instability of that member. Second, there is less soil to oppose applied lateral piling loads, including the flow of the storm surge, wave forces, debris impact, and even the load of the building itself. Third, there is less friction surface to transfer loads between the piling and the ground, and hence less resistance to uplifting by the wind. References 70, 85, 86, and 89 in appendix C provide information on the design of coastal foundations. The goal should be to withstand the 100-year flood and long-term erosion.

FEMA recommends that piling foundations, if these are not controlled by local or state regulations, be embedded to 10 feet below mean sea level in regions subjected to erosion and scour. Shallower depths may be adequate for rocky shorelines or for other soils that resist erosion and scour. A 1997 FEMA publication titled *Building Performance Assessment: Hurricane Fran in North Carolina; Observations, Recommendations, and Technical Guidance* (appendix C, ref. 76) suggests that for ground levels up to 11 feet above the mean sea

Figure 9.19 Tying floors to poles. Supplied by the Southern Pine Association.

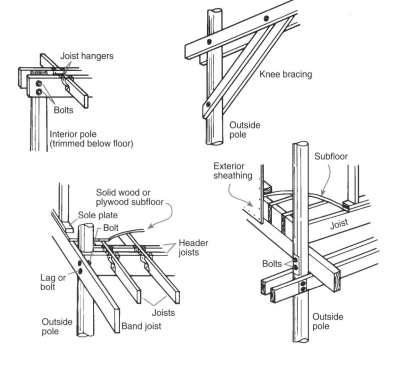

level, the current North Carolina Building Code regulations for foundation embedment depth seemed to be generally successful in warding off foundation failure. However, it may be time for North Carolina to introduce more stringent regulations. A possible revision would be to require embedment depth of 5 feet below mean sea level or 16 feet below ground, whichever is *greater*. The piling foundations for building appendages such as decks, porches, and roof overhangs should be embedded to the same depth as the foundations of the primary structure.

The North Carolina Building Code requires the use of pressure-treated wood for timber foundations. We add an extra caution: Avoid lower-grade lumber that could compromise the strength of timber posts and cross-bracing.

Coastal buildings must be elevated so that water can pass underneath them. Buildings placed in coastal high hazard areas—that is, the V-zones on the National Flood Insurance Program FIRMS—must be constructed so that the lowest floor is at or above the base flood elevation (BFE). Also, there can be no obstructions below the buildings. Buildings with the lowest floor elevated above the BFE are eligible for lower flood insurance rates.

Cross-bracing below elevated buildings can be an obstruction that is counterproductive in terms of structural strength. Piling foundations should be designed to avoid cross-bracing. This may involve using thicker, longer pilings; placing pilings closer together; or utilizing an unroofed deck that increases the building footprint. If cross-bracing cannot be avoided, design it to be adequate for possible wind and water loads, and use as little of it as possible, especially when it might be perpendicular to wave and debris forces.

Solid perimeter masonry foundation walls, which are supported on a continuous footing, are not acceptable in V-zones. Away from the high hazard areas they should be viewed with caution and, as a minimum, be professionally designed. They are susceptible to scour on both seaward and landward faces.

Connection of Pilings to the Floor and Roof

The floor and roof should be securely connected to the poles with bolts or other fasteners. This is especially important if the floor rests on poles that do not extend to the roof. Metal straps are commonly used fasteners. Another method is to attach beams to piles with at least two bolts of adequate size. Unfortunately, builders sometimes simply attach the floor beams to a notched pole with one or two bolts. Hurricanes have proven this method to be unacceptable. During the next hurricane on the North Carolina coast, many houses will be destroyed because of inadequate attachments.

Local building codes may specify the size, quantity, and spacing of the piles, ties, and bracing, as well as the methods of fastening the structure to them. Building codes are often minimal requirements, however, and building inspectors are usually amenable to allowing designs that are equally or more effective.

Corrosion-resistant metal connectors should be employed in building construction, at least at initial locations (figs. 9.11, 9.13, 9.15, 9.17). Information on the installation and upkeep of metal connectors (e.g., truss plates

Figure 9.20 Recommended breakaway wall attachment design. From *Building Performance Assessment: Hurricane Fran in North Carolina* (appendix C, ref. 76).

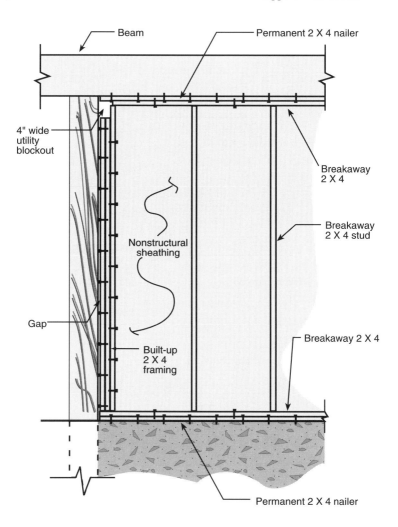

and hurricane straps) is available in an NFIP bulletin titled *Corrosion Protection for Metal Connections in Coastal Areas* (appendix C, ref. 71).

Breakaway Walls below Elevated Buildings

The space under an elevated house, pole type or otherwise, must be kept free of obstructions in order to minimize the impact of waves and floating debris. If walls are constructed below elevated buildings, they should be made of panels that break away when loaded by flood forces. That is, as shown in figure 9.20, breakaway wall panels should be installed so that they can successfully withstand wind loads but will break away under flood loads. It is important, for example, that the exterior wall sheathing not extend over the foundation posts, that it not be placed immediately seaward of cross-bracing, and that it be "weakly" attached to the "permanent" structure.

Concrete Slabs below Elevated Buildings

Slabs below elevated buildings should be designed such that they do not harm the building foundation when subjected to flood forces. These slabs should not be thicker than 4 inches (appendix C, ref. 76), they should be frangible so that they can break into relatively small pieces, and they should not have reinforcing wire mesh extending through joints installed so that the slab is permitted to break into pieces (fig. 9.21). The slab should not be connected to the vertical foundation members, especially if the soil is liable to be affected by erosion and scour.

Utility Systems

On-site utilities, such as air-conditioner/heat pump compressors, electrical meters, and septic systems, must be installed carefully. The local or state health department may have regulations that control the installation of septic systems. Like the building they serve, compressors must be elevated on a platform that is at or above the level of the bfe (fig. 9.22). Make sure utilities do not interfere with breakaway panels and are not placed adjacent to vertical foundation members. As indicated in figure 9.23, service connections, including sewer and water risers, should be located on the landward side of the most landward foundation posts.

Dry Flood-Proofing

NFIP regulations do not permit construction of walls that are impervious to the passage of floodwaters—referred to as "dry flood-proofing"—in coastal

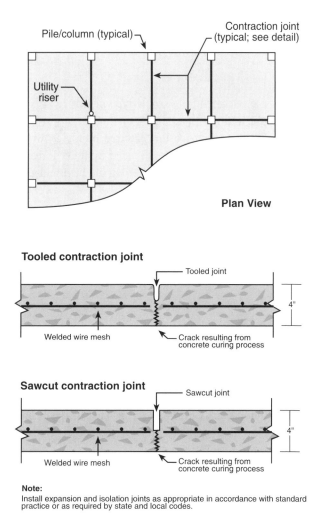

Figure 9.21 Recommended contraction joints for frangible slab-on-grade below elevated building. From *Building Performance Assessment: Hurricane Fran in North Carolina* (appendix C, ref. 76).

high hazard areas (V-zones). However, these regulations do allow dry flood-proofing of nonresidential buildings in A-zones. *Building Performance Assessment: Hurricane Fran in North Carolina* (appendix C, ref. 76) discusses potential problems with dry flood-proofing in North Carolina coastal A-zones.

An Existing House: What to Look for, Where to Improve

If, instead of building a new house, you plan to select a house already built in an area subject to storm surge, waves, flooding, and high winds, consider the following factors: (1) where the house is located; (2) how well the house is built; and (3) how the house can be improved.

Location

Evaluate the site of an existing house using the same principles you would use to evaluate a building site. The elevation of the house, frequency of high water, escape route, and how well the lot drains should be emphasized, but you should go through the complete 14-point site-safety checklist given in chapter 6 (also see table 6.2).

You can modify the house after you have purchased it, but you can't prevent hurricanes or northeasters. First, stop and consider: Do the pleasures and benefits of this location balance the risks and disadvantages? If not, look elsewhere for a home; if yes, then proceed to evaluate the house itself.

How Well Built Is the House?

In general, the principles used to evaluate an existing house are the same as those used in building a new one. Remember that many houses were built prior to the enactment of improved standards that have increased the hur-

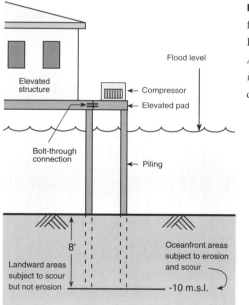

Figure 9.22 Utility platform supported by pilings. From *Building Performance Assessment: Hurricane Fran in North Carolina* (appendix C, ref. 76).

ricane-worthiness of newer buildings. Also, building codes are generally up-dated after devastating storms. Thus, a house built a couple years after Fran will meet stricter hurricane standards than one built before. In the case of an older house, it is up to you, the buyer, to have someone check for deficiencies.

Before you thoroughly inspect the house in which you are interested, look closely at the adjacent homes. If poorly built, they may float against your house and damage it in a flood. You may even want to consider the type of people you will have as neighbors: Will they "clear the decks" in preparation for a storm, or will they leave items in the yard to become

Figure 9.23 Proper location of utilities. From *Building Performance Assessment: Hurricane Fran in North Carolina* (appendix C, ref. 76).

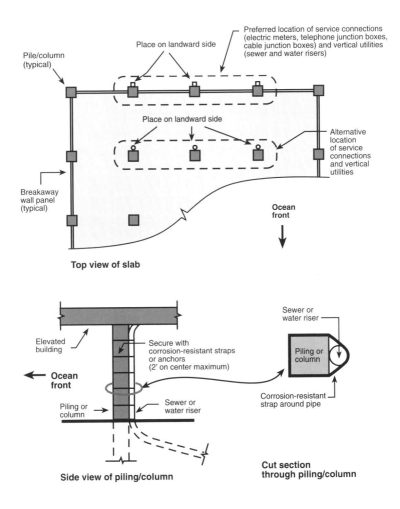

windborne missiles? The house itself should be inspected for the following features.

The house should be well anchored to the ground, and the wall well anchored to the foundation. If the house is simply resting on blocks, rising water may cause it to float off its foundation and come to rest against a neighbor's house or out in the middle of the street. If the house is well built and well braced internally, it may be possible to move it back to its proper location, but chances are great that the house will be too damaged to be habitable.

If the house is on piles, posts, or poles, check to see if the floor beams are adequately bolted to them. If it rests on piers, crawl under the house, if space permits, to see if the floor beams are securely connected to the foundation. *If the floor system rests unanchored on piers, do not buy the house.*

It is difficult to discern whether a house built on a concrete slab is properly bolted to the slab because the inside and outside walls hide the bolts. If you can locate the builder, ask if such bolting was done. Better yet, if you can get assurance that construction of the house complied with the provisions of a building code serving the needs of that particular region, you can be reasonably sure that all parts of the house are well anchored: the foundation to the ground, the floor to the foundation, the walls to the floor, and the roof to the walls.

Be aware that some builders, carpenters, and building inspectors accustomed to traditional construction methods are apt to regard metal connectors, collar beams, and other such devices as newfangled and unnecessary. If consulted, they may assure you that a house is as solid as a rock when in fact that is far from being the case. Nevertheless, it is wise to consult the builder or knowledgeable neighbors when possible.

The roof should be well anchored to the walls to prevent uplifting and separation from the walls. Visit the attic to see if such anchoring exists. Simple toe-nailing (nailing at an angle) is not adequate; metal fasteners are needed. Depending on the type of construction and the amount of insulation laid on the floor of the attic, these connections may or may not be easy to see. If roof trusses or braced rafters were used, it should be easy to see whether the various members, such as the diagonals, are well fastened together. Again, simple toe-nailing will not suffice. Some builders, unfortunately, nail parts of a roof truss just enough to hold it together to get it into place. A collar beam or gusset at the peak of the roof (fig. 9.24) provides some assurance of good construction.

Good-quality roofing material should be well anchored to the sheathing. A poor roof covering will be destroyed by hurricane-force winds, allowing rain to enter the house and damage the ceilings, walls, and contents.

With regard to framing, the fundamental rule to remember is that all the

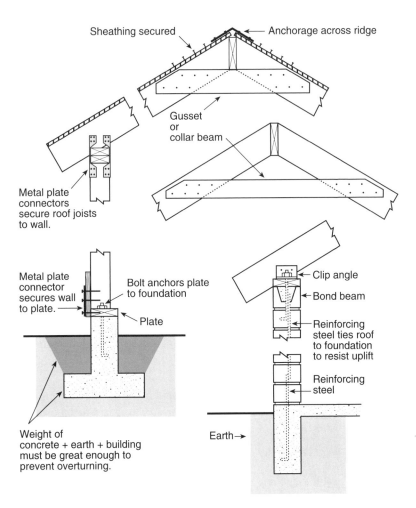

Figure 9.24 Where to strengthen a house.

structural elements should be fastened together and anchored to the ground in such a manner as to resist all forces, regardless of which direction they come from. This prevents overturning, floating off, racking, or disintegration.

Brick, concrete-block, and masonry-wall houses should be adequately reinforced. This reinforcement is hidden from view (fig. 9.24). Building codes applicable to high-wind areas often specify the type of mortar, reinforcing, and anchoring to be used in construction. If you can get assurance that the house was built in compliance with a building code designed for such an area, consider buying it. At all costs, avoid unreinforced masonry houses. Even reinforced masonry structures are not recommended in V-zones.

A poured-concrete bond beam at the top of the wall just under the roof is one indication that the house is well built (fig. 9.25). Most bond beams are formed by putting in reinforcing and pouring concrete in U-shaped concrete blocks. From the outside, however, you can't distinguish these U-shaped blocks from ordinary ones, and therefore you can't be certain that a bond beam exists. The vertical reinforcing should penetrate the bond beam.

Some architects and builders use a stacked bond (one block directly above another) rather than overlapped or staggered blocks because they believe it looks better. The stacked bond is definitely weaker than the overlapped or staggered blocks. Unless you have proof that the walls are adequately reinforced to overcome this lack of strength, you should avoid this type of construction. Some masonry-walled buildings have completely collapsed in hurricanes, resembling the flattened buildings associated with earthquakes.

In past hurricanes, the brick veneer of many houses separated from the wood frame, even when the houses remained standing. Gypsum-board cladding (covered with insulation and stucco) has performed very poorly in past hurricanes, typically suffering wind damage and removal. Such cladding should not be used on any building along the coast of the Carolinas that is more than 30 feet tall. Both brick veneer and wallboard-cladding

Figure 9.25   Reinforced tie beam (bond beam) for concrete-block walls, to be used at each floor level and at roof level around the perimeter of the exterior walls.

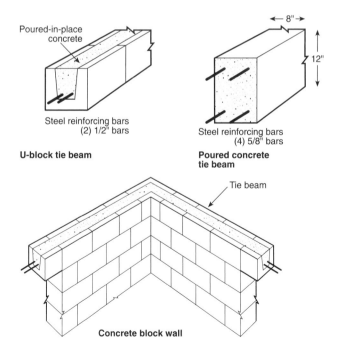

types of construction should be avoided as well. Lightweight preengineered metal walls also do not seem to perform well when subjected to hurricane winds, but these types of materials generally are not used for residential buildings.

Windows and large glass areas should be protected, especially those that face the ocean. Many newer coastal houses have large areas of glazing. Windows and doors can fail when subjected to positive pressures and suction, and often are the weak link in the integrity of a structure. Objects blown through a window during a storm cause dangerous flying glass as well as weakening structural resistance. Wind-blown sand can very quickly frost a window and thereby decrease its aesthetic value. Both of these problems can be avoided if the house has storm shutters. Check to see that they are present and functional.

Consult a good architect or structural engineer for advice if you are in doubt about any aspect of the house. A few dollars spent now for wise counsel may save you from later financial grief.

To summarize, a beach house should have the following:

1. Roof tied to wall, walls tied to foundation, and foundation anchored to the earth (the connections are potentially the weakest link in the structural system)
2. A shape that resists storm forces
3. Shutters for all windows, but especially those facing the ocean
4. Floors sufficiently elevated to be above most storm waters (usually the 100-year still-water flood level plus 3 to 8 feet to account for wave height)
5. Piles that are of sufficient depth or posts embedded in concrete to anchor the structure and withstand erosion
6. Well-braced piling

What Can Be Done to Improve an Existing House?

If you presently own a house or are contemplating buying one in a hurricane-prone area, you will want to know how to improve its ability to protect its occupants. Find the excellent government publication titled *Wind-Resistant Design Concepts for Residences,* by Delbart B. Ward (appendix C, ref. 80). Of particular interest are the sections on building a refuge shelter module within a residence (fig. 9.26). Also noteworthy are two supplements to this publication (appendix C, ref. 81), which deal with buildings larger than single-family residences and may be of interest to the general public, especially residents of urban areas. These works provide a means of checking whether the responsible authorities are doing their jobs to protect schools, office buildings, and apartments. Several other pertinent references are listed in appendix C as well.

Suppose your house is resting on blocks but not fastened to them, and thus is not adequately anchored to the ground. Can anything be done? One solution is to treat the house like a mobile home and screw ground anchors into the ground and then fasten them to the underside of the floor systems. Figures 9.27 and 9.28 illustrate how ground anchors can be used. The number of ground anchors needed will be different for houses and mobile homes, because each is affected differently by the forces of wind and water. Note that recent practice is to put these commercial steel-rod anchors in at an angle in order to align them better with the direction of the pull. If a vertical anchor is used, the top 18 inches or so should be encased in a concrete cylinder about 12 inches in diameter. This prevents the top of the anchor rod from bending or slicing through the wet soil from the horizontal component of the pull.

Diagonal struts, either timber or pipe, may also be used to anchor a house that rests on blocks. This is done by fastening the upper ends of the struts to the floor system, and the lower ends to individual concrete footings substantially below the surface of the ground. These struts must be able to take both tension and compression, and should be tied into the concrete footing with anchoring devices such as straps or spikes.

If the house has a porch with exposed columns or posts, you should be able to install tie-down anchors on their tops and bottoms. Steel straps should suffice in most cases.

Figure 9.26   Bathroom shelter module. From *Wind-Resistant Design Concepts for Residents* (appendix C, ref. 80).

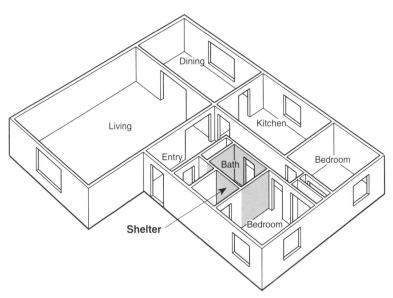

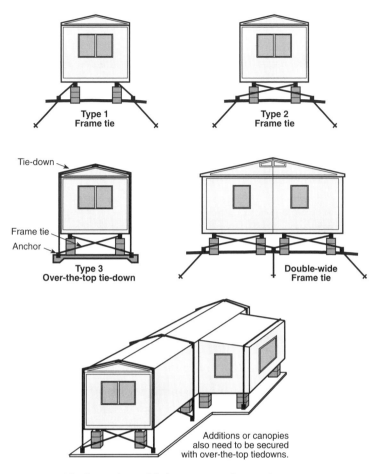

Figure 9.27 Tie-downs for mobile homes. From "Protecting Mobile Homes from High Winds" (appendix C, ref. 93).

When accessible, roof rafters and trusses should be anchored to the wall system. Usually, the roof trusses or braced rafters are sufficiently exposed to make it possible to strengthen joints (where two or more members meet) with collar beams or gussets, particularly at the peak of the roof (fig. 9.24).

A competent carpenter, architect, or structural engineer can review the house with you and help you decide what modifications are most practical and effective. Do not be misled by someone who resists new ideas. One builder told a homeowner, "You don't want all those newfangled straps and anchoring devices. If you use them, the whole house will blow away, but if you build in the usual manner [with members lightly connected], you may lose only part of it." In fact, of course, the very purpose of the straps is to prevent any or all of the house from blowing away. The Standard Building Code (previously known as the Southern Standard Building Code and still frequently referred to by that name, available from the Southern Building Code Congress International, Inc., Birmingham, Alabama) says that "lateral support securely anchored to all walls provides the best and only sound structural stability against horizontal thrusts, such as winds of exceptional velocity." The cost of connecting all elements securely adds very little to the cost of the frame of the dwelling, usually less than 10 percent, and a very much smaller percentage to the total cost of the house.

If the house has an overhanging eave and there are no openings on its underside, it may be feasible to cut openings and screen them. These openings keep the attic cooler (a plus in the summer) and may help to equalize the pressure inside and outside the house during a storm with a low-pressure center.

Another way a house can be improved is to modify one room so that it can be used as an emergency refuge in case you are trapped in a major storm. Please note that this precaution is not an alternative to evacuation before a hurricane! Examine the house and select the best room to stay in during a storm. A small windowless room such as a bathroom, utility room,

Figure 9.28 Hardware for mobile home tie-downs. Modified from "Protecting Mobile Homes from High Winds" (appendix C, ref. 93).

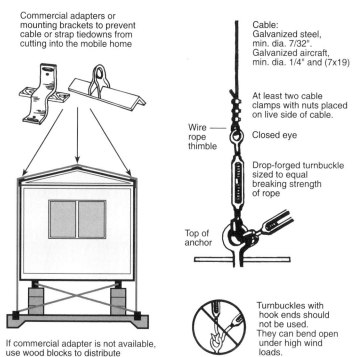

Commercial adapters or mounting brackets to prevent cable or strap tiedowns from cutting into the mobile home

Cable:
Galvanized steel, min. dia. 7/32".
Galvanized aircraft, min. dia. 1/4" and (7x19)

At least two cable clamps with nuts placed on live side of cable.

Wire rope thimble

Closed eye

Drop-forged turnbuckle sized to equal breaking strength of rope

Top of anchor

If commercial adapter is not available, use wood blocks to distribute pressure of cable.

Turnbuckles with hook ends should not be used. They can bend open under high wind loads.

den, or storage space is usually stronger than a room with windows. A sturdy inner room with more than one wall between it and the outside is safest. The fewer doors the better; an adjoining wall or baffle wall shielding the door adds to the protection.

Consider bracing or strengthening the interior walls. This may require removing the surface covering and installing plywood sheathing or strap bracing. Where wall studs are exposed, bracing straps offer a simple way to achieve needed reinforcement against the winds. These straps are commercially produced and are made of 16-gauge galvanized metal with prepunched holes for nailing. These should be secured to studs and wall plates as nail holes permit (figs. 9.11, 9.24). Bear in mind that straps are good only for tension.

If, after reading this, you agree that something should be done to your house, do it now. Do not put off the work until the next hurricane or northeaster is about to hit you!

Mobile Homes: Limiting Their Mobility

Because of their light weight and flat sides, mobile homes are exceptionally vulnerable to the high winds of hurricanes, tornadoes, and severe storms. High winds can overturn unanchored mobile homes or smash them into neighboring homes and property. Some 6 million Americans live in mobile homes today, and the number is growing. Mobile homes account for 20 to 30 percent of the single-family housing produced in the United States. High winds damage or destroy nearly 5,000 mobile homes every year, and the number will surely rise unless protective measures are taken. As one man whose mobile home was overturned in Hurricane Frederic (1979) aptly put it, "People who live in flimsy houses shouldn't have hurricanes." Mobile homes suffered complete destruction during Hugo in areas where wind gusts exceeded 100 miles per hour. An analysis of mobile homes after Hurricane Andrew (1992) showed that, in general, conventional residences suffered less damage than all types of manufactured homes, including mobile homes (appendix C, refs. 96, 97). Manufactured homes built using safe construction standards fared better than those built before the standards were created.

A national standard for mobile and other manufactured home construction was established as a result of the Manufactured Home Construction and Safety Standards (MHCSS) Act of 1974 (appendix C, ref. 95). The federal Department of Housing and Urban Development is responsible for developing and administering standards for all aspects of manufactured home construction, including support and anchoring systems to resist wind loads. Manufactured homes are treated like conventional residential homes by the

NFIP regulations. For example, the NFIP requires manufactured homes to be elevated and anchored so that they are able to withstand flood and wind forces. Particularly high standards are imposed on replacement homes in a mobile home park that has been damaged in a storm.

Several lessons can be learned from past storms. First, mobile homes should be properly located. After Hurricane Camille (1969), observers noted that damage was minimized in mobile home parks surrounded by woods and where the units were close together; the damage was caused mainly by falling trees. In unprotected areas, however, many mobile homes were overturned and destroyed by the force of the wind. The protection afforded by trees outweighs the possible damage from falling limbs. Two or more rows of trees are better than a single row, and trees 30 feet tall or taller give better protection than shorter ones. If possible, position the mobile home so that a narrow side faces the prevailing winds.

Locating a mobile home in a hilltop park greatly increases its vulnerability to the wind. A lower site screened by trees is safer from the wind, but the elevation should be above storm-surge flood levels. Obviously, a location that is too low is subject to flooding. There are fewer safe locations for mobile homes than there are for stilt houses. *Manufactured Home Installation in Flood Hazard Areas* (appendix C, ref. 88) discusses flood hazards and mobile homes.

A second lesson taught by past experience is that the mobile home must be tied down or anchored to the ground so that it will not overturn in high winds (figs. 9.27, 9.28; table 9.1). Simple prudence dictates the use of tie-downs, and in many communities the ordinances require it. Many insurance companies, moreover, will not insure mobile homes unless they are adequately anchored with tie-downs. The traditional single-wide mobile homes are now constructed with built-in tie-down straps. Figure 9.29 shows two types of anchoring systems.

A mobile home may be tied down with cable, rope, or built-in straps, or it may be rigidly attached to the ground by connecting it to a simple wood-post foundation system. A mobile home park may provide permanent concrete anchors or piers to which hold-down ties can be fastened. In general, an entire tie-down system costs a nominal amount.

A mobile home should be properly anchored with both ties to the frame and over-the-top straps; otherwise, it may be damaged by sliding, overturning, or tossing. The most common cause of major damage is the tearing away of most or all of the roof. When this happens, the walls are no longer adequately supported at the top and are more likely to collapse. Total destruction is more likely if the roof blows off, especially if the roof blows off first and then the home overturns. The necessity for anchoring cannot be overemphasized: mobile homes need both over-the-top tie-downs to resist overturning and frame ties to resist sliding off the pier foundations.

It seems that hurricanes and tornadoes are particularly cruel to mobile homes. Hurricane Fran was no exception; the post-hurricane study (appendix C, ref. 76) showed that most mobile homes, including permanently installed RVs, were tied down to foundations of dry-stacked masonry blocks. The anchoring systems were metal straps anchored into the sand with embedded helical anchors, usually 2 feet long with 3-inch helical plates. Fran caused significant damage. Many mobile homes were moved laterally and flipped over by Fran's winds or a combination of wind and flood forces, usually from relatively shallow flood depths (less than 3 feet). The homes shifted because their foundation and tie-down systems failed; namely, localized scour undermined the dry-stack masonry-block piers, leading to collapse of the pier, failure of the strap, and anchor pullout. Corrosion-weakened straps were vulnerable to relatively small tensile loads. Straps can be weakened in a few (less than 6) years if they are exposed to salt spray and are not frequently cleansed by rainfall. Anchor pullout appeared to be related to the saturation of the sand during flooding; the saturated soil could not resist the pullout of the anchors with small-diameter, shallowly embedded helical augers.

As a consequence of the observed Fran damage, it is now recommended that foundations exceed the anticipated scour depths by at least 1 foot. Also, if significant flow is possible in a region without highly dense sand, it is recommended that anchors be at least 4 feet long and 3/4 of an inch in diameter, with helical plates of at least 6 inches diameter.

A study of the tie-down systems after Hurricane Andrew reached the distressing conclusion that most anchoring systems are inadequate (appendix C, refs. 96, 97). In particular, anchors tended to pull out at force levels below

Table 9.1. Mobile Home Tie-down Anchorage Requirements

Wind velocity (mph)	10- and 12-Foot-Wide Mobile Homes				12- and 14-Foot-Wide Mobile Homes	
	30–50 feet long		50–60 feet long		60–70 feet long	
	Number of over-the-top ties	Number of frame ties	Number of frame ties	Number of over-the-top ties	Number of frame ties	Number of over-the-top ties
70	3	2	4	2	4	2
80	4	3	5	3	5	3
90	5	4	6	4	7	4
100	6	5	7	5	8	6
110	7	6	9	6	10	7

Sources: Suggested Technical Requirements for Mobile Home Tie Down Ordinances and *Protecting Mobile Homes from High Winds* (appendix C, refs. 92 and 93).

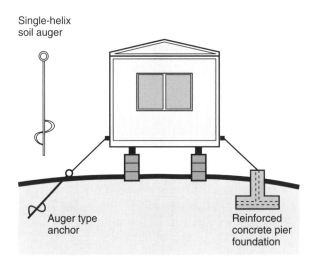

Single-helix
soil auger

Auger type
anchor

Reinforced
concrete pier
foundation

Figure 9.29 Anchoring systems.

values recommended by the standards. Corrective recommendations include conducting anchor pull tests or preloading shallow soil anchors.

There remains a question as to the proper angle at which an anchor
should be set. If anchors are set vertically or at angles not in the direction of
the pull, there can be a tendency for the top of the anchor rod to bend or
"slice" through the soil, especially when the soil is saturated with moisture,
as can occur during a hurricane. Such movement of the anchor rods can
have unfavorable consequences. To limit possible horizontal displacements,
anchors can be placed at an angle so that they are more in line with the direction of pull. See the setting of the auger-type anchor of figure 9.29. There
are some instances when anchors have been set at angles not in the direction
of the pull. The first case is cosmetic, where the anchor is tucked behind the
skirt that is placed around the base of the mobile home. Another case is
when the soil is such that the anchor cannot be properly set.

Mobile-home owners should obtain a copy of the booklet titled *Protecting Mobile Homes from High Winds* (appendix C, ref. 93), which treats the
subject in more detail. The booklet lists specific steps to take on receiving a
hurricane warning and suggests a type of community shelter for a mobile
home park. It also includes a map of the United States that indicates the areas subject to the strongest sustained winds.

High-Rise Buildings: The Urban Shore

Any high-rise you see on the beach was probably designed by an architect
and structural engineer who were presumably well qualified and aware of
the requirements for building on the shoreline. This does not mean that

those requirements were followed! Tenants of such a building should not assume it is invulnerable to storms. Many people living in two- and three-story apartment buildings in Mississippi were killed when the buildings were destroyed by Hurricane Camille in 1969. Storms have smashed five-story buildings in Delaware. Hugo did extensive damage to moderate- and high-rise buildings in 1989. The larger high-rises have yet to be thoroughly tested by a major hurricane.

The first aspect of high-rise construction a prospective apartment dweller or condo owner must consider is the type of piling used. High-rises near the beach should be built so that the building will remain standing even if the foundation is severely undercut during a storm. It is well known in construction circles that less scrupulous builders sometimes take short-cuts and do not drive the piling deep enough. Just as important as driving the piling deep enough to support the load it must carry is the need to fasten piles securely to the structure they support. The connections must resist horizontal loads from winds and waves during a storm and also resist uplift from the same sources. It is the joint responsibility of builders and building inspectors to make sure the job is done right. In 1975, Hurricane Eloise exposed the foundation of a high-rise under construction and revealed that some of the piling was not attached to the building. This happened in Panama City, Florida, but such problems probably exist everywhere that high-rises crowd the beaches.

Despite the assurances that come with an engineered structure, life in a high-rise has definite drawbacks that prospective tenants should take into consideration. They stem from high winds, high water, and poor foundations.

Pressure from the wind is greater near the shore than it is inland, and it also increases with height. If you are living inland in a two-story house and plan to move to the eleventh floor of a high-rise on the shore, you should expect five times more wind pressure than you are accustomed to. It can be a great and possibly devastating surprise. The high wind pressure can actually cause unpleasant motion of the building. Before you buy, check with current residents of the high-rise to find out if it has undesirable motion characteristics. Residents of some buildings claim the swaying is enough to cause motion sickness. A more serious problem is that high winds can break windows and damage other property. People can be hurt, and tenants of severely damaged buildings have to relocate until repairs are made.

Those interested in researching the subject further, and even the knowledgeable engineer or architect who is engaged to design a structure near the shore, should obtain a copy of *Structural Failures: Modes, Causes, Responsibilities* (appendix C, ref. 74). Of particular importance is the chapter titled "Failure of Structures Due to Extreme Winds," which analyzes wind damage to engineered high-rise buildings from the storms at Lubbock and Corpus Christi, Texas, in 1970.

Another occurrence that affects a multifamily high-rise building more seriously than a low-occupancy structure is a power failure or blackout. Power failures are more likely along the coast than inland because of the more severe weather conditions associated with coastal storms. It is not difficult to imagine the many inconveniences that can be caused by a power failure in a multistory building. For example, people can be caught between floors in an elevator. Think of the mental and physical distress after several hours of confinement, compounded by the roaring winds of a hurricane whipping around the building.

Fire is particularly hazardous in high-rises. Even recently constructed buildings seem to have problems. A number of hotel fires have occurred over the last few years. Fire department equipment reaches only so high, and many areas along the coast are too sparsely populated to be able to afford high-reaching equipment. Fire and smoke travel along ventilation ducts, elevator shafts, corridors, and similar passageways. The situation can be corrected and the building made safer, however, especially if the building is new. Sprinkler systems should be operated by gravity water systems rather than by powered pumps (because of possible power failure); gravity systems use water from tanks located high up in the building. Battery-operated emergency lights that come on when the other lights fail, better fire walls and automatic sealing doors, pressurized stairwells, and emergency-operated elevators in pressurized shafts all contribute to occupants' safety. Unfortunately, these improvements cost money, and that is why they are often omitted unless required and enforced by the building code.

If you own a condominium, you should encourage your homeowners' association to have the building inspected. The inspector should be a qualified engineer with experience in coastal construction codes and a knowledge of water and wind loading. The inspector should be able to propose corrective retrofits to improve the safety of the building.

Modular Unit Construction: Prefabricating the Urban Shore

The method of building a house, duplex, or larger condominium structure by fabricating modular units in a shop and assembling them at the building site is becoming popular in shoreline developments. The largest prefabricated structures are commonly two to three stories tall and may contain a large number of living units.

Modular construction makes good economic sense, and there is nothing inherently wrong in this approach to coastal construction. The same methods have been used in the manufacturing of mobile homes for years, although final assembly of mobile homes is done in the shop rather than in the field. Doing as much of the work as possible in a shop can save considerable labor and cost. The workers are not affected by outside weather conditions; they can be paid by piecework, enhancing their productivity; and shop work lends itself to labor-saving equipment such as pneumatic nailing guns, overhead cranes, and assembly lines.

If the manufacturer desires it, shop fabrication can permit a higher-quality product. Inspection and control of the whole construction process are much easier in the shop. For instance, there is less hesitation about rejecting a poor piece of lumber when a good supply is nearby than when there is just the right amount of lumber available on the building site. On the other hand, because so much of the work is done out of the sight of the buyer, the manufacturer has the opportunity to take shortcuts if so inclined.

The following points are very important. Were the wiring, plumbing, heating and air conditioning, and ventilation installed at the factory or at the building site? Were the installers licensed and certified? Was the work inspected both at the factory and on the construction site?

Most important, is the modular dwelling unit built to provide safety in the event of a fire? Just a few of the many fire safety features that should be present are two or more exits, stairs remote from each other, masonry fire walls between units, noncombustible wall sheeting, and compartmentalized units so that any fire that does occur will be confined to one unit.

In general it is very desirable to check the reputation and integrity of the manufacturer just as you would when hiring a contractor to build your individual house on-site. Approach the acquisition of a modular unit with the same caution you use for other structures. If you are contemplating purchasing a modular dwelling unit, you are well advised to take the following steps:

1. Check the reputation and integrity of the developer and manufacturer.
2. Check to see if the developer has a state contractor's license.
3. Check the state law to find out who is required to approve and to certify the building.
4. Check that building codes are enforced.
5. Check to make sure the state fire marshal's office has indicated that the dwelling units comply with all applicable codes. Also check to see if this office makes periodic inspections.
6. Check to see that smoke alarms have been installed, that windows are the type that can be opened, that the bathroom has an exhaust fan, and that the kitchen has a vent through the roof.

As with all other types of structures, you should also consider site safety and escape route(s) for the location.

What Should Be Done to Protect Property along the North Carolina Coast?

The public's growing desire for less "big government" and less regulation has left coastal property more and more vulnerable—not just to natural hazards but also to weak or unenforced building codes, to construction cost reduction through the use of low-quality materials that at best meet minimum code requirements, and to rushed construction and use of unsupervised and inexperienced labor, which leads to poor-quality workmanship or, even worse, to shortcuts that render buildings unsafe. The adage "Buyer beware!" goes double for coastal property.

Coastal property owners and residents should insist that state and local governments follow the recommendations of postdisaster investigation teams. For example, most of the post-Andrew recommendations (appendix C, ref. 75) apply to the Carolinas, particularly the following:

1. The quality of workmanship needs to be improved. Both the construction industry and the building inspection and enforcement people need to be sure their personnel are properly trained.
2. Building codes must be improved and better enforced.
3. Guidance on correct methods of transferring loads must be provided to building contractors.
4. Licensed design professionals should have more participation in the inspection of construction.
5. Inspector supervision and accountability should be improved.

These activities should be ongoing and evaluated after each storm. Many of the same recommendations made after Hurricane Andrew had been made—and ignored—after earlier hurricanes. When will we learn?

10 Earthquake Potential and Damage Mitigation

Earthquakes in North Carolina? Surely not; earthquakes happen somewhere else. Think again. Not only does North Carolina have a history of earthquakes and earthquake risk, but the coast in particular has a unique place in the history of public response to earthquake predictions.

In 1975, a geology professor at the University of North Carolina predicted the likelihood of earthquakes in the Wilmington area, based on the presence of "bulges" in the local geology, although the key data for his prediction were ultimately shown to be false. The professor went further and decided to bring a California psychic into the picture. After the professor and the psychic carried out a series of surveillance tours by airplane and car, the psychic predicted a number of earthquakes for the Carolina coast, the largest of which would be a magnitude 8 on the Richter scale (a great earthquake) in the Wilmington and Southport areas. The public fright and concern that ensued are legendary. Some people rushed to buy earthquake insurance and emergency supplies. Stores ran "earthquake sales."

As a result of that episode, the Seismological Society of America issued rules and procedures about earthquake predictions designed to ensure their scientific basis and credibility. Inaccurate predictions without scientific basis still occur, of course. For example, at least one interpretation of a Nostradamus quatrain has predicted that an earthquake would occur in southern California. Residents of the central Mississippi Valley (the New Madrid area in particular) were panicked in late 1990 by a prediction that an earthquake would occur because of higher than usual tidal loading on the earth's crust! The predicted events did not take place, but these areas are nevertheless at risk, as is North Carolina.

Earthquake Hazards and Risks in North Carolina

Earthquakes are commonly measured in terms of either the Richter scale or the Modified Mercalli Intensity (MMI) scale. Events of magnitude 7 or above on the Richter scale are considered great earthquakes (e.g., the Northridge, California, quake of January 17, 1994, which measured 7.1 on the Richter scale). The Richter scale is logarithmic; thus there is a tenfold difference between magnitudes of 6 and 7, and again between 7 and 8, and so on. Seismologists state that each full number increase on the Richter scale equals an energy release about 31 times greater. The MMI scale reflects the effect or amount of damage of an earthquake to a geographic area and is expressed in whole Roman numerals, I through XII. An intensity VII or greater quake can cause structural damage. An intensity VIII earthquake can cause considerable damage to poorly designed or built structures; chimneys can fall and panels can be tossed out of their frames.

Notwithstanding the exaggerations of a psychic or two, the North Carolina coast is at risk for earthquakes. The risk comes from three sources: (1) a zone of seismicity in the western portion of the state that is capable of producing an earthquake in the range of 6 on the Richter scale; (2) a seismic zone near Charleston, South Carolina, which produced an earthquake on August 31, 1886, that is estimated to have been about magnitude 7 and caused ground shaking in North Carolina as high as VIII on the MMI scale in some places; and (3) there is the potential for a "background," or commonplace, seismic event anywhere in the state and along the coast with around a Richter 5 magnitude that could cause damage.

There was a magnitude 3.6 quake in Pamlico County in 1994. Not much damage to structures was reported, although some nonstructural loss (e.g., falling dishes and wall hangings) probably occurred. In 1995, a similar-sized event (ca. 3.9 on the Richter scale) occurred in the Charleston area, resulting in about $125,000 in damage to school buildings. Thus, the earthquake threat is real.

Also important to the perception of earthquake hazards in North Carolina are two aspects of the ground beneath us: (1) the general character of eastern geology versus the general geological characteristics of the more seismically active western portions of the United States, and (2) the tendency of the surface geology along the coast to amplify ground shaking by as much as two to four times. Bedrock in the West tends to be less rigid than bedrock in the East. The more flexible western bedrock dampens the travel of the damaging seismic waves that go through the earth after an earthquake. Although earthquakes occur in the East much less often than in the

West, when they do occur, they affect a much larger area because the eastern bedrock is a better conductor of earthquake energy. If equally sized events were to occur in California and North Carolina, the area of shaking in North Carolina could be three to five times greater.

The geologic character of North Carolina's Coastal Plain and Atlantic shelf also contributes to the severity of earthquake impact. The soft sediments of the Coastal Plain amplify ground shaking in a way similar to that seen in the 1985 Mexico City quake or in the Marina district of San Francisco during the Loma Prieta earthquake of 1989. Such amplification may account for some of the damage attributed to the 3.9 magnitude quake that occurred in South Carolina in 1995. The extreme end result of ground shaking in unconsolidated sediments is soil liquefaction such as that which occurred in the 1886 Charleston earthquake. Note that the Charleston quake occurred well before the advent and growth of development along the North Carolina coast. How would our dense housing developments of today respond to such an earthquake?

Reducing the Earthquake Threat

Despite the geologic conditions that intensify ground shaking in North Carolina, measures can be taken to reduce earthquake damage. The danger to human life is most severe in large, engineered buildings. North Carolina has adopted and enforces the Standard Building Code, which incorporates design and construction parameters that address the earthquake hazard. The principles on which those parameters are based are discussed in further detail below. But in addition, you should keep a few facts in mind: there are buildings in North Carolina constructed before the building codes were adopted; codes in local jurisdictions do not all have earthquake mitigation requirements for single-family homes or other less engineered structures such as shopping malls or condominiums; and building codes that are not complied with or enforced do not offer much protection.

Fortunately, some of the measures that increase a structure's ability to resist coastal storms increase ground motion resistance as well (see chapter 9). As an example, many homes along the coast are elevated to deal with floodwaters and to avoid water damage to residences and vacation cottages. As noted in chapter 9, prudent use of between-stilt cross-bracing may be necessary for some types of hurricane-resistant construction. Such cross-bracing is exactly what is needed for a building to resist earthquake ground motions as well.

Few builders will claim they can build an earthquake-proof house. If certain fundamentals of design and construction are applied, however, the likelihood and extent of damage from earthquake forces will be significantly reduced. The information that follows provides a basic under-standing of how structures react to earthquake forces and points out design and construction concepts that should be considered or understood by any-one purchasing or constructing a house in an area potentially subject to ground shaking. Again, many of these techniques are applicable to and complement the design requirements for high wind and other coastal haz-ards. In most cases, application of these techniques is not very costly and re-sults in a better-built structure with a longer life expectancy.

How Buildings React to Earthquake Forces

Earthquakes create forces in structures because of inertia, the tendency for a body at rest (in this case the house or building) to resist motion, and for a body in motion to remain in motion. The forces that act on the structure depend on the direction of the ground motion caused by the earthquake. They may act from side to side (horizontal), up and down (vertically), or both. When an earthquake begins, a structure resists the initial movement of the ground, but as the ground shaking continues, the structure eventu-ally begins to move back and forth with the ground until the shaking stops and the earthquake is over. The larger earthquake-related forces are usually horizontal or lateral forces acting parallel to the ground. In houses, the ef-fects of vertical forces are normally considered to be offset by the weight of the building. Figure 10.1 shows the inertial effects on a building frame caused by back-and-forth motion parallel to the ground. Similar effects would occur if the ground was stationary and a horizontal force was ap-plied back and forth at the roof line.

Elements of Earthquake-Resistant Design and Construction

Siting

Structures in the North Carolina coastal zone are subject to collateral earth-quake hazards beyond ground shaking. Besides the obvious damage that can be caused by ground shaking, buildings face the problems of ground liquefaction and subsidence, both of which occurred in the 1886 Charleston earthquake mentioned above. We have no record of how these earthquake processes affected the barrier islands, but it is critical that anyone building or buying a home on a barrier island understand the nature of the ground under and around the house. Site evaluation often requires professional guidance and consultation, but it can be worth the cost and effort. Obvious areas to avoid are marshes and other water-saturated soils, organic fills and alluvium, and loose, shifting soils. The sandy soils of barrier islands with shallow water tables may liquefy in an earthquake.

The best building sites are on stable and solid rock formations, but these are not generally available along the North Carolina coast. Inland, deep bedrock provides the least hazardous conditions and minimizes earthquake damage to dwellings. Natural sites that consist of firm, consolidated deposits of well-drained soil, either flat or sloping, and stable hillside slopes are desirable.

Design and Construction

Dr. Karl Steinbrugge, the father of modern earthquake engineering, coined the phrase that has become the standard opening line for many an earthquake speech: "Earthquakes don't kill people, buildings do." Attention to earthquake-resistant design and use of good construction techniques can reduce injury and property loss as well as loss of life.

In general, one- and two-family dwellings, because of their design characteristics and materials, tend not to collapse in earthquakes. Wood-frame buildings perform better in earthquakes than buildings of unreinforced masonry and other materials, although this is not to say that a wood-frame building will escape significant damage. And such damage often makes the structure uninhabitable, causing both economic and social trauma to the occupants.

Most conventional homes can resist the horizontal forces of earthquakes (or wind) because they are built in a boxlike configuration. The simpler the design, the more stable the structure. The box configuration provides resistance by means of roof and floors (horizontal) and walls (vertical). Roofs and floors are considered to be horizontal diaphragms. A horizontal diaphragm can be compared to a steel beam that has a top and bottom flange and web, with the web oriented in a horizontal plane. In house construction, the exterior wall's top plates act as flanges and the roof sheathing functions as the web (fig. 10.2). For the roof to act most effectively as a horizontal diaphragm, it should be of a simple, regular shape with unbroken planes. A flat, pitched, or gabled roof is the best configuration.

Floor diaphragms are also most effective when they are simple in shape and designed in a geometric pattern. Shape and design are particularly important in a first-floor diaphragm spanning a basement opening and on cripple-wall foundations. (Cripple walls are usually wooden-stud walls built on top of an exterior foundation to support a house and create the crawl space.) It is best to apply a conventional design combined with a corresponding symmetrical pattern for the shear walls or shear panels (walls that resist horizontal forces; see below).

Floors and roofs often have to be penetrated for practical purposes such as duct shafts, and for aesthetic purposes such as skylights. The size and lo-

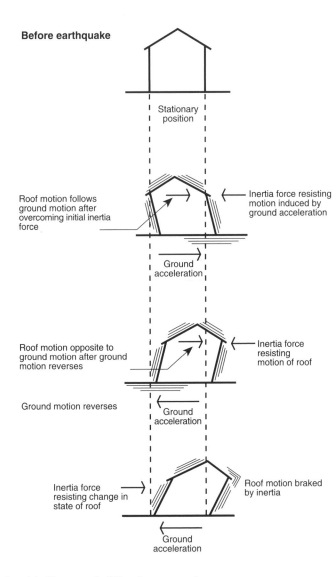

Before earthquake

Stationary
position

Roof motion follows
ground motion after
overcoming initial inertia
force

Inertia force resisting
motion induced by
ground acceleration

Ground
acceleration

Roof motion opposite to
ground motion after ground
motion reverses

Inertia force
resisting
motion of roof

Ground motion reverses

Ground
acceleration

Inertia force
resisting change in
state of roof

Roof motion braked
by inertia

Ground
acceleration

Figure 10.1   The inertial effects on a building frame caused
by back-and-forth motion parallel to the ground.

cation of such openings must be carefully considered because they can have
a critical impact on how effectively the diaphragm will function during an
earthquake or severe windstorm. Floors and roofs must be securely anchored to walls at the perimeter and at intermediate locations.

Walls that resist horizontal forces are known as shear walls or shear panels, the latter being resistant elements that might be part of a longer wall.
Shear walls can be viewed as upright beams on a fixed base comparable to a

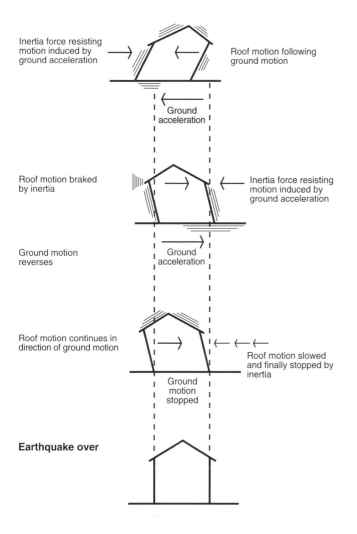

Inertia force resisting motion induced by ground acceleration

Roof motion following ground motion

Ground acceleration

Roof motion braked by inertia

Inertia force resisting motion induced by ground acceleration

Ground motion reverses

Ground acceleration

Roof motion continues in direction of ground motion

Roof motion slowed and finally stopped by inertia

Ground motion stopped

Earthquake over

vertical cantilever beam (a beam supported at one end only), with the end studs of the sheathed portion acting as flanges and the sheathing between end studs acting as the web. During an earthquake, ground motions enter the structure and create inertial forces that move the floor diaphragms. This movement is resisted by the shear walls, and the forces are transmitted back down to the foundation.

The shape and size of the shear walls are important design criteria. Walls that are too tall or too narrow tend to tip over before they slide. Because

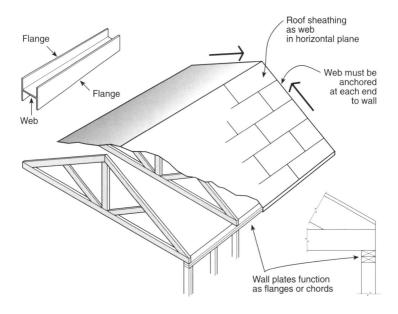

Figure 10.2 In house construction, the exterior walls' top plates
act as flanges and the roof sheathing functions as the web.

earthquakes can create forces in any direction, hold-downs must be placed
at each end of a shear wall or panel. Shear wall patterns are configured so
that opposite and parallel pairs of walls resist loads in a single direction, and
the exterior walls help the house resist twisting or racking (fig. 10.3). To be
effective, shear walls must be located at or near the boundaries of the roof
and floor diaphragms; that is, at each exterior wall.

In order to ensure that construction is earthquake resistant, it is essential
to provide a continuous load path from roof to foundation in order to dissipate earthquake forces. Good connections between the resisting elements
provide the continuity to ensure an uninterrupted path and tie the building
components together (figs. 10.4, 9.15).

One of the most common types of earthquake damage to houses occurs
when an improperly anchored structure shifts off its foundation. This dis-
placement can rupture gas lines, resulting in fire, and can cause exterior
damage to walls and windows as well as interior damage to contents. Further, it is very expensive to lift a house and put it back on its foundation.

In order to keep the house from sliding off its foundation, all the structural components (roof, shear walls, and floors) must be securely tied to the
foundation (fig. 10.5). Such structural integrity is most effectively achieved
by anchoring the sill plate to the foundation. (The sill plate is the wooden
board that sits directly on top of the foundation and secures the house to

the foundation.) The anchor bolts must be located accurately on the center line of the mud sills, and the mud sill plates must be secured to and consistently spaced along the foundation. To check whether a house is properly anchored, look in the crawl space for the heads of the anchor bolts. You should be able to see them installed every 4 to 6 feet along the sill plate. Other forms of connectors, such as steel plates, may have been used to connect the frame to the foundation.

Houses on foundations of unreinforced masonry such as brick or concrete block also tend to move off their foundations during earthquake shaking. Brick foundations should have visible anchor bolts or steel reinforcing bars between the inner and outer faces. Concrete-block foundations should be reinforced with anchored steel bars embedded in the grout fill of the blocks. If the cells of the concrete blocks are hollow, the foundation is probably unreinforced and is likely to fail, allowing the house to shift during an earthquake.

Building design or construction that incorporates cripple walls does not perform well in earthquake-prone areas if the walls are not properly braced. Plywood panels or diagonal wood sheathing form the best braces for cripple walls.

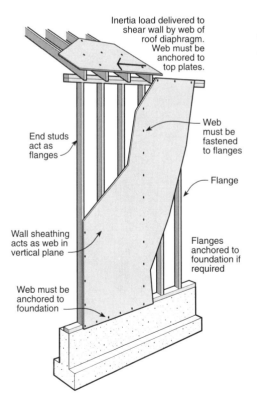

Figure 10.3 The exterior walls help the house resist twisting or racking.

Houses built on concrete slabs are generally considered to include a degree of seismic resistance because they do not have cripple walls and are bolted to the foundation. In most cases, such houses have foundation anchor bolts installed during construction, and these anchor bolts are usually visible. If they are not visible, you can usually tell if the bolts are there by examining the walls connecting the garage to the house.

Masonry chimneys are extremely vulnerable to earthquake forces. These heavy and brittle structures are usually constructed to be free standing above the roof line and pose special problems when used with flexible buildings such as wood-frame homes. The chimney should be vertically supported on a reinforced concrete pad, and the chimney walls should have a minimum of horizontal and vertical reinforcing. Separation of the chimney from the structure during ground shaking is the predominant damage pattern. To prevent this, the chimney should be anchored to the house framing at every diaphragm level (floor, ceiling, and roof) with ties that are embedded in the masonry and strapped around the vertical reinforcing.

Figure 10.4 Good connections between the resisting elements provide the continuity to ensure an uninterrupted path and tie the building components together.

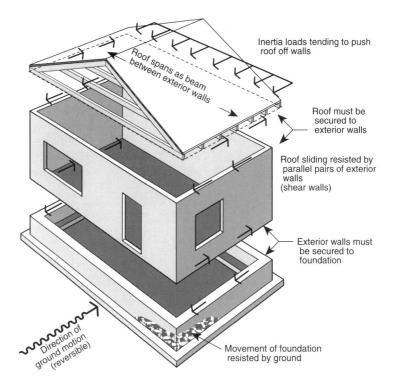

Depending on the size and height of the chimney relative to the frame, additional ties may be needed. Also, consider replacing masonry chimneys with metal flues. Determining whether a chimney is susceptible to earthquakes is not easy. Tall, slender chimneys that dramatically exceed the plane of the roof tend to be the most vulnerable. Inspection by a professional is often necessary.

Nonstructural Components

The loose contents inside your home may be a greater threat to your safety during an earthquake than collapsing walls and roof. Few people bother to consider fixtures, appliances, bookcases, and other objects that can fall over and cause personal injury or a fire hazard. Several excellent documents are available for assessing interior hazards around your home. Two in particular are *Checklist of Nonstructural Earthquake Hazards* and *Reducing the Risks of Nonstructural Earthquake Damage: A Practical Guide* (appendix C, refs. 101 and 100). Both documents are available free of charge.

Two particularly important nonstructural hazards are improperly braced water heaters and free-standing stoves. Water heaters not securely fastened to the wall may topple over during an earthquake and cause extensive water damage. Fires can be ignited when the connecting gas or electric lines break. Ensuring that such accidents do not happen is relatively simple and inexpensive. Metal straps or braces should encircle the heater and be secured by bolts to the wall. These bolts should go into studs or concrete, but not into drywall, which cannot support the weight of the heater during intense ground shaking. Also, flexible pipes connecting the gas and water lines perform better during ground shaking than more rigid aluminum or copper pipes.

Free-standing stoves are common sources of residential heat. In most cases, fire codes set the requirements for the construction and siting of these units. One of the requirements is for significant clearance around the stove. This often means that the stove is unsupported on all four sides, making it extremely vulnerable to sliding or overturning during an earthquake. To prevent a fire hazard, the stove should be anchored to the floor, and the stovepipe sections secured to prevent separation. The materials used for this anchoring and bracing must be heat resistant.

Manufactured Homes

Manufactured homes are seldom destroyed by earthquakes, but even a moderate earthquake can separate a mobile home from its foundation or piers and cause significant damage to awnings, decks, steps, skirting, and other attached accessory structures. Mobile homes often rotate on their foundations in an earthquake so that the doorway no longer opens onto the deck, porch, or steps. More than one resident has survived a quake only to step out the door into unexpected space and take a short fall to injury. Fires often result when gas line connections to the structure or to the inside appliances rupture. Reinstallation of damaged mobile homes can be quite expensive.

Figure 10.5 A secondary effect of earthquake forces is overturning of walls. This is best resisted by hold-downs, anchors to the foundation.

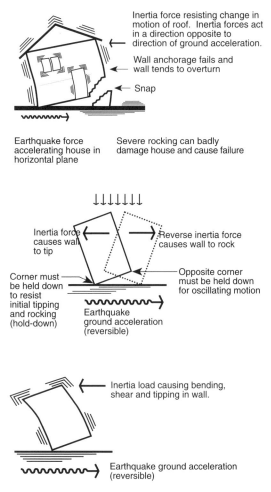

Bracing systems are available to secure the manufactured home so that it will not fall to the ground. To prevent earthquake-related fires, install flexible gas lines and secure all gas-burning appliances in place with strapping to ensure that they won't be dislocated by the ground shaking.

Codes and Current Practices

The foregoing concepts represent the very basics of earthquake-resistant design for residential buildings. Residential design and construction is one of the most rapidly changing and innovative industries in the nation today. The frequent changes in construction technology for the housing market make it especially important for buyers and residents alike to review local building codes carefully and consult the reference materials included in appendix C.

Incorporating earthquake resistance into the design and construction of a residence most often requires specialized advice, and we encourage you to utilize the services of design and engineering professionals. Contact FEMA for the most recent earthquake-resistant construction guidelines. In addition, recent actions on the part of the model code groups indicate that they are considering adopting the Council of American Building Officials (CABO) One and Two Family Dwelling Code as the nationally accepted code for such construction. The seismic provisions of the CABO code should be substituted for the current provisions included in the Standard Building Code, the model building code applied in North Carolina.

A final point about earthquakes, hurricanes, or any other risk confronting coastal Carolina. Awareness of natural hazards is a matter of vital interest to individuals as well as communities. Every person, business, and public servant in the community should take responsibility for reducing the risks associated with such hazards. Mitigation is accomplished during the siting, design, and construction of buildings, and the safety of our hospitals, schools, theaters, and public buildings is a function of public awareness. Public expressions of interest and concern make everyone more sensitive to natural hazards and more interested in taking the proper actions to reduce the associated risks (see appendixes A and C).

Appendix A
Hazard Safety Checklists

Natural disasters such as those described in this book can strike at any time, and without warning. Even with modern hurricane and flood prediction and warning capabilities, so many uncertainties remain that it is impossible to make perfect watch, warning, and evacuation calls every time. For example, Hurricane Hugo's forward speed and absolute strength grew so rapidly during the last few hours before it made landfall that the coast from Virginia to Florida was still preparing for a category 3 storm when Hugo rammed South Carolina as a category 4 storm.

With respect to the uncertainties involved in preparing for natural disasters, we include in this appendix several safety checklists with guidelines to preparing for, riding out, and recovering from natural disasters. Several precautions and preparations are the same for all disasters, and these are included as the "General Disaster Preparation Guide." Specifics for hurricanes, floods, and earthquakes follow the general information. Keep these checklists handy and use them to protect your family and property.

Inland dwellers may be at risk, too. There is always a possibility of heavy rains and flooding inland when a hurricane strikes the coast. The widespread inland wind damage associated with Hurricanes Hugo and Fran is a case in point. Unfortunately for inland residents whose property was damaged by Hugo and Fran, the construction people had gone to the coast to repair and rebuild. Power, water, and telephone services were interrupted for a longer time in some inland areas than at the coast. Be prepared.

Also mentioned in this appendix are several publications you may want to include in your home library. In most cases the publications are free and are readily available with just a phone call or postcard.

General Disaster Preparation Guide

Find out what natural hazards are likely to affect your community (or vacation rental site). Check your phone book for the local evacuation route, or call the nearest town, township, or county office. Learn the evacuation route. Have a plan.

Do hurricanes occur here? Tornadoes? Are earthquakes possible? Are they likely? Are you located on a floodplain, and have heavy rains been predicted or have they recently occurred? Have you moved your family into your dream vacation home right on the oceanfront just as a tropical disturbance is forming or intensifying out to sea?

One of the best all-around sources of information on disaster preparedness is the book *Are You Ready?* by FEMA (revised in September 1993). This 86-page publication is extensive in its coverage of natural and technological (nuclear, toxic spills) disasters. Write to FEMA and ask for publication H-34. You may also want to contact the North Carolina Sea Grant and ask for publication number UNC-SG-BP-92-03, *Hurricane Safety Checklist* (see appendix B for addresses).

You should have a disaster supply kit already put together that contains the essentials needed for any emergency from power outages to hurricanes.

Stock adequate supplies:
—battery-powered radio
—weather radio with alarm function for direct National Weather Service broadcasts
—fresh batteries
—flashlights
—portable halogen lamp (you'll need more light than just the emergency flashlight when the power goes off)
—hammer
—boards (for securing windows and doors against hurricanes)
—pliers
—hunting knife
—tape
—first-aid kit
—prescribed medicines
—candles
—matches
—nails
—ax (to cut an emergency escape opening if you go to the upper floor or attic of your home)
—rope (for escape to the ground when water subsides)
—plastic drop cloths, waterproof bags, and ties
—containers of water
—canned food, juices, and soft drinks
—enough food for at least three days and enough water for more than three days (select food that does not require cooking or refrigeration)
—water purification tablets
—insect repellent
—chewing gum, candy
—life jackets
—charcoal bucket, charcoal, and charcoal lighter
—buckets of sand
—disinfectant
—hard-top headgear
—fire extinguisher
—can openers and utensils (knives, forks, spoons, cups)

Make sure you know how to shut off electricity, gas, and water at main switches and valves. Know where the gas pilots are and how the heating system works. Be ready and able to secure your property before you leave so your belongings won't cause harm to others and you will be able to reenter your home safely.

Make a record of your personal property. Photograph or videotape your belongings, and store the record in a safe place.

Keep insurance policies, deeds, property records, and other important papers in a safe place away from your home.

Hurricane Safety Checklist

When (or before) a Hurricane Threatens

—Most important, know the *official evacuation route* for your area. You will not be asked to evacuate unless your life is in danger, so *evacuate as directed* by local emergency preparedness officials. Do not react to rumors.

—Many local telephone books contain community information about hurricane preparedness and evacuation. Check to see if the information is there and make sure everyone in the house is familiar with it.

—Read your newspaper and listen to radio and television for official weather reports and announcements.

—Secure reentry permits if necessary. Some communities allow only property owners and residents with proper identification or tags to return in the storm's immediate wake.

—Pregnant women, the ill, and the infirm should call a physician for advice.

—Be prepared to turn off gas, water, and electricity where it enters your home.

—Make sure your car's gas tank is full.

—Secure your boat. Use long lines to allow for rising water.

—Secure movable objects on your property:

   —doors and gates
   —outdoor furniture
   —shutters
   —garden tools
   —hoses
   —garbage cans
   —bicycles or large sports equipment
   —barbecues or grills
   —other

—Board up or tape windows, glassed-in areas, and glazing. Close storm shutters. Draw drapes and window blinds across windows and glass doors, and remove furniture in their vicinity.

—Check mobile home tie-downs.

—Your primary line of defense is *early evacuation*. If you are unable to evacuate, you should also do the following:

   —Know the location of the nearest emergency shelter. Go there if directed by emergency preparedness officials.

   —When a flood or hurricane is imminent, fill tubs and containers with water enough for one week (a minimum of one quart per person per day).

Special Precautions for Apartments/Condominiums

—Designate one person as the building captain to supervise storm preparations.

—Know your exits.

—Count stairs on exits: you may be evacuating in darkness.

—Locate safest areas for occupants to congregate.

—Close, lock, and tape windows.

—Remove loose items from your terrace (and from your absent neighbors' terraces).

—Remove (or tie down) loose objects from balconies or porches.

—Assume other trapped people may wish to use the building for shelter.

Special Precautions for Mobile Homes

—Pack breakables in padded cartons and place on floor.
—Remove bulbs, lamps, and mirrors, and put them in the bathtub (you are leaving, so the bathtub will not be a water reservoir).
—Tape windows.
—Turn off water, propane gas, electricity.
—Disconnect sewer and water lines.
—Remove awnings.
—*Leave.* Don't stay inside for *any* reason unless you can absolutely ascertain that the hazards from rising floodwaters are greater than those from wind.

Special Precautions for Businesses

—Take photographs of your building and merchandise before the storm.
—Assemble insurance policies.
—Move merchandise away from plate glass.
—Move merchandise to the highest location possible.
—Cover merchandise with tarps or plastic.
—Remove outside display racks and loose signs.
—Take out file drawers, wrap them in trash bags, and store them in a high place.
—Sandbag spaces that may leak.
—Take special precautions with reactive or toxic chemicals.

If You Remain at Home

—*Never* remain in a mobile home; seek official shelter.
—Stay indoors. Remember, the first calm may be the hurricane's eye. Do not attempt to change your location during the eye unless absolutely necessary. Remain indoors until an official all-clear is given.
—Stay on the *downwind* side of the house. Change your position as the wind direction changes.
—If your house has an inside room (away from all outdoor walls), it may be the most secure part of the structure. Stay there.
—Monitor *official* information on radio and television continuously.
—Keep calm. Your ability to meet emergencies will help others.

If Evacuation Is Advised

—Leave as soon as you can. Follow official instructions only. Ignore rumors.
—Follow predesignated evacuation routes unless those in authority direct you to do otherwise.
—Take these supplies:
   —reentry permit
   —change of warm, protective clothes
   —first-aid kit
   —baby formula
   —identification tags: include name, address, next of kin (wear them!)
   —flashlight
   —food, water, gum, candy

- —rope, hunting knife
- —waterproof bags and ties
- —can opener and utensils
- —disposable diapers
- —special medicine
- —blankets and pillows, in waterproof casings
- —battery-powered radio
- —fresh batteries (for radio and flashlight)
- —bottled water
- —purse, wallet, valuables
- —life jackets
- —games and amusements for children
- —Disconnect all electric appliances except refrigerator and freezer; their controls should be turned to the coldest setting and the doors kept closed.
- —Leave food and water for pets. Seeing-eye dogs are the only animals allowed in the shelters.
- —Shut off water at the main valve (where it enters your home).
- —Lock windows and doors.
- —Keep important papers with you:
  - —driver's license and other identification
  - —insurance policies
  - —property inventory
  - —Medic Alert or other device to convey special medical information

During the Hurricane

- —Stay indoors and away from windows and glassed areas.
- —If you are advised to evacuate, do so at once.
- —Listen for weather bulletins and official reports.
- —Use your telephone only in an emergency.
- —Follow official instructions only. Ignore rumors.
- —Keep a window or door *open* on the side of the house opposite the storm winds.
- —Beware the eye of the hurricane. A lull in the winds does not necessarily mean the storm has passed. Remain indoors unless emergency repairs are necessary. Be cautious. Winds may resume suddenly, in the opposite direction and with greater force than before. Remember, if the wind direction does change, the open window or door must be changed accordingly.
- —Be alert for rising water. Stand on furniture if necessary.
- —If electric service is interrupted, note the time. Take the following steps when the electricity goes out:
  - —Turn off major appliances, especially air conditioners.
  - —Do not disconnect refrigerators or freezers. Their controls should have been turned to the coldest setting and the doors kept closed to preserve food for as long as possible.
  - —Keep away from fallen wires. Report location of such wires to the utility company.

If You Detect Gas

- —Do not light matches or cigarette lighters or turn on electrical equipment, not even a flashlight.

—Extinguish all flames.

—Shut off gas supply at the meter. Gas should be turned back on only by a gas service professional or licensed plumber.

Water

—The only *safe* water is the water you stored before it had a chance to come in contact with floodwaters.

—Should you require more water, be sure to boil water for 30 minutes before using.

—If you are unable to boil water, treat it with water purification tablets. These are available at camping stores.

Note: An official announcement will proclaim tap water safe. Boil or treat all water except stored water until you hear the announcement.

After the Hurricane Has Passed

—Listen for official word that the danger has passed. Don't return to your home until officially directed to do so.

—Watch out for loose or hanging power lines as well as gas leaks. People have survived storms only to be electrocuted and burned. Fire protection may be nonexistent because broken power lines and fallen debris in the streets are blocking access.

—Walk or drive carefully through storm-damaged areas. Streets will be dangerous because of debris, undermining by washout, and weakened bridges. Traffic lights may not work; street signs may have been blown down. Approach every intersection as if it had a stop sign.

—Watch out for animals that may act irrationally after being driven out by floodwaters.

—Looting may be a problem in certain areas. Police protection may be nonexistent. Do not participate in such illegal acts and do not try to stop others. Wait for police, National Guard, or other officials to arrive.

—Eat nothing and drink nothing that has been touched by floodwaters.

—Place spoiled food in plastic bags and tie them securely.

—Dispose of all mattresses, pillows, and cushions that have been in floodwaters.

—Contact relatives as soon as possible.

—If you use an electric generator for home power, make sure your house's main circuit breaker switch is off. This will prevent your home-generated electricity from "leaking" out to the main power lines. After Hurricane Hugo in 1989, several power line repairers were electrocuted by electricity from the home generators of thoughtless individuals. Save a life! Make sure your main circuit breaker is off!

Note: If you are stranded, signal for help by waving a flashlight at night or white cloth during the day. If you have no cloth to wave, wave both arms (waving just one arm is an "OK" greeting).

Riverine and Flash Flood Safety Checklist

What to Do Before a Flood

—Know the terminology:
  —*Flood watch: flooding is possible.*
    —Stay tuned to NOAA weather radio or commercial radio or television.
  —*Flash flood watch: flash flooding, which can result in raging waters in just a few minutes, is possible.*

—Move to higher ground, a flash flood could occur without any warning.

—Stay tuned to radio or television.

—*Flood warning: flooding is occurring, or will occur soon.*

—If evacuation is advised, do so immediately.

—*Flash flood warning: a flash flood is occurring.*

—Seek higher ground on foot immediately.

—Find out from your local emergency management office whether your property is in a flood-prone area. Learn the elevation of your area. Learn about the likely flooding scenario of your lot/neighborhood/community.

—Identify dams in your area and determine if they pose a hazard.

—Purchase flood insurance (flood losses are not covered under your homeowner's insurance policy); it is widely available through the NFIP. Your local private insurance agent can direct you to find proper coverage. Have your agent also advise you on complete insurance coverage even if you do not live on a river floodplain.

—Prepare a family plan:

—Have a portable radio, flashlight, and emergency supplies.

—Be prepared to evacuate.

—Learn local evacuation routes.

—Choose a safe area in advance.

—Plan a family meeting place in case you are separated and cannot return home.

During a Flood

—Flood watch (2–3 days for flood; 2–12 hours for flash flood)

—*If you have time*, bring outdoor garden equipment and lawn furniture inside or tie it down.

—*If you have time*, move furniture and other items to higher levels (for flood).

—Fill your car's gas tank (for flood).

—Listen to radio or TV for up-to-the-minute information.

—Flood warning (24–48 hours for flood; 0–1 hour for flash flood)

—Evacuate, if necessary, when flood warning indicates, and follow instructions.

—Do not walk or drive through floodwaters.

—Stay off bridges covered by water.

—Heed barricades blocking roads.

—Keep away from waterways during heavy rain; if you are driving in a canyon area and hear a warning, get out of your car and get to high ground immediately.

—Keep out of storm drains and irrigation ditches.

—Listen to radio or TV for up-to-the-minute information.

After a Flood

—Stay away from floodwaters, they could be contaminated.

—Stay away from moving water.

Earthquake Safety Checklist

Before an Earthquake

—Have a plan of action, and know what to do afterward.

—Have a family reunion plan.

—Have an out-of-state family contact.

—Have supplies on hand such as water, a flashlight, a portable radio, food, a fire extinguisher, and tools.

—Bolt down bookshelves and water heaters, secure cabinets.

During an Earthquake

—Get under a heavy table or desk and hold on, or sit or stand against an inside wall.

—Keep away from windows.

—If you are indoors, stay indoors.

—If you are outdoors, stay outdoors, away from falling debris, trees, and power lines.

—If you are in a car, stay in the car.

—Don't use elevators.

After an Earthquake

—Expect aftershocks.

—Check gas, water, and electrical lines and appliances for damage.

—Use a flashlight (not a match!) to inspect for damage. Do not use even a flashlight if you smell gas!

—Turn off main gas and electricity valves.

—Don't venture into damaged areas.

—Don't use telephones except in emergencies.

—Don't use vehicles except in emergencies.

—Use a portable radio for information.

Postdisaster Recovery

Both coastal and inland residents should prepare an emergency handbook or plan for postdisaster recovery: what to do and how to do it. Start with a disaster addendum to your phone book. List contact numbers not just of relatives and disaster agencies, but also the names of contractors you will need to do repair work (e.g., utilities, water, house repairs, tree clearance, etc.).

Unfortunately, the postdisaster period is a time of social "hazards." People are dazed, confused, and in need of help that is in short supply. Unscrupulous individuals may appear at your door in the guise of construction or clearance contractors. Numerous people, particularly the elderly, were bilked after Fran. Do not accept bids for work unless the contractor provides evidence that the company is bonded and insured (it's best to have established contact with known contractors in advance).

Your telephone service is likely to be out. Know in advance where you might go to find a public phone that is in service (e.g., there's usually a public phone at or near fast-food restaurants or quick-marts). Have enough gasoline to get there (gas stations generally do not have mechanical pumps; when the electricity is off, so are the pumps). When communications are out, rumor takes over. Word-of-mouth rumors spread misinformation, and people feel out of touch. Don't listen to or act on rumors. Get the "official" word. A limited number of radio or TV stations may be in service after the disaster. Make sure you have a portable radio or TV with fresh batteries.

Water may be your greatest need. Store water before the storm (see checklists above), and know in advance where emergency supplies are likely to be available. Power outages and flooding may result in contaminated water supplies for days. In the case of flooding, everything that has come in contact with the floodwater is likely to be contaminated (i.e., household furniture and other belongings may not be salvageable).

Debris clearance and disposal is one of the biggest poststorm problems. After Fran, many people expected government help in the cleanup, but the U.S. Army Corps of Engineers and FEMA cannot go on private property to remove debris. Most likely, there will be no place immediately available for private individuals to put debris. Expect the cleanup to take weeks, more likely months, after the storm or flood.

Finally, people are not the only creatures displaced by these events. You may have to deal with some unwanted invaders. Be particularly cautious in regard to poisonous snakes, fire ants, bees, and other venomous, poisonous, or stinging animals. Dogs and cats also are more likely to bite or scratch when displaced, frightened, and disoriented.

Appendix B
Guide to Federal, State, and Local Agencies
Involved in Coastal Development

Numerous agencies at all levels of government are engaged in planning, regulating, or studying coastal development in North Carolina. These agencies issue permits for various phases of construction and provide information on development to the homeowner, developer, or planner. Following is an alphabetical list of topics related to coastal development; under each topic are the names of agencies to consult for information on that topic. Where possible, we have also provided World Wide Web addresses for those with Internet access. Please keep in mind that in the ever-changing world of the Internet, these addresses may have changed.

Aerial Photography, Orthophoto Maps, and Remote-Sensing Imagery

Persons interested in aerial photography, remote-sensing techniques, or agencies that supply aerial photographs or images should contact:

> North Carolina Department of Transportation
> Division of Highways
> Photogrammetry Unit
> 1020 Birch Ridge Drive
> Raleigh, NC 27611
> Phone: (919) 250-4170

An index photograph of your part of the coast is available for $10–30 from the Photogrammetry Unit at the above address and phone number.

> Earth Science Information Center
> U.S. Geological Survey
> 12201 Sunrise Valley Drive
> Reston, VA 22092
> Phone: (703) 860-6045; for book and map sales, (703) 648-6892
> http://info.er.usgs.gov

Erosion-rate aerial photographs are available from local Coastal Area Management Act permitting offices.

Beach Erosion

Information on beach erosion, inlet migration, floods, and high winds is available from:

Marine, Earth, and Atmospheric Sciences
North Carolina State University
Box 8208
Raleigh, NC 27695
Phone: (919) 515-3711
http://www2.ncsu.edu/ncsu/pams/meas/meas_home.html

Duke University Division of Earth and Ocean Sciences
Program for the Study of Developed Shorelines
341 Old Chemistry
Box 90228
Durham, NC 27708-0228
Phone: (919) 684-4238
http://www.geo.duke.edu/psds.htm

District Engineer
U.S. Army Corps of Engineers
P.O. Box 1890
Wilmington, NC 28401
Phone: (910) 251-4000

North Carolina Department of Environment, Health, and Natural Resources
Division of Coastal Management
P.O. Box 27687
Raleigh, NC 27611-7687
Phone: (919) 733-2293
http://www.ehnr.state.nc.us/EHNR/

Bridges and Causeways

The U.S. Coast Guard has jurisdiction over the issuing of permits to build bridges or causeways that will affect navigable waters. Information is available from:

Commander, 7th Coast Guard District
909 S.E. 1st Avenue
Miami, FL 33130
Phone: (305) 536-4108

Building Codes and Zoning

The North Carolina State Building Code contains special provisions for building in hurricane-prone areas. Check to be sure that the property in which you are interested is zoned for your intended use, and that adjacent property zones do not conflict with your plans. For information, contact the city or county building inspector, or:

North Carolina Department of Insurance
P.O. Box 26387
Raleigh, NC 27611
Phone: (919) 733-3901 (ask for either the building code consultant or the deputy commissioner)

Coastal Area Management Act, North Carolina (CAMA)

The Coastal Resources Commission designates Areas of Environmental Concern (AECs) where special environmental, historical, or scientific factors must be considered in development. Permits from the state for major developments or from local government (if it chooses to act as a permit-letting agency) for minor development are required to develop land in these areas. Learn where AECs are in relation to your property. For further information, write or call:

North Carolina Department of Environment, Health, and Natural Resources
Division of Coastal Management
P.O. Box 27687
Raleigh, NC 27611-7687
Phone: (919) 733-2293
http://www.ehnr.state.nc.us/EHNR/
or
National Oceanic and Atmospheric Administration
Office of Ocean and Coastal Resources Management
1305 E-W Highway
Silver Spring, MD 20910
Phone: (301) 713-3115

Construction

American Society of Civil Engineers (ASCE)
1801 Alexander Bell Drive
Reston, VA 20191-4400
(800) 548-2723 (ASCE)
http://www.pubs.asce.org

Disaster Assistance

Federal Disaster Assistance Administration
1371 Peachtree Street
Atlanta, GA 30309
Phone: (404) 853-4300

American National Red Cross
Emergency Services
Washington, DC 20006
Phone: (202) 728-6400

District Engineer
U.S. Army Corps of Engineers
P.O. Box 1890
Wilmington, NC 28401
Phone: (910) 251-4000

North Carolina Department of Environment, Health, and Natural Resources
Division of Emergency Management
116 W. Jones Street
Raleigh, NC 27603

Phone: (919) 733-3867 or (919) 733-3767
http://www.ehnr.state.nc.us/EHNR/

U.S. Department of Housing and Urban Development Services
Phone: (202) 708-1422

Federal Emergency Management Agency (FEMA) Disaster Services
Phone: (800) 262-9029

FEMA Main Office
Phone: (202) 646-2500 or (800) 427-4661

Dredging, Filling, and Construction in Coastal Waterways

North Carolina law requires all those who wish to dredge, fill, or otherwise alter marsh-lands, estuarine bottoms, or tidelands to apply for a permit from the state Division of Commercial and Sports Fisheries. For information, write or call:

North Carolina Department of Environment, Health, and Natural Resources
Division of Coastal Management
P.O. Box 27687
Raleigh, NC 27611-7687
Phone: (919) 733-2293
http://www.ehnr.state.nc.us/EHNR/

North Carolina Department of Environment, Health, and Natural Resources
Division of Marine Fisheries
Permit Section
P.O. Box 769 (or 3441 Arendell Street)
Morehead City, NC 28557
Phone: (919) 726-7021 or (800) 682-2632
http:// www.ncfisheries.net/

Federal law requires any person who wishes to dredge, fill, or place any structure in navigable water (almost any body of water) to apply for a permit from the U.S. Army Corps of Engineers. Information is available from:

Permits and Statistics Branch
U.S. Army Corps of Engineers
P.O. Box 1890
Wilmington, NC 28402-1890
Phone: (910) 251-4008

The American Shore and Beach Preservation Association publishes a quarterly journal, *Shore and Beach,* which features articles concerned with dredging and construction along the U.S. coasts. For more information, write:

American Shore and Beach Preservation Association
1724 Indian Way
Oakland, CA 94611

Dune Alteration

North Carolina law prohibits the destruction, damaging, or removal of any sand dune or dune vegetation. Individual counties usually have ordinances pertaining to dune alteration as well. Permits for certain types of alteration may be obtained from the local dune-protection officer. For information, call or write your local county courthouse.

Geologic Information

Earth Science Information Center
U.S. Geological Survey
12201 Sunrise Valley Drive
Reston, VA 22092
Phone: (703) 860-6045
(Request *Geologic and Water-Supply Reports and Maps, North Carolina,* index.)

U.S. Geological Survey
Water Resources Division
3916 Sunset Ridge Road
Raleigh, NC 27607
Phone: (919) 571-4000

North Carolina Department of Environment, Health, and Natural Resources
Division of Land Resources
P.O. Box 27687
Raleigh, NC 27611-7687
Phone: (919) 733-3833
http://www.ehnr.state.nc.us/EHNR/DLR/scro.htm

Coastal Education and Research Foundation (CERF)
P.O. Box 21087
Royal Palm Beach, FL 33421
Phone: (561) 753-7557

Hazards (see also *Beach Erosion* and *Insurance*)

Literature describing natural hazards on barrier islands is available from:

UNC Sea Grant College Program
Box 8605
North Carolina State University
Raleigh, NC 27695-8605
Phone: (919) 515-2454
http://www2.ncsu.edu/ncsu/CIL/sea_grant/index.html

National Oceanic and Atmospheric Administration
Office of Ocean and Coastal Resources Management
1305 E-W Highway
Silver Spring, MD 20910
Phone: (301) 713-3115

Information on all types of hazard research can be obtained from:

Natural Hazards Research and Applications Information Center
Institute of Behavioral Science #6
University of Colorado at Boulder

Campus Box 482
Boulder, CO 80309-0482
Phone: (303) 492-6818
http://adder.colorado.edu/~hazctr/Home.html

Health (see also *Sanitation* and *Septic-System Information*)

Your local Department of Health is in charge of issuing home septic tank permits. Questions may be directed to the officer of the local county health department.

History and Archaeology

North Carolina Department of Archives and History
109 E. Jones Street
Raleigh, NC 27601-2807
Phone: (919) 733-3952

National Ocean Survey
Distribution Division (c-44)
National Oceanic and Atmospheric Administration
Riverdale, MD 20840
Phone: (301) 436-6990

North Carolina in Maps (1966), a book containing historic maps and descriptive text of North Carolina, is available for $25 plus $3 shipping and handling from:

North Carolina Department of Cultural Resources
Historic Publications Section
109 E. Jones Street
Raleigh, NC 27601-2807
Phone: (919) 733-7442

Housing (see *Subdivisions*)

Hurricane Information

The National Oceanic and Atmospheric Administration (NOAA) is the best agency from which to request information on hurricanes. NOAA prepares storm evacuation maps for vulnerable areas. To find out whether a map for your area is available, call or write your local civil defense agency.

National Hurricane Center
11691 S.W. 17th Street
Miami, FL 33165-2149
Phone: (305) 229-4470
http://www.nhc.noaa.gov/

National Oceanic and Atmospheric Administration
Office of Ocean and Coastal Resources Management
1305 E-W Highway
Silver Spring, MD 20910
Phone: (301) 713-3155

Insurance

In coastal areas, special building requirements must often be met in order to obtain flood or windstorm insurance. To find out the requirements for your area, check with your insurance agent or the Kemper Insurance Company, which services the National Flood Insurance Program in North Carolina. Further information is available from:

Kemper Insurance Company
2709 Water Ridge Parkway
Charlotte, NC 28217
Phone: (704) 329-2200

Federal Insurance Administration
National Flood Insurance Program
Department of Housing and Urban Development
500 C Street S.W.
Washington, DC 20472
Phone: (202) 646-2500

State Coordinating Agency for Flood Insurance
Division of Emergency Management
North Carolina Department of Environment, Health, and Natural Resources
116 W. Jones Street
Raleigh, NC 27603
Phone: (919) 733-5392
http://www.ehnr.state.nc.us/EHNR/

For V-zone coverage or structure rating contact:
National Flood Insurance Program
ATTN: V-Zone Underwriting Specialist
P.O. Box 6468
Rockville, MD 20849-6468
Phone: (800) 638-6620

For flood maps, etc., contact:
Federal Emergency Management Agency
Flood Map Distribution Agency
6930 (A-F) San Thomas Road
Baltimore, MD 21227-6627
Phone: (800) 358-9616

Other agencies:
FEMA Main Office
Phone: (202) 646-2500 or (800) 427-4661

FEMA Disaster Services
Phone: (800) 262-9029

Department of Housing and Urban Development Services
Phone: (202) 708-1422

Information on the state building code, regulations governing mobile homes, and related areas is available from:

North Carolina Department of Insurance
P.O. Box 26387
Raleigh, NC 27611
Phone: (919) 733-3901

Property loss information is available from:
Institute for Business and Home Safety (IBHS)
(formerly the Insurance Institute for Property Loss Reduction)
73 Tremont Street, Suite 510
Boston, MA 02108-3910
Phone: (617) 722-0200

Land Acquisition

When acquiring property or a condominium—whether or not it is in a subdivision—check into the following: (1) Owners of property next to dredged canals should make sure the canals are designed for adequate flushing to keep the canals from becoming stagnant. Requests for federal permits to connect extensive canal systems to navigable water are frequently denied! (2) Description and survey of land in coastal areas is very complicated. Old titles granting fee-simple rights to property below the high-tide line may not be upheld in court; a title should be reviewed by a competent attorney before it is transferred. A boundary described as the high-water mark may be impossible to determine. (3) Ask about the provision of sewage disposal and utilities, including water, electricity, gas, and telephone. (4) Be sure any promises of future improvements, access, utilities, additions, and common property rights are in writing. (5) Be sure to visit the property and inspect it carefully before buying it. (See *Planning* and *Subdivisions* below.)

Maps

Maps are useful to planners and managers and may be of interest to individual property owners. Topographic, geologic, and land-use maps and orthophoto quadrangles are available from:

Earth Science Information Center
U.S. Geological Survey
12201 Sunrise Valley Drive
Reston, VA 22092
Phone: (703) 860-6045; for book and map sales, (703) 648-6892
http://info.er.usgs.gov/

Request a free index to the type of map desired (e.g., the "Index to Topographic Maps of North Carolina"), and then use it for ordering specific maps.

North Carolina Department of Environment, Health, and Natural Resources
Division of Land Resources
P.O. Box 27687
Raleigh, NC 27611
Phone: (919) 733-3833
http://www.ehnr.state.nc.us/EHNR/DLR/scro.htm

Flood-zone maps: see *Insurance.*

Planning maps: Call or write your local county commission.

Soil maps and septic suitability: see *Soil.*

County highway base maps are available from:
North Carolina Department of Transportation
Division of Highways
P.O. Box 25021
Raleigh, NC 27611
Phone: (919) 733-7600
(County maps are $0.25 each, highway maps are free.)

Nautical charts in several scales contain navigation information on North Carolina's coastal waters. A nautical chart index map is available from:
Distribution Branch N/CG 33
National Ocean Service
National Oceanic and Atmospheric Administration
Riverdale, MD 20737-1199
Phone: (301) 436-6990

Marine and Coastal-Zone Information

North Carolina has three state aquaria. Located conveniently along the coast, they are designed as learning laboratories and serve a variety of functions. Exhibits, aquaria, and various displays are open year-round, and there are lectures, seminars, and film series as well. Each center has a professional staff available to answer questions, and many Sea Grant publications that are free or inexpensive. State aquaria are located at the following addresses:

North Carolina Aquarium
Roanoke Island
Manteo, NC 27954
Phone: (919) 473-3493
http://www.aquariums.state.nc.us/Aquariums/

North Carolina Aquarium (located near Fort Fisher)
2201 Fort Fisher Boulevard; S Box 1
Kure Beach, NC 28449
Phone: (910) 458-8257
http://www.aquariums.state.nc.us/Aquariums/

North Carolina Aquarium (located on Bogue Banks)
P.O. Box 580
Atlantic Beach, NC 28512
Phone: (919) 247-4003
http://www.aquariums.state.nc.us/Aquariums/

Other sources of information on the coastal zone include:
National Sea Grant Depository
Pell Library Building
University of Rhode Island
Narragansett Bay Campus
Narragansett, RI 02882-1197
Phone: (401) 792-6114
E-mail: cmurray@gsosunl.uri.edu

UNC Sea Grant College Program
North Carolina State University
Box 8605
Raleigh, NC 27695-8605
Phone: (919) 515-2454
http://www2.ncsu.edu/ncsu/CIL/sea_grant/index.html
The Sea Grant Program distributes a monthly newsletter and other publications.

Coast Alliance
210 D Street, S.E.
Washington, DC 20003
Phone (202) 546-9554

Marine, Earth, and Atmospheric Sciences
North Carolina State University
Box 8208
Raleigh, NC 27695
Phone: (919) 515-3711
http://www2.ncsu.edu/ncsu/pams/meas/meas_home.html

Coastal Marine Advisories
Phone: (910) 458-5780

Duke University Marine Laboratory
135 Duke Marine Lab Road
Beaufort, NC 28516-9721
Phone: (919) 504-7503 for Information; (919) 504-7583 for Oceanography.

Parks and Recreation

North Carolina Department of Environment, Health, and Natural Resources
Division of Parks and Recreation
P.O. Box 27687
Raleigh, NC 27611
Phone: (919) 733-4181
http://www.ehnr.state.nc.us/EHNR/

Cape Hatteras National Seashore Headquarters
Route 1, Box 675
Manteo, NC 27954
Phone: (919) 473-2111
http://www.nps.gov/caha/

Cape Lookout National Seashore Headquarters
131 Charles Street
Harkers Island, NC 28531
Phone: (919) 728-2250
http://www.nps.gov/calo/

Planning and Land Use (see also *Coastal Area Management Act*)

North Carolina Department of Environment, Health, and Natural Resources
Division of Coastal Management

P.O. Box 27687
Raleigh, NC 27611
Phone: (919) 733-2293
http://www.ehnr.state.nc.us/EHNR/

Center for Urban and Regional Studies
University of North Carolina at Chapel Hill
Campus Box 3410
Chapel Hill, NC 27599-3410
Phone: (919) 962-3074
Ask for publication list on development and planning.

North Carolina Department of Environment, Health, and Natural Resources
Division of Land Resources
P.O. Box 27687
Raleigh, NC 27611
Phone: (919) 733-3833
E-mail: Charles_Gardner@mail.ehnr.state.nc.us
http://www.ehnr.state.nc.us/EHNR/DLR/scro.htm

For specific information on your area, check with your local town or county commission. Many local governments have planning boards that answer to the commission and have available copies of existing or proposed land-use plans.

Roads and Property Access

The North Carolina Department of Transportation is not required to furnish access to all property owners. Before buying property, make sure access rights and roads will be provided. Permits to connect driveways from commercial developments to state-maintained roads must be obtained from the district engineer of the Division of Highways.

Subdivision roads and privately built roads, including those serving seasonal residences, must meet specific standards in order to be eligible for addition to the state highway system. Information on these requirements may be obtained from the district engineer or the secondary roads officer of the local Division of Highways office. Further information is available from:

Secondary Roads Department
Division of Highways
North Carolina Department of Transportation
P.O. Box 25201
Raleigh, NC 27611
Phone: (919) 733-3250

Sanitation

Improvement permits for septic tanks must be obtained from your local Department of Health before construction permits can be issued. Improvement permits are based on soil suitability for septic tank systems and apply to conventional homes and mobile homes outside mobile-home parks, in areas that are not served by public or community sewage systems and generate less than 3,000 gallons of effluent per day.

A permit must be obtained from the North Carolina Division of Water Quality for any discharge into surface water and for wastewater treatment systems of design capacities that exceed 3,000 gallons per day. Septic tank systems will not be approved in high-density areas (those producing more than 1,200 gallons of wastewater per acre per day, or those containing more than three residential units per acre).

More information may be obtained from your county health department or:

North Carolina Department of Environment, Health, and Natural Resources
Division of Water Quality
Northeastern Field Office
1424 Carolina Avenue
Washington, NC 27889
Phone: (919) 946-6481

North Carolina Department of Environment, Health, and Natural Resources
Division of Water Quality
Southeastern Field Office
127 Cardinal Drive
Wilmington, NC 28405
Phone: (910) 395-3900

A permit for the construction of a sewage disposal unit or any other structure in navigable waters must be obtained from the U.S. Army Corps of Engineers. More information is available from:

Permits and Statistics Branch
U.S. Army Corps of Engineers
P.O. Box 1890
Wilmington, NC 28402-1890
Phone: (910) 251-4000

A permit for any discharge into navigable waters must be obtained from the U.S. Environmental Protection Agency. Recent judicial interpretation of the Federal Water Pollution Control Amendments of 1972 extends federal jurisdiction above the mean high-water mark for protection of wetlands. Federal permits may now be required to develop land that is occasionally flooded by water draining indirectly into a navigable waterway. Information may be obtained from:

Water Management Division
U.S. Environmental Protection Agency
Region IV
345 Courtland Street N.E.
Atlanta, GA 30365
Phone: (404) 347-4450

North Carolina Department of Environment, Health, and Natural Resources
Division of Marine Fisheries
P.O. Box 769
Morehead City, NC 28557
Phone: (919) 726-7021
http://www.ncfisheries.net/

Septic-System Information and Permits
(see also *Sanitation* and *Water Resources*)

General information may be obtained from:

UNC Sea Grant College Program
North Carolina State University
Box 8605
Raleigh, NC 27695-8605
Phone: (919) 515-2454
http://www2.ncsu.edu/ncsu/CIL/sea_grant/index.html

Department of Soil Science
Box 7619
North Carolina State University
Raleigh, NC 27695
Phone: (919) 515-2655
http://www.soil.ncsu.edu

Water Management Division
U.S. Environmental Protection Agency
345 Courtland Street N.E.
Atlanta, GA 30365
Phone: (404) 347-4450

On-site soil information is available from your local conservation district office, county extension office, or private consultants. Home system permits may be obtained from your local health department. Business or industrial system permits may be obtained from the regional office of the Department of Natural Resources and Community Development.

Soils (see also *Septic-System Information* and *Vegetation*)

Soil type is important in terms of (1) the type of vegetation it can support, (2) the type of construction it can withstand, (3) its drainage characteristics, and (4) its ability to accommodate septic systems. Ultimately, soil reports including maps and ratings of soil types will be available for most of the North Carolina coast. The following agencies cooperate to produce a variety of reports that are useful to property owners:

U.S. Department of Agriculture
Soil and Water Conservation Service
P.O. Box 27307
Raleigh, NC 27611
Phone: (919) 715-6102 (715-6103 after 2:00 P.M.)

Publishes maps and reports; supplies information to Soil and Water Conservation district offices; operates annual "beach clinics" in conjunction with the soil- and water-conservation districts.

North Carolina Department of Environment, Health, and Natural Resources
Division of Soil and Water
P.O. Box 27687
Raleigh, NC 27611-7682
Phone: (919) 733-2302
Cooperates in publication of soil reports and maps.

Department of Soil Science
Box 7619
North Carolina State University
Raleigh, NC 27695
Phone: (919) 515-2655
http://www.soil.ncsu.edu

Persons seeking information on soil should check first with the Soil and Water Conservation district office. The white pages of the local phone directory and local community or county health departments can also provide information.

Subdivisions

Subdivisions containing more than 50 lots and offered in interstate commerce must be registered with the Office of Interstate Land Sales Registration (as specified by the Interstate Land Sales Full Disclosure Act). Prospective buyers must be provided with a property report. This office also produces a booklet entitled *Get the Facts . . . Before Buying Land* for people who wish to invest in land. Information on subdivision property and land investment is available from:

Office of Interstate Land Sales Registration
U.S. Department of Housing and Urban Development
451 7th Street S.W.
Room 9160
Washington, DC 20410
Phone: (202) 708-0502

Vegetation

Information on vegetation may be obtained from the local Soil and Water Conservation district office. For information on the use of grass and other plantings for stabilization or aesthetics, consult the publications listed in appendix C under "Vegetation." *Seacoast Plants of the Carolinas for Conservation and Beautification* is particularly useful.

Videos

Several videos are available for sale from:

UNC Sea Grant College Program
North Carolina State University
Box 8605
Raleigh, NC 27695-8605
Phone: (919) 515-2454
http://www2.ncsu.edu/ncsu/CIL/sea_grant/index.html
Videos include *North Carolina Coastal Plain: A Geologic and Environmental Perspective, Lucas and Its Aftermath,* and *The Death of a Whale.*

Several videos on coastal processes, pollution, coastal land loss, and related topics are available for sale from:

Environmental Media
P.O. Box 99
Beaufort, SC 22901

Phone: 1 (800) 368-3382
Fax: (803) 986-9093
http://www.envmedia.com
Videos include *Living on the Edge* (a guide to buying or building on the coast), *The Challenge on the Coast, Vanishing Lands, The Beaches Are Moving,* and *Underwater Oases: The Science of Hardbottoms.*

Videos are also available from NOAA, FEMA, and IBHS. Call or write for recent publication lists:

FEMA Main Office
Phone: (202) 646-2500 or (800) 427-4661

Institute for Business and Home Safety (IBHS)
(formerly the Insurance Institute for Property Loss Reduction)
73 Tremont Street, Suite 510
Boston, MA 02108-3910
Phone: (617) 722-0200

The Nature Conservancy's film *The Atlantic's Last Frontier* is available from:
The Nature Conservancy
1815 N. Lynn Street
Arlington, VA 22209
Phone: (703) 841-5300

The North Carolina Lighthouse Tour is a video available from:
Southern Lights Productions
4301 Waterleaf Court
Greensboro, NC 27410

Water Resources (see also *Dredging, Filling, and Construction in Coastal Waterways* and *Sanitation*)

Several agencies are concerned with water quality and availability. The following will answer questions on this subject:

Water Management Division
U.S. Environmental Protection Agency
345 Courtland Street N.E.
Atlanta, GA 30365
Phone: (404) 347-4450

U.S. Geological Survey
Water Resources Division
3916 Sunset Ridge Road
Raleigh, NC 27607
Phone: (919) 571-4000

Water Resources Research Institute
124 Riddick Building
North Carolina State University
Raleigh, NC 27607
Phone: (919) 515-2815

North Carolina Department of Environment, Health, and Natural Resources
Division of Water Quality
Northeastern Field Office
1424 Carolina Avenue
Washington, NC 27889
Phone: (919) 946-6481
http://pluto.ehnr.state.nc.us/index.html

North Carolina Department of Environment, Health, and Natural Resources
Division of Water Resources
P.O. Box 27687
Raleigh, NC 27611-7687
Phone: (919) 733-4064
http://www.dwr.ehnr.state.nc.us/home.htm

Weather

General information may be obtained from:

National Weather Service, North Carolina Climatologic Data
585 Stewart Avenue
Garden City, NY 11530
Phone: (516) 924-0517

Southeastern Regional Climate Center
1201 Main Street, Suite 1100
Columbia, SC 29201
Phone: (803) 737-0849

Hurricane information is available from:

National Oceanic and Atmospheric Administration
Office of Ocean and Coastal Resources Management
1305 E-W Highway
Silver Spring, MD 20910
Phone: (301) 713-3115

Public Affairs Division
National Hurricane Center
11691 S.W. 17th Street
Miami, FL 33165-2149
Phone: (305) 229-4470
http://www.nhc.noaa.gov/

Internet users may also find the following web sites useful for information about weather and hurricanes:

The Weather Channel: http://www.weather.com

Purdue University Weather Processor:
http://wxp.atms.purdue.edu/

NOAA's weather page:
http://www.esdim.noaa.gov/weather_page.html

For current weather information, listen to your local radio and television stations.

Appendix C
101 Useful References

The following publications are listed by subject and arranged in the approximate order in which they appear in the text. Sources are included for readers who would like more information on a particular subject. Many of the references listed are either inexpensive or free. For scientific literature (books and journal articles), university libraries are the best bet. Popular books should be available at general bookstores. If not, your local bookstore should be able to locate them for you. Government publications are available from the agency that produced them or from the U.S. Government Printing Office. See appendix B for addresses. Another source of information is the "information superhighway." More and more agencies and organizations are creating their own home pages on the World Wide Web.

The original North Carolina shore book, *From Currituck to Calabash: Living with North Carolina's Barrier Islands,* by Orrin Pilkey and others, was published in 1982 by Duke University Press, Durham, North Carolina. It contains an appendix that lists several classic references on pioneering work along the North Carolina coast, books on barrier island processes in general, and references of historical interest that are not listed here. The older book should still be available in libraries.

Abbreviations used in this appendix or in the text are given below:

AEC   Area of Environmental Concern
AIRAC   All-Industry Research Advisory Council
ASBPA   American Shore and Beach Preservation Association
ASCE   American Society of Civil Engineers
BFE   Base Flood Elevation
CABO   Council of American Building Officials
CAMA   Coastal Area Management Act
CBRS   Coastal Barrier Resources System
CCC   Civilian Conservation Corps
CERC   Coastal Engineering Research Center
CERF   Coastal Education and Research Foundation
CRC   Coastal Resources Commission
CZMA   Coastal Zone Management Act
DCM   Division of Coastal Management
FEMA   Federal Emergency Management Agency
FIA   Federal Insurance Administration

FIRM	Federal Insurance Rate Map
IBHS	Institute for Business and Home Safety
MHCSS	Manufactured Home Construction and Safety Standards Act
MMI	Modified Mercalli Intensity Scale
MSL	Mean Sea Level
NAS	National Academy of Sciences
NCDEM	North Carolina Division of Emergency Management
NFIP	National Flood Insurance Program
NHRAIC	Natural Hazards Research and Applications Information Center
NIST	National Institute of Standards and Technology
NMFS	National Marine Fisheries Service
NOAA	National Oceanic and Atmospheric Administration
NPDES	National Pollution Discharge Elimination System
NPS	National Park Service
NRC	National Research Council
NTIS	National Technical Information Service
UNC	University of North Carolina
USACOE	U.S. Army Corps of Engineers
USGS	U.S. Geological Survey

History

1. *The Cape Hatteras Lighthouse: Sentinel of the Shoals,* by Dawson Carr, 1991, gives a full history of the historic lighthouse and the recent attempts to preserve it. Published by the University of North Carolina Press ([800] 848-6224), http://sunsite.oit.unc.edu/uncpress/text_index.html.

2. *Mapping the North Carolina Coast: Sixteenth-Century Cartography and the Roanoke Voyages,* by William P. Cumming, 1988, is an interesting introduction to the oldest known existing maps of the Carolina coast and the spots where the early European explorers may have been. The author traces the history of the maps likely to have been the basis for Sir Walter Raleigh's efforts to establish an English colony in North Carolina. Implicit in the story is the opening and closing of inlets, major storms, and coastal erosion on the islands in the sounds. The 143-page paperback was published by the Division of Archives and History, N.C. Department of Cultural Resources (see appendix B).

3. *The Outer Banks of North Carolina, 1584–1958,* by David Stick, 1958. This classic history of the Outer Banks is recommended to all residents of coastal North Carolina, particularly in Carteret, Hyde, and Currituck Counties. Contains storm history, accounts of the origins of most points of interest, and examples of early development. Published by the University of North Carolina Press, Chapel Hill.

4. *Saving Cape Hatteras Lighthouse from the Sea: Options and Policy Implications,* Committee on Options for Preserving Cape Hatteras Lighthouse; Board on Environmental Studies and Toxicology; Commission on Physical Sciences, Mathematics, and Resources; National Research Council. Produced by the National Research Council and published by the National Academy of Sciences Press in 1988, this book explores the options available to preserve the tallest lighthouse on the Atlantic coast, including relocation inland. It is available from the NRC Board on Environmental Studies and Toxicology.

5. *Islands, Capes, and Sounds, the North Carolina Coast,* by Thomas J. Schoenbaum, 1982, is a history of the Outer Banks and the early settlements along Albemarle and Pamlico Sounds. Published by John F. Blair, 1406 Plaza Drive, Winston-Salem, NC 27103.

6. *Eastern North Carolina Hurricane Evacuation Study,* appendix A, Inundation Maps, by the North Carolina Division of Emergency Management (NCDEM), 1987, shows low-lying coastal areas vulnerable to flooding during hurricanes.

7. *"Hurricane!" A Familiarization Booklet,* by NOAA, 1993, 36 pp. A descriptive and nontechnical overview of U.S. hurricanes. Includes sections on hurricane anatomy, storm surge, forecasting, and lists of the most intense and destructive hurricanes through 1992. Hurricane checklist is provided. Available through NOAA as document NOAA PA 91001.

8. *The Weather Book,* by Jack Williams, 1992, explains weather phenomena in easily understood language, with many diagrams and photographs. Published by Vintage Books, New York.

9. *North Carolina's Hurricane History,* by Jay Barnes, 1995, published by the University of North Carolina Press, is an interesting narrative supported by numerous photos, maps, and diagrams that outline the state's memorable hurricanes in chronological order through Emily in 1993. It is highly recommended for all North Carolinians and visitors to the state's shores. In addition, this 206-page book discusses northeasters, the next great hurricane, and tips for storm survival.

10. *The Deadliest, Costliest, and Most Intense United States Hurricanes of This Century (and Other Frequently Requested Hurricane Facts),* by Paul J. Hebert and Glenn Taylor, 1988 (updated in 1997), is NOAA Technical Memorandum NWS-TPC-1. This pamphlet contains a discussion of hurricane facts and several tables summarizing deaths, costs, and hurricane intensities. Available from NOAA, National Weather Service.

11. "Surface Wind Fields in 1996 Hurricanes Bertha and Fran at Landfall," 1997, by Sam Houston and others, contains some interesting hindcast data about Bertha and Fran. Specifically, Topsail Island, although farther from the storm's eye than Wrightsville Beach, experienced hurricane-force winds for seven hours longer. Provides a great reality check about the unpredictability of devastating storms. American Meteorological Society, 22nd Conference on Hurricanes and Tropical Meteorology, May 19–23, 1997, Fort Collins, Colorado.

12. "Soundside Impacts of a Northward Tracking Tropical Cyclone: Hurricane Emily (31AUG93), Cape Hatteras Area, North Carolina," by David M. Bush and others, is a scientific paper published in the *Journal of Coastal Research,* vol. 12, no. 1 (1996), pp. 229–239. Although Hurricane Emily never made landfall, the eye of this category 3 hurricane came within 25 miles of the Outer Banks, and its effects provide an example of wind setup in the sounds. Flooding came from the back sides of the islands, and the sound-side shores were eroded by debris carried against the landward side of the dunes. Finger canals funneled floodwaters into the island's interior.

13. *Impacts of Hurricane Hugo: September 10–22, 1989,* edited by Charles W. Finkl and Orrin H. Pilkey, 1991, was published by the CERF as *Journal of Coastal Research* Special Issue 8. Its 356 pages contain 24 scientfic papers describing various aspects of Hugo's meteorology and effects. Available from CERF, 4310 N.E. 25th Avenue, Fort Lauderdale, FL 33308. Includes "Beach Scraping in North Carolina with Special Reference to Its Effectiveness during Hurricane Hugo," by John T. Wells and Jesse McNinch, pp. 249–263.

14. "Nor'easters," by Robert E. Davis and Robert Dolan, is one the best and most thorough treatments of winter storms available. It includes a scale for ranking these storms patterned somewhat on the Saffir/Simpson scale for hurricanes. Information on storm formation and tracking is included, along with good historical accounts.

Published in *American Scientist*, vol. 81 (1993), pp. 428–439.

15. "New Respect for Nor'easters," by Ben Watson, was published in *Weatherwise*, vol. 46, no. 6 (December 1993), pp. 18–23. This article summarizes new research into the genesis and impacts of winter storms. *Weatherwise* contains a great deal of interesting meteorological information understandable by the layperson.

16. *The Ash Wednesday Storm, March 7, 1962*, by David Stick, 1987, is an excellent and colorful account of the greatest winter northeaster of the twentieth century. Highly recommended for visitors and residents of the northern Outer Banks. Published by Gresham Publications, P.O. Drawer 807, Kill Devil Hills, NC 27948, (919) 441-5091.

Barrier Islands and Beaches

17. *The Beaches Are Moving: The Drowning of America's Shoreline*, by Wallace Kaufman and Orrin Pilkey, 1979. This account of the state of America's coastline explains natural processes at work at the beach, provides a historical perspective of human-shoreline relations, and offers practical advice on how to live in harmony with the coastal environment. Published by Duke University Press, Durham, N.C.

18. *Ribbon of Sand: The Amazing Convergence of the Ocean and the Outer Banks*, by John Alexander and James Lazell, 1992, provides a casual view of barrier island environments in North Carolina. Published by Algonquin Books, Chapel Hill, N.C. 238 pp.

19. *Using Common Sense to Protect the Coasts*, by Michael Weber, 1990. This brief document (24 pp.) contains basic information on the geology and ecology of barrier islands, the destructive effects of development, and legislation passed concerning the islands' protection and management. Produced and distributed by The Coast Alliance, 218 D Street S.E., Washington, DC 20003.

20. *Living with the South Carolina Coast*, by Gered Lennon and others, 1996, published by Duke University Press, Durham, N.C., provides valuable lessons learned from Hurricane Hugo and the 1886 Charleston earthquake.

21. *At the Sea's Edge: An Introduction to Coastal Oceanography for the Amateur Naturalist*, by W. T. Fox, 1983. Excellent nontechnical, richly illustrated introduction to coastal processes, meteorology, environments, and ecology, published by Prentice-Hall, Englewood Cliffs, N.J.

22. "Rip Currents," poster available free from UNC Sea Grant, publication UNC-SG-95-03.

23. *Coastal Environments—An Introduction to the Physical, Ecological and Cultural Systems of Coastlines*, by R. W. G. Carter, 1988, is an excellent text for almost all aspects of the coastal zone, although management of coastal environments is its emphasis. Published by Academic Press, New York.

24. *Coasts: An Introduction to Coastal Geomorphology*, by Eric C. F. Bird, 3d ed., 1984. This introduction to coastal types and their classifications discusses tides, waves, and currents; changing sea levels; cliffed coasts; beaches, spits, and barriers; coastal dunes; estuaries and lagoons; deltas; and coral reefs and atolls. Published by Basil Blackwell, London.

25. *Waves and Beaches*, by Willard Bascom, 1964, discusses beaches and coastal processes based on World War II research to assist amphibious landings. This classic may be the original coastal text. Updated periodically, it is a "must read" for beginners. Published by Anchor Books/Doubleday, Garden City, N.Y.

26. *North Carolina Long-Term Erosion Rates Updated through 1992*, by the N.C. Division of Coastal Management, published by the N.C. Department of Health, Environment, and Natural Resources, Raleigh, shows every stretch of the North Carolina coast and the rate at which each stretch is eroding.

27. *Barrier Island Ecosystems of Cape Lookout National Seashore and Vicinity, North Carolina,* by P. J. Godfrey and M. M. Godfrey, 1977. The Godfreys studied Core Banks for several years, particularly the processes of overwash, plant response, and dune and marsh development. Scientific Monograph series no. 13 from the National Park Service, Washington, D.C.

Recreation and Nature

28. If you live or travel in North Carolina's coastal zone, check out the University of North Carolina Press publications on the subject, especially the following three useful references:

    Dirk Frankenberg, professor of marine sciences at UNC, authored the companion set *The Nature of the Outer Banks,* 1995, and *The Nature of North Carolina's Southern Coast: Barrier Islands, Coastal Waters, and Wetlands,* 1997, which provide an ecologic view of a range of coastal and estuarine environments, including guides to specific field sites. Both books are a good read and great field companions. Also from UNC Press is Glenn Morris's *North Carolina Beaches: A Guide to Coastal Access,* 1993.

29. *Seashells Common to North Carolina,* by Hugh Porter and Jim Tyler, 1981, is an excellent handbook, written for the layman, describing and illustrating seashells. An essential reference for Carolina shell collectors. Available from UNC Sea Grant (see appendix B).

30. *Seacoast Life,* by Judith M. Spitsbergen, 1980, published by UNC Press, provides good descriptions and illustrations of flora and fauna typically found on barrier islands in North Carolina.

31. *The Audubon Society Field Guide to North American Seashells,* by Harold A. Rehder, 1995. This well-illustrated reference is an excellent handbook for the serious shell collector. Published by Alfred A. Knopf, New York.

32. *A Field Guide to Southeastern and Caribbean Seashores: Cape Hatteras to the Gulf Coast, Florida, and the Caribbean,* by Eugene H. Kaplan, 1988. One of the Peterson Field Guide series, sponsored by the National Audubon Society and the National Wildlife Federation, this 425-page guide describes most of the wildlife you are likely to encounter in North Carolina. Published by Houghton Mifflin, Boston.

33. *The Audubon Society Field Guide to North American Fishes, Whales, and Dolphins,* by H. Boschung, J. Williams, D. Gotshall, D. Caldwell, and M. Caldwell, 1983, provides detailed species accounts for fishes and marine mammals of North America. Published by Alfred A. Knopf, New York.

34. *The Audubon Society Field Guide to North American Seashore Creatures,* by N. Meinkoth, 1995, gives detailed species descriptions and an overview of the taxonomy of major shore animals of North America. Illustrated with color photographs. Published by Alfred A. Knopf, New York.

35. *Birds and Mammals of the Cape Hatteras National Seashore: Thirty-five Years of Change,* publication UNC-SG-92-01, available from UNC Sea Grant.

36. *1993 Atlas of Colonial Waterbirds of North Carolina Estuaries,* available from UNC Sea Grant, publication UNC-SG-95-02.

Shoreline Engineering and Beach Replenishment

37. *The Corps and the Shore,* by Orrin H. Pilkey and Katherine L. Dixon, 1996, delves into the role of the U.S. Army Corps of Engineers in U.S. beach management, including

beach nourishment, and points out the need for external checks on Corps activities. Published by Island Press, Washington, D.C. 272 pp.

38. *The Effects of Seawalls on the Beach,* edited by Nicholas C. Kraus and O. H. Pilkey Jr., appeared as Special Issue 4 of the *Journal of Coastal Research.* This technical volume explores the nature of seawalls' impacts on beaches. See the paper by Pilkey and Wright titled "Seawalls versus Beaches," which discusses how seawalls cause the narrowing of beaches and clearly demonstrates that the problem is not *whether* seawalls negatively affect beaches, but *how* they do.

39. *A Homeowner's Guide to Estuarine Bulkheads,* publication UNC-SG-81-11 available from UNC Sea Grant.

40. "An Analysis of Replenished Beach Design Parameters on U.S. East Coast Barrier Islands," by Lynn Leonard, Tonya Clayton, and Orrin Pilkey. This scientific paper published in the *Journal of Coastal Research,* vol. 6, no. 1 (1990), pp. 15–36, concludes that replenished beaches north of Florida generally have life spans of less than five years; storm frequency is a major factor. The authors document overestimates of beach life by the USACOE.

41. "A 'Thumbnail Method' for Beach Communities: Estimation of Long-Term Beach Replenishment Requirements," by Orrin H. Pilkey. This short paper demonstrates that current methods of estimating long-term volume requirements for replenished beaches are inadequate. The long-term volume required can be estimated by assuming that the initial restoration volume must be replaced at prescribed intervals depending on location. Published in *Shore and Beach,* vol. 56, no. 3 (July 1988), pp. 23–31, by ASBPA.

42. *Shoreline Erosion Control Using Marsh Vegetation and Low-Cost Structures,* publication UNC-SG-92-12, available from UNC Sea Grant.

Hazard Evaluation

43. *Citizen's Guide to Geologic Hazards,* by Edward B. Nuhfer and others, 1993. Written for the general public, this book discusses geologic hazards in understandable terms. Available from the American Institute of Professional Geologists, 7828 Vance Drive, Suite 103, Arvada, CO 80003-2124, (303) 431-0831.

44. *Coastal Hazards: Perception, Susceptibility, and Mitigation,* edited by Charles W. Finkl Jr., 1995, published as Special Issue 12 of the *Journal of Coastal Research.* Features papers on coastal hazard issues such as hazard recognition and evaluation, sea level rise, storms, tsunamis, effects of humans on coastal environments, effects of coastal hazards on natural features, and hazard mitigation. Published by the CERF.

45. *Living by the Rules of the Sea,* by David M. Bush, William J. Neal, and Orrin H. Pilkey, 1996, is the umbrella volume for the Living with the Shore series. Published by Duke University Press, Durham, N.C., this 179-page book discusses coastal hazards, risk assessment, and property damage mitigation. If you are interested in what your community can do now to reduce the impact of the next storm, we recommend this guide.

46. *The Citizen's Guide to North Carolina's Shifting Inlets,* by Simon Baker, 1977, is a guide to inlet history. Contains excellent aerial photographs of each inlet in the state. Two historic shoreline positions are marked in red on each photograph. Allows readers to compare historic and present inlet-shoreline positions and illustrates their instability. Brief explanatory text accompanying the photographs raises questions that should concern all coastal residents and taxpayers. Published by UNC Sea Grant and available through your library.

47. "Potential Inlet Zones on the North Carolina Coast from Virginia to Cape Hatteras,"

by Lisa L. Lynch and Stephen B. Benton, 1985, is an unpublished report prepared for the N.C. Department of Health, Environment, and Natural Resources, Division of Coastal Management, Raleigh.

48. *Catastrophic Earthquakes: The Need to Insure against Economic Disaster,* by the National Committee on Property Insurance, 1989. As a working document of the Earthquake Project, a coalition of insurance companies and their trade associations, this 120-page report (plus 188 pages of appendixes) addresses the national threat of a catastrophic earthquake's impact on the U.S. economy and the insurance industry's role in preparation and response. The estimated 6.5–7.0 magnitude 1886 Charleston earthquake is discussed, as well as other central and eastern U.S. events. No matter where the "big one" occurs, the projected impact on the national and local economies is sobering. Prepared by the National Committee on Property Insurance (subsequently the Insurance Institute for Property Loss Reduction, now the Institute for Business and Home Safety). Available from IBHS, 73 Tremont Street, Suite 510, Boston, MA 02108-3910.

Vegetation

49. *Seacoast Plants of the Carolinas for Conservation and Beautification,* by K. E. Braetz, 1973, is an excellent discussion of natural plants of our beach and dune environments. Includes suggestions for plantings to stabilize and protect dunes and landscape the beach; descriptions and illustrations of various natural and ornamental plants. Available from UNC Sea Grant.

50. *A Guide to Salt Marsh Plants Common to North Carolina,* publication UNC-SG-81-04. Available from UNC Sea Grant.

51. *An Assessment of the Maritime Forest Resources on the North Carolina Coast,* by Michael J. Lopazanski and others, 1988, was published by the N.C. Department of Natural Resources and Community Development, Division of Coastal Management, Raleigh.

52. *A Guide to Protecting Maritime Forests through Planning and Design,* by Larry Zucchino, 1990, 24 pp., is an excellent booklet describing North Carolina's maritime forests and their function, relations to water resources, and how construction disrupts the protective role of vegetation. Human impact is "cumulative and largely irreversible," but the booklet sets down guidelines for property owners, developers, and local planners to conserve this threatened resource and, in some cases, restore forest cover. Published by and available from the N.C. Department of Environment, Health, and Natural Resources, Division of Coastal Management, Raleigh.

53. *Building and Stabilizing Coastal Dunes with Vegetation* (UNC-SG-82-05) and *Planting Marsh Grasses for Erosion Control* (UNC-SG-81-09), by S. W. Broome, W. W. Woodhouse Jr., and E. D. Seneca, 1982. These publications on using vegetation as stabilizers may still be available from UNC Sea Grant.

54. *A Guide to Ocean Dune Plants Common to North Carolina,* by Jean Wilson Kraus, is a concise illustrated handbook of the most frequently encountered dune flora. Available from UNC Sea Grant, publication UNC-SG-87-01.

55. "These Dunes Aren't Made for Walking," poster available free from UNC Sea Grant, publication UNC-SG-94-04.

Site Analysis

56. *Questions and Answers on Purchasing Coastal Real Estate in North Carolina,* available free from UNC Sea Grant, publication UNC-SG-96-10.

Water Resources

57. *Understanding Septic Systems,* available free from UNC Sea Grant, publication UNC-SG-BP-83-01.

Coastal Management

General

58. *Introduction to Coastal Management,* by Timothy Beatley, David J. Brower, and Anna K. A. Schwab, published in 1994 by Island Press of Washington, D.C. (210 pp.), is a reference book for anyone working or interested in coastal management.
59. *Coastal Zone Management Handbook,* by John R. Clark, is a very detailed manual and reference source for coastal resources planners and managers. This 694-page book was published in 1996 by CRC Press, 2000 Corporate Boulevard N.W., Boca Raton, FL 33431, (800) 272-7737. You will find everthing you want to know about the coast here, from development impacts, to beach management, to biotoxins, to sewage treatment. Not for the casual reader, but recommended for your coastal community's reference library.
60. *Managing Coastal Erosion,* by the Committee on Coastal Erosion Zone Management for the NRC, 1990, is a 182-page report on coastal erosion and its management written by a blue-ribbon panel of experts. Chapters include "Coastal Erosion: Its Causes, Effects, and Distribution"; "Management and Approaches"; "The National Flood Insurance Program"; "State Programs and Experiences"; and "Predicting Future Shoreline Changes." Available from the National Academy of Sciences, National Academy Press, Washington, D.C.

Storm Damage Mitigation

61. "Hurricanes Gilbert and Hugo Send Powerful Messages for Coastal Development," by E. R. Thieler and D. M. Bush, 1991. This article, which appeared in the *Journal of Geological Education,* vol. 39 (1991), pp. 291–299, compares the characteristics and impacts of Hugo and Gilbert and discusses how types and designs of buildings contributed to the damage.
62. *Catastrophic Coastal Storms: Hazard Mitigation and Development Management,* by D. R. Godschalk, D. J. Brower, and T. Beatley, 1989, contains extensive information on mitigation and development management in at-risk coastal locations. Published by Duke University Press, Durham, N.C.

Coastal Law and Public Involvement

63. *Cities on the Beach, Management Issues of Developed Coastal Barriers,* edited by Rutherford Platt, Sheila Pelczarski, and Barbara Burbank, 1987. The 28 essays in this book concern barrier island development. Available from the Department of Geography, University of Chicago, 5828 S. University Avenue, Chicago, IL 60637-1583, as Research Paper 224.
64. *Protecting Coastal Resources from Cumulative Impacts: An Evaluation of the North Carolina Coastal Area Management Act,* available free from UNC Sea Grant, publication UNC-SG-96-12.

Coastal Flooding

65. *Projected Impact of Relative Sea Level Rise on the National Flood Insurance Program,* by FEMA, 1991, concludes that coastal flood-hazard areas will require periodic mapping if we are to stay abreast of the impact of the sea level rise, but elevation requirements of the present nfip program provide at least a 20-year cushion (to 2010) for study and adjustment of construction elevation requirements. This 72-page report includes projections of numbers of households in the coastal floodplains through the year 2010. Produced by FEMA, Federal Insurance Administration, Washington, D.C.

66. *How to Use a Flood Map to Protect Your Property. A Guide for Interested Private Citizens, Property Owners, Community Officials, Lending Institutions, and Insurance Agents,* 1994. A 22-page tabloid-sized publication designed to help readers understand Flood Insurance Rate Maps (FIRMS), which establish the extent of flood hazard within a flood-prone community. Available from FEMA, publication FEMA-258.

67. *Questions and Answers on the National Flood Insurance Program,* by FEMA, 1983 (updated March 1992). Pamphlet explaining basics of flood insurance and providing addresses of FEMA offices. Available from the regional office of FEMA as publication FIA-2.

68. *Saving Money on Flood Insurance for Coastal Property Owners,* 1989, is available from UNC Sea Grant, publication UNC-SG-89-05.

Coastal Construction

General Design

69. *Blue Sky Ten Year Strategic Plan, Southern Shores, North Carolina, 1995* outlines the local plan to upgrade construction quality and retrofit older homes to withstand high wind and water forces. Blue Sky is a program initiated in the town of Southern Shores that has since been adopted elsewhere on the East Coast, with the help of funding from FEMA, state, local, and private sources. Also see *Wind Load Engineering Design Guidelines,* 1996, Blue Sky. This is a continuing effort to develop construction guidelines for wind-loaded buildings in North Carolina. Contact Blue Sky Program Manager, Town of Southern Shores, 6 Skyline Road, Southern Shores, NC 27949, (919) 261-2394.

70. *Free of Obstruction: Requirements for Buildings Located in Coastal High Hazard Areas,* NFIP Technical Bulletin 5, considers the prevention of damage to coastal buildings resulting from obstructions underneath the buildings. Complies with National Insurance Program requirements. Available from FEMA.

71. *Corrosion Protection for Metal Connections in Coastal Areas,* NFIP Technical Bulletin 8. Provides guidance on selection, installation, and maintenance of metal connectors. Available from FEMA.

72. *Hurricane-Resistant Construction for Homes,* by Todd L. Walton Jr. and Michael R. Barnett, 1991, provides guidelines for wood-frame, masonry, and brick construction; pole houses; and special considerations such as roofs, doors, glass, shutters, and siding. Available as bulletin 16 (MAP-16) from Florida Sea Grant College Program, University of Florida, Gainesville, FL.

73. *Surviving the Storm: Building Codes, Compliance and the Mitigation of Hurricane Damage,* by the All-Industry Research Advisory Council, 1989. Available from AIRAC, Oak Brook, IL.

74. *Structural Failures: Modes, Causes, Responsibilities,* 1973. See especially the chapter

titled "Failure of Structures Due to Extreme Winds," pp. 49–77. Available from the Research Council on Performance of Structures, American Society of Civil Engineers, 345 E. 47th Street, New York, NY 10017.

75. *Building Performance: Hurricane Andrew in Florida; Observations, Recommendations, and Technical Guidance,* by FEMA and FIA, 1992, is an illustrated booklet including background information about the storm, on-site observations of the damaged area, and recommendations for reducing future damage. Available from FEMA, publication FIA-22.

76. *Building Performance Assessment: Hurricane Fran in North Carolina; Observations, Recommendations, and Technical Guidance,* by FEMA, 1997, assesses the problems that occurred during Hurricane Fran in North Carolina. Particularly useful are the recommendations on how to avoid these problems in the future. Available from FEMA, publication FEMA-290.

Wind Resistance

77. *Against the Wind,* 1993, is a 6-page brochure with summary information about protecting your home from hurricane wind damage. Developed jointly by the American Red Cross, FEMA, Home Depot, the National Association of Home Builders of the United States, and the Georgia Emergency Management Agency, it briefly discusses roof systems, exterior doors and windows, garage doors, and shutters. Available from the American Red Cross (publication ARC-5023) and FEMA (publication FEMA-247).

78. "Wind Conditions in Hurricane Hugo and Their Effect on Buildings in Coastal South Carolina," by P. R. Sparks, is a contribution to the *Journal of Coastal Research* Special Issue 8 on Hurricane Hugo (pp. 12–24). Insured property owners should read this paper because the author gives a good evaluation of how and why buildings failed in Hurricane Hugo, and why the Standard Building Code's wind-resistance requirements were inadequate. Available through university libraries.

79. *The Hurricanes Are Coming,* 1996, by Charles R. Calhoun and Laszlo G. Fulop. This booklet uses simple diagrams to explain methods for retrofitting and building homes in coastal regions to withstand hurricane wind forces. Available from Callaz Research Alliance, P.O. Box 15046, Wilmington, NC 28403.

80. *Wind-Resistant Design Concepts for Residents,* by Delbart B. Ward. Displays, with vivid sketches and illustrations, construction problems and methods of tying structures to the ground. Offers recommendations for strengthening houses and relatively inexpensive modifications that will increase the safety of homes subject to severe winds. Available as TR-83 from the Civil Defense Preparedness Agency, Department of Defense, The Pentagon, Washington, DC 20301; or from the Civil Defense Preparedness Agency, 2800 Eastern Boulevard, Baltimore, MD 21220.

81. *Interim Guidelines for Building Occupant Protection from Tornadoes and Extreme Winds* (TR-83A) and *Tornado Protection: Selecting and Designing Safe Areas in Buildings* (TR-83B) are supplements to reference 80 and are available from the same addresses.

82. "Glazed Opening Design for Windborne Debris Impact," by J. Minor, in *Proceedings of the Conference on Natural Disaster Reduction,* 1996, American Society of Civil Engineers.

83. "Progress of the ASTM Standard on Fenestration Relative to Windstorms and Its Relationship to Building Codes," by D. Hattis, in *Proceedings of the Conference on Natural Disaster Reduction,* 1996, American Society of Civil Engineers.

84. *Wooden Wind Anchors for Hurricane-Resistant Construction Near the Ocean,* available free from UNC Sea Grant, publication UNC-SG-BP-94-03.

85. *Minimum Design Loads for Buildings and Other Structures,* 1995, American Society of Civil Engineers. Standard ASCE 7-95, contains criteria for calculating flood loads and for combining these with other loads. This standard meets, and in some cases exceeds, the NFIP requirements. Builders and design engineers should be familiar with this highly technical set of standards for construction. Available from the American Society of Civil Engineers (see appendix B for address).

86. *Coastal Construction Manual,* prepared by Dames & Moore and Bliss & Nyitray, Inc., for FEMA, 1986. Guide to the coastal environment with recommendations on site and structure design relative to the NFIP. Includes discussions of the program, building codes, coastal environments, and examples. The second edition includes a chapter on the design of large structures at the coast and recommends that pilings be embedded to a depth of 10 feet below mean sea level. Appendixes include design tables, bracing examples, design worksheets, equations and procedures, construction costs, and a list of references. Also includes engineering computer program listings and a sample construction code for use by coastal municipalities. Available from the U.S. Government Printing Office as publication FEMA-55 and from FEMA offices. Note: At the time of this writing, the Coastal Construction Manual was being revised for a new edition to be published in 1998 or 1999.

87. *Mitigation of Flood and Erosion Damage to Residential Buildings in Coastal Areas,* by FEMA, 1994. This report on flood-proofing includes a couple of case studies from the Carolinas and is a good starting point to review flood-proofing techniques; includes additional reading list. Available from FEMA, publication FEMA-257.

88. *Manufactured Home Installation in Flood Hazard Areas,* prepared by the National Conference of States on Building Codes and Standards for FEMA, 1985, is a 110-page guide to design, installation, and general characteristics of manufactured homes with respect to coastal and flood hazards. Anyone contemplating buying a manufactured home or already living in one should read this publication and follow its suggestions to lessen potential losses from flood, wind, and fire. Available from the U.S. Government Printing Office as publication 1985-529-684/31054; or from FEMA as publication FEMA-85.

89 *Flood Resistant Design and Construction Practices,* 1997, ASCE standard. This standard provides recommendations for design and construction of buildings to resist flood loadings. These recommendations meet or exceed the minimum requirements of the NFIP. Available from the ASCE.

North Carolina Codes

90. *North Carolina Uniform Residential Building Code,* prepared by the North Carolina Building Inspectors' Association, 1997 edition. For coastal regions, two sections are particularly appropriate: (1) appendix D, "Windstorm Resistive Construction," specifies the type of anchoring required in areas subject to winds greater than 75 miles per hour. Includes details on framing, masonry, walls, roof structures, and roof coverings. (2) Section 3.0 of appendix D, "Piles Required" (the Sand Dune Ordinance), specifies that all buildings erected within 150 feet of the high-water mark of the Atlantic Ocean must be constructed on pile-type foundations. Includes details on the piles and the methods of fastening the structure to them. Published by the North Carolina Building Code Council. Available from the N.C. Department of Insurance, Engineering Division, P.O. Box 26387, Raleigh, NC 27611.

Pole-House Construction

91. *Elevated Residential Structures,* prepared by the American Institute of Architects Foundation (1735 New York Avenue N.W., Washington, DC 20006) for FEMA, 1984, is an excellent outline of coastal and riverine flood hazards and the need for proper planning and construction. Discusses the NFIP, site analysis and design, design examples and construction techniques; includes illustrations, glossary, references, and worksheets for estimating building costs. Available as stock no. 1984-0-438-116 from the U.S. Government Printing Office; also available from FEMA as FEMA-54.

Mobile Homes

92. *Suggested Technical Requirements for Mobile Home Tie Down Ordinances,* prepared by the Civil Defense Preparedness Agency, 1974 (TR-73-1); should be used in conjunction with TR-75 (ref. 93). Available from the U.S. Army Publication Center, Civil Defense Branch, 2800 Eastern Boulevard (Middle River), Baltimore, MD 21220.

93. *Protecting Mobile Homes from High Winds* (TR-75), prepared by the Civil Defense Preparedness Agency, 1974. This excellent 16-page booklet outlines methods of tying down mobile homes and means of protection such as positioning and windbreaks. Publication 1974-0-537-785, available from the U.S. Government Printing Office; or from the U.S. Army Publications Center, Civil Defense Branch, 280 Eastern Boulevard (Middle River), Baltimore, MD 21220.

94. *North Carolina Manufactured/Mobile Home Regulations,* published by the N.C. Department of Insurance, 1995 edition. A compilation of state regulations pertaining to mobile homes. Contains special requirements governing homes in hurricane areas. Available from the N.C. Department of Insurance, Box 26837, Raleigh, NC 27611.

95. *Manufactured Home Construction and Safety Standards,* 1992, 24 Code of Federal Regulations, chap. 20, pt. 3280, pp. 196–233.

96. *Wind Load Provisions of the Manufactured Home Construction and Safety Standards—A Review and Recommendations for Improvement,* by R. D. Marshall, 1993, contains the results of a study of wind-load design criteria for manufactured homes based on the effects of Hurricane Andrew (1992), performed by the National Institute of Standards and Technology (NIST) with the support of the Department of Housing and Urban Development (HUD). Manufactured homes built after the Manufactured Home and Construction and Safety Standards and accompanying HUD labels were issued experienced less damage than did units constructed before these standards. In general, conventional residential homes fared better than manufactured homes, including those with HUD labels. The report concludes that ASCE standard 7-95 is the most logical reference to provide a basis for wind-load design criteria. Available as NISTIR 5189 from the National Technical Information Service (NTIS), 5285 Port Royal Road, Springfield, VA 22161 (phone: [800] 553-6847).

97. *Manufactured Homes—Probability of Failure and the Need for Better Windstorm Protection through Improved Anchoring Systems,* by R. D. Marshall, 1994, contends that the anchoring system is responsible for many failures. The anchor system load capacity implied by the current standards for the installation of manufactured homes is rarely achieved in practice. Available from NTIS, NISTIR 5370.

98. *Recommended Performance-Based Criteria for the Design of Manufactured Home Foundation Systems to Resist Wind and Seismic Loads,* by R. D. Marshall, 1995, is another NTIS report that questions whether the current practice for anchor systems for manufactured homes is adequate for wind-load protection. Available from NTIS, NISTIR 5664.

Earthquake-Resistant Construction

99. *The Home Builder's Guide for Earthquake Design,* by FEMA, 1992. Available from FEMA, FEMA-232.

100. *Reducing the Risks of Nonstructural Earthquake Damage: A Practical Guide,* by FEMA. Available from FEMA, FEMA-74.

101. *Checklist of Nonstructural Earthquake Hazards,* Bay Area Regional Earthquake Preparedness Project (BAREPP), 101 8th Street, Suite 152, Oakland, CA 94607.

Other Publications and Newsletters

Publications List, Coastal Engineering Research Center (CERC) and Beach Erosion Board (BEB), by the U.S. Army Corps of Engineers. List (updated periodically) of published research by the U.S. Army Corps of Engineers. Free from the USACOE. Lists of earlier publications are available from the same library.

FEMA *Publications Catalog,* by FEMA, 1996, is a booklet listing more than 300 publications available from FEMA to assist everyone from individual property owners to emergency managers. Request publication FEMA-20 from FEMA.

Publications of the Natural Hazards Research and Applications Information Center, in Boulder, Colorado. Hundreds of publications are available—most for a very nominal charge—covering all aspects of natural hazard preparedness, response, mitigation, and planning. A monthly magazine, *Natural Hazards Observer,* contains a wealth of information. Contact the NHRAIC Publications Clerk, Campus Box 482, University of Colorado, Boulder 80309-0482, (303) 492-6818.

As part of the National Earthquake Hazards Reduction Program (NEHRP), FEMA has developed more than 100 publications in its Earthquake Hazards Reduction series. A list of these publications, which are available free, may be requested by writing to FEMA, P.O. Box 70274, Washington, DC 20024.

The *Earthquake Education Center Newsletter* is available from the Earthquake Education Center, Charleston Southern University, P.O. Box 118087, Charleston, SC 29423-8087. The newsletter provides useful information on seismic hazards, calendars of workshops and meetings, summaries of earthquake events, and related stories. The center produced an information brochure titled *South Carolina Earthquakes.* A 10-minute video, *Earthquake Awareness and Preparedness,* is available from the center for a fee.

Coastwatch (bimonthly magazine) from UNC Sea Grant provides a wide range of information on the coastal zone and should be of interest to anyone living on a North Carolina beach.

Index

National Academy of Engineering, 6
National Academy of Sciences, 6
National Flood Insurance Act of 1968, 204
National Flood Insurance Program (NFIP), 113, 203, 206, 207, 208, 222, 234, 239, 250
National Flood Insurance Reform Act of 1994, 207
National Flood Mitigation Fund, 207
National Hurricane Center, 22, 221
National Marine Fisheries Service (NMFS), 106
National Oceanic and Atmospheric Administration (NOAA), 22
National Park Service, 6, 103, 104
National Pollution Discharge Elimination System (NPDES), 84
National Weather Service, 22, 24, 221
Nature Conservancy, 147
Neuse River, 53, 67, 68, 76, 85, 126
Neuse River estuary, 82
New Bern, 85
New Currituck Inlet, 139
New Jersey, 12, 14, 15, 23, 88, 91, 93, 94
New Jerseyization, 13, 14, 15, 127
Newport estuary, 64
New River estuary, 64
New River Inlet, 171, 174
New River Inlet Road, 174
New Topsail Inlet, 178, 179, 181, 182
NFIP. *See* National Flood Insurance Program
No Name Island, 120, 183
Norfolk, Virginia, 94, 143
North Carolina Building Code, 212, 215, 237
North Carolina Coastal Area Management Act (CAMA), 119, 130, 190, 208–212
North Carolina Department of Transportation, 122
North Carolina Division of Coastal Management (DCM), 208
North Carolina State Highway: No. 12, 89, 137, 150, 152, 153, 155, 161; No. 50, 178; No. 58, 165, 166; No. 64, 150; No. 210, 173, 175
Northeasters, 14, 19, 30, 31; 1962 Ash Wednesday storm, 31, 145, 150, 156; 1987 New Year's Day Storm, 31; 1988 storm, 19; 1991 Thanksgiving Day Storm, 31; 1991 Halloween Storm, 19, 147, 153; 1992 No-Name Storm, 31; 1993 Storm of the Century, 19, 32

North estuary, 64
North River estuary, 69
North Shore Drive, 177
North Topsail Beach, 10, 14, 29, 30, 115, 120, 137, 174, 175, 177, 206
Notches in dunes, 16
Nourishment, 99, 100. *See also* Beach: nourishment

Oak Island, 44, 116, 192, 194
Ocean erodible area, 209
Ocean hazard areas, 209
Ocean Isle, 116, 199
Ocean Isle Beach, 124, 197, 198, 201
Ocean View Railroad, 13
Ocracoke, 12, 13, 26, 53, 125, 150, 159, 161
Ocracoke Inlet, 12, 13, 159, 160
Ocracoke Island, 26, 132, 139, 159, 161
Off-shore bar, 58
Offshore breakwaters, 93, 209. *See also* Shoreline: engineering, stabilization
Old Currituck Inlet, 139
Old Nags Head, 148
Old Topsail Inlet, 183
Onslow Bay, 42
Onslow Beach, 13, 51, 54, 81, 120, 171
Onslow County, 124
Oregon Inlet, 4, 47, 51, 53, 89, 104, 106, 121, 137, 139, 150, 152
Oregon Inlet jetty, 106
Organic shorelines, 71, 74
Outer Banks, 1, 4, 12, 13, 26, 27, 28, 43, 51, 53, 63, 82, 102, 104, 119, 127, 137, 139, 145, 150, 154, 155, 159, 161
Outlaw family house, 102
Outstanding Resource Waters, 208
Overwash, 16, 17, 22, 35, 46, 47, 109, 115, 139, 182, 194; fan, 44, 47, 120; passes, 16, 120; sand, 30, 38; terraces, 120
Oyster shells, 43, 54, 163

Pamlico County, 260
Pamlico River, 67, 68, 76, 85
Pamlico River estuary, 82
Pamlico Sound, 27, 39, 48, 51, 65, 66, 69, 76, 77, 81, 150, 153, 156, 158
Panama City, Florida, 254
Pasquotank estuary, 69
Pea Island, 50, 103

Contributors

Jane Bullock is the Chief of Staff at the Federal Emergency Management Agency, Washington, D.C.

David M. Bush is an Assistant Professor of Geology at State University of West Georgia, Carrollton, Georgia.

Brian A. Cowan is the Director of the Disaster Resistant Community Project, FEMA, Washington, D.C.

William J. Neal is a Professor of Geology at Grand Valley State University, Allendale, Michigan.

Deborah F. Pilkey is a graduate student in the Department of Engineering Science and Mechanics at Virginia Polytechnic Institute and State University, Blacksburg, Virginia.

Orrin H. Pilkey is James B. Duke Professor of Geology at Duke University, Durham, North Carolina.

Stanley R. Riggs is a Professor of Marine Geology at East Carolina University, Greenville, North Carolina.

Craig A. Webb is a research assistant in the Division of Earth and Ocean Sciences at Duke University, Durham, North Carolina.

Library of Congress Cataloging-in-Publication Data
The North Carolina Shore and Its Barrier Islands : restless ribbons of sand / by Orrin H. Pilkey ... [et al.].
p.   cm.-- (Living with the shore)
Includes bibliographical references and index.
ISBN 0-8223-2208-0 (cloth : alk. paper).
ISBN 0-8223-2224-2 (paper : alk paper).
1. Shore protection — North Carolina. 2. Coastal zone management — North Carolina. 3. Beach erosion — North Carolina. 4. Barrier islands — North Carolina. I. Pilkey, Orrin H., 1934– . II. Series.
TC224.N8N67 1998 333.91'75'097561 — dc21 98-4578 CIP